Estudos de Direito Internacional e da União Europeia
Essays on International and European Union Law

2019

Ana Maria Guerra Martins
Professora Associada com Agregação
da Faculdade de Direito da Universidade de Lisboa

ALMEDINA

ESTUDOS DE DIREITO INTERNACIONAL E DA UNIÃO EUROPEIA
ESSAYS ON INTERNATIONAL AND EUROPEAN UNION LAW

AUTOR
Ana Maria Guerra Martins
EDITOR
EDIÇÕES ALMEDINA, S.A.
Rua Fernandes Tomás, nºs 76, 78 e 80
3000-167 Coimbra
Tel.: 239 851 904 · Fax: 239 851 901
www.almedina.net · editora@almedina.net
DESIGN DE CAPA
FBA.
PRÉ-IMPRESSÃO
EDIÇÕES ALMEDINA, S.A.
IMPRESSÃO E ACABAMENTO
PENTAEDRO, LDA.

Maio, 2019
DEPÓSITO LEGAL
455671/19

ALMEDINA | GRUPOALMEDINA

BIBLIOTECA NACIONAL DE PORTUGAL – CATALOGAÇÃO NA PUBLICAÇÃO
MARTINS, Ana Maria Guerra, 1963-
Estudos de direito internacional e da União Europeia, essays on international and European Union law. – (Monografias)
ISBN 978-972-40-7933-2
CDU 341

ÍNDICE

ÍNDICE 5
ABREVIATURAS 11
NOTA PRÉVIA 15

PARTE I
QUESTÕES CONSTITUCIONAIS E INSTITUCIONAIS DA UNIÃO EUROPEIA

I. THE IMPACT OF BREXIT ON THE EU'S CONSTITUTIONAL NATURE AND ON ITS FOUNDING TREATIES 19
1. Introduction 19
2. Declaration of interest: the *constitutionalism beyond the State* theory 21
2.1. General remarks 21
2.2. EU Constitutional Law and the EU's Constitutional Nature 21
3. Article 50 TEU and EU Constitutional Law 25
3.1. The background of Article 50 TEU 26
3.1.1. The discussion on a Member State's withdrawal before the Treaty of Lisbon 26
3.1.2. The introduction of a withdrawal clause in the TECE 27
3.2. Impact of Brexit on the constitutional law of the EU ... 29
3.2.1. The rhetoric of sovereignty and democracy 29
3.2.2. Inevitable changes in EU constitutional law as a result of Brexit 32
3.2.2.1. Constitutional impact of Brexit on the territorial clause 34

3.2.2.2. Constitutional Impact of Brexit on the EU's Institutional Framework ... 34
3.2.2.3. Constitutional Impact of Brexit on the EU's objectives and policies ... 37
3.2.2.4. Constitutional Impact of Brexit on the EU Fundamental Rights and EU Citizenship ... 39
4. Can Brexit enhance the constitutional nature of EU Law? ... 42
5. Some (un)conclusive remarks ... 44
Abstract ... 44

II. A REVISÃO DOS TRATADOS E O ALARGAMENTO DOS PODERES DOS ÓRGÃOS DA UE ... 47
a) Article 48 ... 47
b) Article 352 ... 57
c) Article 353 ... 62

III. DIREITO INSTITUCIONAL DA UNIÃO EUROPEIA ... 65
A) Parlamento Europeu ... 65
1. O modo de designação dos membros do PE ... 65
2. O estatuto dos membros do PE ... 65
3. A composição do PE ... 65
4. A organização e o funcionamento do PE ... 66
5. Os poderes do PE ... 67
Bibliografia ... 69
B) Conselho Europeu ... 69
1. A génese do Conselho Europeu ... 69
2. A composição e a organização do Conselho Europeu ... 70
3. A presidência do Conselho Europeu ... 71
4. O modo de funcionamento do Conselho Europeu ... 71
5. A competência do Conselho Europeu ... 72
Bibliografia ... 72

PARTE II
A PESSOA HUMANA NO DIREITO DA UNIÃO EUROPEIA

IV. O PRINCÍPIO DA DIGNIDADE DA PESSOA HUMANA ... 77
Bibliografia ... 80

V. A CIDADANIA DA UNIÃO EUROPEIA. 30 ANOS DEPOIS DA ADESÃO DE PORTUGAL À UNIÃO EUROPEIA 83
1. Introdução 83
2. A cidadania da União Europeia – antecedentes, criação pelo Tratado de Maastricht e impacto na Constituição Portuguesa ... 84
2.1. Antecedentes 84
2.2. A introdução da cidadania da União no Tratado de Maastricht . 85
2.2.1. As dificuldades inerentes à natureza da União 85
2.2.2. As consequências da utilização do critério da nacionalidade na atribuição da cidadania da União.. 88
2.2.3. Os limites dos poderes dos Estados em sede de atribuição da nacionalidade 90
2.2.4. Nota crítica 91
2.3. O impacto da cidadania da União na Constituição Portuguesa.. 92
3. Os direitos (e deveres) das portuguesas e dos portugueses inerentes à cidadania da União 93
3.1. As bases jurídicas dos direitos de cidadania da União 93
3.2. Os direitos decorrentes da cidadania da União 95
3.3. Apreciação crítica do estatuto de cidadão da União 97
3.4. A faceta excludente da cidadania da União 97
4. A jurisprudência do Tribunal de Justiça da União Europeia no domínio da cidadania 99
4.1. Uma jurisprudência casuística e ambivalente............... 99
4.2. O impacto da jurisprudência do Tribunal de Justiça da União Europeia no Tribunal Constitucional Português – estudo de caso 102
5. Síntese conclusiva 103

VI. AS DECISÕES DO TJUE NOS CASOS *ACHBITA E BOUGNAOUI*: A NÃO DISCRIMINAÇÃO EM FUNÇÃO DA RELIGIÃO NO EMPREGO 105
1. Introdução 105
2. As decisões do TJUE 107
2.1. Matéria de facto 107
2.2. As questões prejudiciais colocadas pelos tribunais nacionais. 109
2.3. A decisão do Tribunal de Justiça no caso *Achbita*........... 111
2.4. A decisão do Tribunal no caso *Bougnaoui* 113
3. Apreciação crítica de ambas as decisões do TJUE............... 114

3.1. O direito a não ser discriminada/o em função da religião.... 115
3.2. O silêncio do TJ quanto à discriminação múltipla........... 119
3.3. A eventual justificação da medida e o princípio da proporcionalidade.................................... 120
3.4. A ponderação dos direitos em confronto: a liberdade religiosa e a liberdade de empresa.............. 123
3.5. Os limites do diálogo dos juízes do Luxemburgo com os de Estrasburgo 124
4. Conclusões.. 126

PARTE III
O MIGRANTE, O REFUGIADO E O TRABALHADOR NO DIREITO INTERNACIONAL

VII. A IGUALDADE E A NÃO DISCRIMINAÇÃO COMO FUNDAMENTO DOS DIREITOS DOS MIGRANTES E DOS REFUGIADOS NO DIREITO INTERNACIONAL................................ 131
1. Introdução 131
1.1. Objeto do presente estudo 131
1.2. Indicação de sequência 132
2. A herança cultural comum europeia em matéria de igualdade e de não discriminação – breve nota 132
2.1. Da Antiguidade ao liberalismo............................ 133
2.2. Do liberalismo à atualidade 140
3. As diferentes vertentes da igualdade e a não discriminação na atualidade.. 143
3.1. A igualdade formal e a igualdade substancial............... 146
3.2. A discriminação negativa e a vertente positiva da igualdade... 149
3.3. A discriminação direta e a discriminação indireta........... 159
4. A igualdade e a não discriminação como base dos direitos fundamentais dos migrantes e dos refugiados no direito internacional....................................... 162
4.1. A igualdade e a não discriminação no direito internacional dos direitos humanos em geral 163
4.2. O direito internacional relativo à igualdade e à não discriminação dos migrantes e dos refugiados....... 165

VIII. A ORGANIZAÇÃO INTERNACIONAL DO TRABALHO E A UNIÃO EUROPEIA 171
1. Introdução 171
1.1. Razões da escolha do tema 171
1.2. O objeto do presente estudo 174
1.3. Indicação de sequência 175
2. Breve referência aos objetivos da UE e da OIT 176
2.1. Os objetivos da UE 176
2.2. Os objetivos da OIT 177
3. O estatuto da União Europeia no seio da OIT 178
4. As atribuições da União Europeia no domínio de atuação da OIT .. 180
4.1. Os princípios 180
4.2. As categorias de atribuições da União 181
4.3. As atribuições externas da União nos domínios de atuação da OIT 185
4.3.1. Questão prévia: a subjetividade internacional da União Europeia 185
4.3.2. O princípio do paralelismo de atribuições internas e externas 186
4.3.3. O direito de celebração de convenções internacionais após o Tratado de Lisboa 187
4.3.4. As dificuldades inerentes às convenções da OIT 188
5. Os eventuais conflitos entre as convenções da OIT e o direito da UE 189
6. Conclusões 191

PARTE IV
A CONVENÇÃO EUROPEIA DOS DIREITOS DO HOMEM

IX. OPINION 2/13 OF THE EUROPEAN COURT OF JUSTICE IN THE CONTEXT OF MULTILEVEL PROTECTION OF FUNDAMENTAL RIGHTS AND MULTILEVEL CONSTITUTIONALISM REVISITED .. 195
I. Introduction 196
A. The background of Opinion 2/13 196
B. Scholars' Reactions 198
C. Purpose of the Present Study 200
II. Multilevel Protection of Fundamental Rights in the Context of Multilevel Constitutionalism 201

A. Multilevel Protection of Fundamental Rights and EU Accession to the ECHR 201
B. Multilevel Constitutionalism 203
III. Summary of CJEU Opinion 2/13 207
A. Violation of the integrity and autonomy of EU Law 211
B. Institutional Innovations 213
C. CJEU Jurisdiction over Common Foreign and Security Policy 213
IV. Opinion 2/13 from the perspective of multilevel constitutionalism 214
A. General Framework 214
1. Principle of a Higher Protection of Fundamental Rights 221
a) Coordination between Article 53 of the Charter and Article 53 ECHR 222
b) Area of Freedom, Security and Justice 224
c) Jurisdiction over Common Foreign and Security Policy 225
2. Principle of Common Values between the EU Member States, the EU, the Council of Europe and its Member States 226
3. Principle of Cooperative Judicial Dialogue 227
4. Principle of Sincere Cooperation and Mutual Trust ... 230
V. Concluding Remarks 231

X. TRIBUNAL EUROPEU DOS DIREITOS DO HOMEM 231
1. Introdução 231
2. Composição, estrutura e funcionamento do Tribunal Europeu dos Direitos do Homem 231
3. A competência do Tribunal Europeu dos Direitos do Homem ... 232
3.1. Competência *ratione personae* 233
3.2. Competência *ratione loci* 233
3.3. Competência *ratione materiae* 234
3.4. A decisão do TEDH 234
Bibliografia 235

ABREVIATURAS

AAVV	*Autores vários*
Ac.	*Acórdão*
ACP	*África, Caraíbas e Pacífico*
Act. Dr.	*Actualités de Droit*
AFDI	*Annuaire Français de Droit International*
AJDA	*Actualité Juridique – Droit Administratif*
AJIL	*The American Journal of International Law*
AöR	*Archiv des öffentlichen Rechts*
AUE	*Acto Único Europeu*
Aussenwirt.	*Aussenwirtschaft*
Austr. Rev. Int. Eur. Law	*Austrian Review of International and European Law*
AWD	*Aussenwirtschafsdienst des Betriebs-Beraters*
BEUR	*Boletín europeo de la Universidad de La Rioja*
BFDUC	*Boletim da Faculdade de Direito da Universidade de Coimbra*
Bol. CE	*Boletim das Comunidades Europeias*
Bul. CE	*Bulletin des Communautés Européennes*
BVerfG	*Bundesverfassungsgericht*
CambridgeYELS	*Cambridge Yearbook of European Legal Studies*
CDE	*Cahiers de Droit Européen*
CDFUE	*Carta dos Direitos Fundamentais da União Europeia*
CE	*Comunidade Europeia*
CECA	*Comunidade Europeia do Carvão e do Aço*
CEDH	*Convenção Europeia dos Direitos do Homem*
CEDS	*Comité Europeu dos Direitos Sociais*
CEE	*Comunidade Económica Europeia*
CEEA	*Comunidade Europeia da Energia Atómica*
CFREU	*Charter of Fundamental Rights of the European Union*
CIG	*Conferência Intergovernamental*

CJAI	*Cooperação Judiciária e em matéria de Assuntos Internos*
CMLR	*Common Market Law Review*
CNU	*Carta das Nações Unidas*
Col.	*Colectânea de Jurisprudência do Tribunal de Justiça e do Tribunal de Primeira Instância*
Colum. J. Eur. L.	*The Columbia Journal of European Law*
Columb. J. Transnat'l L.	*Columbia Journal of Transnational Law*
Cons.	*Considerando*
CPJP	*Cooperação Policial e Judiciária Penal*
CRP	*Constituição da República Portuguesa*
DCDSI	*Diritto Comunitario e degli Scambi Internazionali*
Dir. Pub.	*Diritto Pubblico*
Dir. Pubb. Comp. Eur.	*Diritto Pubblico Comparato Europeo*
Dir. Un. Eur.	*Il Dirittto dell'Unione Europea*
DöV	*Die öffentliche Verwaltung*
DUDH	*Declaração Universal dos Direitos Humanos*
DVBl	*Deutsches Verwaltungsblatt*
EADLR	*European Anti-Discrimination Law Review*
ECHR	*European Convention of Human Rights*
ECtHR	*European Court of Human Rights*
ECL	*European Current Law*
EEE	*Espaço Económico Europeu*
EFTA	*European Free Trade Association (Associação Europeia de Comércio Livre)*
EHRLR	*European Human Rights Law Review*
EJIL	*European Journal of International Law*
EJML	*European Journal of Migration and Law*
ELJ	*European Law Journal*
ELR	*European Law Review*
EPL	*European Public Law*
ERPL/REDP	*European Review of Public Law/Revue Européenne de Droit Public*
EU	*European Union*
EuConst	*European Constitutional Law Review*
EuGRZ	*Europäische Grundrechte – Zeitschrift*
EuR	*Europarecht*
Fordham Int'l L. J.	*Fordham International Law Journal*
GATT	*Acordo Geral sobre Tarifas e Comércio*
GG	*Grundgesetz*

GJ	*Gaceta juridica de la CE y de la competencia*
Harv. J. L. & Pub.Pol'y	*Harvard Journal of Law and Public Policy,*
ILJ	*Industrial Law Journal*
Int.	*Integration*
IYIL	*Italian Yearbook of International Law*
JOCE	*Jornal Oficial das Comunidades Europeias/Journal officiel des Communautés européennes*
JOUE	*Jornal Oficial da União Europeia*
JT – Dr. Eur.	*Journal des Tribunaux – Droit européen*
JZ	*Juristenzeitung*
Miami Int. & Comp. L. R.	*Miami International & Comparative Law Review*
Minn. L. Rev.	*Minnesota Law Review*
MJ	*Maastricht Journal of Comparative and International Law*
MLR	*Modern Law Review*
MNE	*Ministro dos Negócios Estrangeiros*
NATO	*Organização do Tratado do Atlântico Norte*
NJW	*Neue Juristische Wochenschrift*
NYIL	*Netherlands Yearbook of International Law*
OIT	*Organização Internacional do Trabalho*
OMC	*Organização Mundial do Comércio*
ONU	*Organização das Nações Unidas*
PCC	*Política Comercial Comum*
PCSD	*Política Comum de Segurança e Defesa*
PE	*Parlamento Europeu*
PECO's	*Países da Europa Central e Oriental*
PESC	*Política Externa e de Segurança Comum*
PL	*Public Law*
PSDC	*Política de Segurança e Defesa Comum*
RAE	*Revue des Affaires Européennes*
RCADI	*Recueil des Cours de l'Académie de Droit International*
RDP	*Revue de Droit Public et de la Science Politique en France et à l'Étranger*
RDUE	*Revue de Droit de l'Union européenne*
Rec.	*Recueil de Jurisprudence de la Cour de Justice des Communautés Europénnes*
Rec. Dalloz	*Recueil Dalloz*
REDC	*Revista Española de Derecho Constitucional*
Rev. Der. Com. Eur.	*Revista de Derecho Comunitario Europeo*
RFDUL	*Revista da Faculdade de Direito da Universidade de Lisboa*

RFDUNL	*Revista da Faculdade de Direito da Universidade Nova de Lisboa*
Riv. Dir. Eur.	*Rivista di Diritto Europeo*
Riv. Ital. Dir. Pub. Com.	*Revista Italiana di Diritto Pubblico Comunitario*
RMC	*Revue du Marché Commun*
RMCUE	*Revue du Marché Commun et de l'Union Européenne*
RMUE	*Revue du Marché Unique Européen*
RTDE	*Revue Trimestrielle de Droit européen*
RTDH	*Revue Trimestrielle des Droits de l'homme*
RUDH	*Revue universelle des droits de l'homme*
SEAE	*Serviço Europeu de Ação Externa*
STEUA	*Supremo Tribunal dos Estados Unidos da América*
TCE	*Tratado institutivo da Comunidade Europeia*
TCECA	*Tratado institutivo da Comunidade Europeia do Carvão e do Aço*
TCEE	*Tratado institutivo da Comunidade Económica Europeia*
TCEEA	*Tratado institutivo da Comunidade Europeia da Energia Atómica*
TECE	*Tratado que estabelece uma Constituição para a Europa*
TEDH	*Tribunal Europeu dos Direitos do Homem*
TEU	*Treaty on European Union*
TFEU	*Treaty on Functioning of the European Union*
TFUE	*Tratado sobre o Funcionamento da União Europeia*
TG	*Tribunal Geral*
TIJ	*Tribunal Internacional de Justiça*
Tilburg Foreign L. Rev.	*Tilburg Foreign Law Review*
TJ	*Tribunal de Justiça*
TJUE	*Tribunal de Justiça da União Europeia*
TL	*Tratado de Lisboa*
TPI	*Tribunal de Primeira Instância*
TUE	*Tratado da União Europeia*
UE	*União Europeia*
UEM	*União Económica e Monetária*
VerfBlog	*Verfassungsblog*
Vol.	*Volume*
YEL	*Yearbook of European Law*
ZaöRV	*Zeitschrift für ausländisches öffentliches Recht und Völkerrecht*
ZeuS	*Zeitschrift für Europarechtliche Studien*

NOTA PRÉVIA

O presente livro, intitulado ***Estudos de Direito Internacional e da União Europeia – Essays on International and European Union Law****, reúne um conjunto de textos, em língua portuguesa e inglesa, publicados, em obras coletivas, revistas jurídicas, comentários e enciclopédias, nos últimos três anos, em Portugal e no estrangeiro. Incluem-se igualmente alguns estudos ainda inéditos, mas em vias de publicação.*

Apesar de a maior parte dos escritos terem sido elaborados em resposta a solicitações que nos foram sendo feitas, todos obedecem a um mesmo fio condutor, qual seja o de colocar o ser humano no centro das preocupações e das discussões que atualmente se travam no seio do direito internacional e do direito da União Europeia.

Tendo em conta que uma das principais missões do professor universitário consiste na divulgação dos resultados da sua investigação perante a comunidade científica, os estudantes e a sociedade civil, o objetivo primeiro desta obra é tornar acessíveis artigos que se encontram dispersos.

O livro divide-se em quatro partes.

A primeira parte trata de Questões constitucionais e institucionais da União Europeia*, iniciando-se com um dos temas mais prementes da atualidade, ou seja, o impacto constitucional do Brexit na União Europeia e nos seus Tratados fundacionais. Em seguida, prossegue com um tópico que nos tem acompanhado, desde os nossos primeiros passos na investigação, qual seja o da revisão dos Tratados e o alargamento de poderes dos órgãos da União Europeia. A finalizar, incluem-se dois textos sobre questões institucionais.*

A segunda parte incide sobre A pessoa humana no direito da União Europeia*, iniciando-se com o princípio da dignidade da pessoa humana. Seguidamente, analisa-se o impacto, em Portugal, da cidadania da União Europeia trinta anos* *depois da adesão, e, por último, procede-se a um comentário das decisões do TJUE nos casos Achbita e Bougnaoui no domínio da não discriminação em função da religião no emprego.*

A terceira parte debruça-se sobre O migrante, o refugiado e o trabalhador no direito internacional, *começando por estudar a igualdade e a não discriminação como fundamento dos direitos dos migrantes e dos refugiados no direito internacional, continuando com as relações que se estabelecem entre a Organização Internacional do Trabalho e a União Europeia em prol dos direitos dos trabalhadores.*

Finalmente, a quarta parte intitula-se A Convenção Europeia dos Direitos do Homem *e contém uma análise crítica do Parecer 2/13 do Tribunal de Justiça da União Europeia relativo à adesão da União à CEDH na ótica da proteção multinível dos direitos fundamentais assim como um estudo acerca do Tribunal Europeu dos Direitos do Homem.*

Antes de terminar, gostaríamos de expressar o nosso mais veemente desejo de que esta obra mais do que estimular o estudo das matérias que trata, contribua para aprofundar a discussão de temas tão atuais como o Brexit, os direitos dos migrantes, dos refugiados e dos trabalhadores no direito internacional, a cidadania e a não discriminação em função de todas as categorias suspeitas.

Parte I

Questões Constitucionais e Institucionais da União Europeia

I

The Impact of Brexit on the EU's Constitutional Nature and on its Founding Treaties[*]

1. Introduction

The formal inclusion of a withdrawal clause – Article 50 of the Treaty on the European Union (TEU)[1] – into the TEU through the Treaty of Lisbon opened a Pandora's box with consequences that no one predicted. As the negotiations of Brexit,[2] the draft agreement that ensued,[3] and its rejection

[*] This article is the written version of the Author's presentation in the first section of the annual reunion of the European Public Law Group in Legraina last September. The Author warmly thanks the comments and suggestions of the participants in that conference. However, the opinions expressed are only her own.

[1] According to Article 50 TEU, any Member State may decide to withdraw from the Union in accordance with its own constitutional requirements. The Member State, which decides to leave the Union, shall notify the intention of withdrawal to the European Council. The Union shall negotiate and conclude an agreement with that Member State, which shall be concluded on behalf of the Union by the Council, by a qualified majority with the consent of the European Parliament;
The Treaties shall cease to apply to the State in question from the date of entry into force of the withdrawal agreement or, failing that, two years after the notification above referred, unless the European Council, in agreement with the Member State concerned, unanimously decides to extend this period.
If a State, which has withdrawn from the Union, asks to rejoin, its request shall be subject to the accession procedure.

[2] The documents related to the negotiations of Brexit are available at the website https://europa.eu/newsroom/highlights/special-coverage/brexit_en

[3] Draft Agreement on the withdrawal of the United Kingdom of Great Britain and Northern Ireland from the European Union and the European Atomic Energy Community, as agreed

by the House of Commons[4] have shown, it is rather difficult to overcome the obstacles that came out of that opened box.

Currently, we are in a deadlock. Nobody knows what will happen in the near future: another referendum in the UK? The renegotiation of the draft agreement? Another agreement? An extension of the 29 March 2019 deadline? An exit without an agreement? All scenarios are possible and none of them is entirely desirable.

The withdrawal of a Member State from the European Union (EU) raises so many constitutional, legal, political, and financial questions that it is impossible to address all of them within the scope of a review's article. As a result, the subject of our contribution is confined to the impact of Brexit on the constitutional nature of the EU and on its Founding Treaties.

Before proceeding, we ought to make a declaration of interest – the choice of this topic is a rather selfish option. On the one hand, it does not depend on the outcome of the current Brexit process, which is by now rather uncertain, and, on the other hand, it presupposes the acceptance of the *constitutionalism beyond the State* theory, which has been one of the author's research areas during the last twenty years.

Given the divergent understandings of this theory, it is important to begin by explaining our point of departure and by addressing the question of whether Article 50 TEU does fall within the Constitutional Law of the EU (section 2). Furthermore, we study the impact of Brexit on the EU's constitutional law (section 3). Finally, we raise the question of whether Brexit may contribute to enhance the constitutional nature of the EU and of its constitutional law (section 4).

at negotiators' level on 14 November 2018, available at https://ec.europa.eu/commission/files/draft-agreement-withdrawal-united-kingdom-great-britain-and-northern-ireland-european-union-and-european-atomic-energy-community-agreed-negotiators-level-14-november-2018_en

[4] The Draft Withdrawal Agreement was rejected at 15 January 2019.

2. Declaration of interest: the *constitutionalism beyond the State* theory

2.1. General remarks

As mentioned above, our point of departure is the *constitutionalism beyond the state* theory, which appears nonsensical for those still faithful to state constitutionalism.[5] For them, Article 50 TEU and Brexit are the expression of States' sovereignty – full stop.

By contrast, for those who sustain that the current constitutionalism does not identify itself – nor does it operate – exclusively within the territorial scope of the State, due to the existence of political decision centers located outside of, and on a wider scale than the State – be those global or regional –, Article 50 TEU and Brexit need to be explained within the scope of a constitutional theory.

As a matter of fact, constitutionalism currently has as many levels as the centers of exercise of political power. These multiple and multilevel centers overlap and compete with the State.

The most evident example of *constitutionalism beyond the State* undoubtedly includes the former European Communities – currently the European Union – and their respective treaties.

2.2. EU Constitutional Law and the EU's Constitutional Nature

Currently, the European Union is much more than an international organization. There is no other international organization in the world with a parliament elected by its citizens, as is the case with the European Union. There is no supranational assembly with as many powers as the European Parliament. There is no international organization whose laws affect its citizens so profoundly and in such a wide array of areas. There is no international organization whose rules directly apply to citizens in such a large scale.

Having said that, it is important to note that, while the EU is much more than an international organization, it is also less than a State. It is some sort of a new compound entity, created by its Member States, whose authority derives, firstly, from them and, secondly, from its citizens. We

[5] See René Barents, "The Fallacy of Multilevel Constitutionalism", in Matej Avbelj/Jan Komárek (eds), *Constitutional Pluralism in the European Union and Beyond* (2012) 153 et seq.

have sustained for more than twenty years that the European Union is a union of States and citizens.[6]

The European Union does not intend to – and it actually cannot – eliminate the authority of its Member States. By contrast, it is based on the ideas of cooperation, mutual influence and interdependence.[7]

In short, the European Union is a multilevel constitutional[8] and political entity[9].

The current EU Founding Treaties, and the former EC Founding Treaties, or, at least, the basic provisions thereof, are of a substantially constitutional nature due to the following reasons:

- They contain a set of rules and principles concerning, *inter alia*, the aims of the Union, which in many aspects coincide with the aims of the State, its values, which include, among others, human dignity, the rule of law, democracy and the respect for human rights – in short, the values of the European democracies.
- The human being plays a determinant role in the Union, either as citizen or as holder of fundamental rights directly derived from EU law provisions.
- The institutional system represents the Member States and the citizens and seeks a balance between all of the institutions and powers.
- The Court of Justice is the guarantor of the Union's law, including fundamental rights.
- The relationship between the European Union's law and the internal law of Member States is based on the principles of primacy, direct effect and direct applicability, which contribute to place the human being within the center of the European project, as well as

[6] See one of our latest books, Ana Maria Guerra Martins, *Manual de Direito da União Europeia* (2017) 229 et seq.

[7] See Ingolf Pernice, "The Treaty of Lisbon: Multilevel Constitutionalism in Action", *The Columbia Journal of European Law* 15 (2009) 383.

[8] On our perspective of the insertion of the European Union in the multilevel constitutional theory see Ana Maria Guerra Martins, "Opinion 2/13 of the Court of Justice in the Context of Multilevel Protection of Fundamental Rights and Multilevel Constitutionalism" *Zeitschrift für öffentliches Recht/Journal of Public Law* (2016), 33 et seq.

[9] Since 2000 we have sustained that the EU is a new form of aggregation of political power and ever since we have not changed our opinion. See Ana Maria Guerra Martins, *A natureza jurídica da revisão do Tratado da União Europeia* (2000) 303 et seq.

to enhance the interaction and interdependence between both legal dimensions.

As a result, the current European constitutionalism can no longer be solely anchored in the State, but shall also include the EU and its treaties. Concerning the field of fundamental rights, it is also and, at least partially, anchored in the Council of Europe, particularly in the European Convention on Human Rights (ECHR).

The corpus of EU law order shall therefore be included in the purview of a broader constitutional theory.

Although this study is not the most adequate forum to elaborate on that theory, new concepts, including transnational constitutionalism,[10] constitutional pluralism,[11] multilevel constitutionalism,[12] or, more recen-

[10] See Ana Maria Guerra Martins, "Opinion 2/13 of the Court of Justice in the Context of Multilevel Protection of Fundamental Rights and Multilevel Constitutionalism" 32 et seq; Marcelo Neves, *Transconstitucionalismo* (2009) 83 et seq; Ana Maria Guerra Martins, *A natureza jurídica da revisão do Tratado da União Europeia* (2000) 303 et seq; Idem, *Curso de Direito Constitucional da União Europeia* (2004) 119 et seq; Idem, *A igualdade e a não discriminação dos nacionais de Estados terceiros legalmente residentes na União Europeia – Da origem na integração económica ao fundamento na dignidade do ser humano* (2010) 22 and 23; Idem, *Manual de Direito da União Europeia* 229 et seq.

[11] For further reading on constitutional pluralism, see Matej Avbelj/Jan Komárek (eds), *Constitutional Pluralism in the European Union and Beyond* (2012); J. H. H. Weiler, "Prologue: global and pluralist constitutionalism – some doubts", in Gráinne de Búrca/J. H. H. Weiler, *The Worlds of European Constitutionalism* (2012) 8 et seq; Daniel Halberstam, "Local, global and plural constitutionalism: Europe meets the world", in Gráinne de Búrca/J. H. H. Weiler, *The Worlds of European Constitutionalism* (2012) 150 et seq; Nico Krisch, "The case for pluralism in postnational law", in Gráinne de Búrca/J. H. H. Weiler, *The Worlds of European Constitutionalism* (2012) 203 et seq; Miguel Poiares Maduro, *A Constituição Plural – Constitucionalismo e União Europeia* (2006) 15 et seq.

[12] On multilevel constitutionalism see, above all, Ingolf Pernice, "Multilevel Constitutionalism and the Crisis of Democracy in Europe", *European Constitutional Law Review* 11 (2015) 541 et seq; Idem, "The Treaty of Lisbon: Multilevel Constitutionalism in Action" 349–407; Idem, "Multilevel Constitutionalism in the European Union", *European Law Review* 27 (2002) 511–529; Idem, Multilevel Constitutionalism and the Treaty of Amsterdam: European Constitution-Making Revisited?, *Common Market Law Review* 36 (1999) 707 et seq.

tly, global constitutionalism,[13] have emerged in the last decades and have rapidly circulated in the post-Westphalian world.

In spite of the lack of consensus regarding the definition and scope of these new concepts, which we are not going to discuss further in this study, it is important to underline that, currently, in Europe, a complete constitutional theory shall include different constitutional systems. Departing from the constitutional law of the Member States of the EU and also of the Council of Europe's Member States, the inclusion of, at least, part of European Union law and part of the law of the European Convention on Human Rights is crucial, since these three levels of constitutionalism are in permanent interdependency and are reciprocal influential parts of one single body.[14]

The correlation between national and European law (including the EU and the ECHR law) from the perspective of both States and citizens means that European constitutionalism has an impact both in the States and in their citizens, and that the Member States' constitutional law also has an impact in the EU and in the Council of Europe, namely in the ECHR.

From this reciprocal impact comes a new set of convergent and transnational values, rules and principles, especially in the domains of fundamental rights and rule of law, which constitute the core of European constitutionalism.

In the context of European constitutional law, the EU plays a very significant role as it is "an instrument of the states and their peoples for meeting new challenges and for achieving certain common political goals".[15]

Before finalizing this section, one has to point out that admitting the European constitutionalism theory does not mean asserting that the EU has a constitution in a formal and positivist meaning. Currently, it remains problematic to identify one or more formal documents that codify the European Union's constitutional law, as well as a constitutional power

[13] On global constitutionalism see, above all, Neil Walker, "Constitutionalism and Pluralism in Global Context", in Matej Avbelj/Jan Komárek (eds), *Constitutional Pluralism in the European Union and Beyond* (2012) 17 et seq.

[14] For further reading see Ana Maria Guerra Martins, *Manual de Direito da União Europeia* 48 et seq. as well as the bibliography quoted therein.

[15] Ingolf Pernice, "The Treaty of Lisbon: Multilevel constitutionalism in action" 376.

emerging from a *demos*. In addition, the potential superiority of the European Constitution is not anchored on a hierarchy.

However, as many scholars pointed out,[16] the functional approach of what is understood by a Constitution includes the creation of institutions and the attribution of competences and powers to them on the basis of the principle of institutional balance, the determination of the fundamental objectives, principles and orientation of the institutions (in substantive and value-related dimensions such as the rule of law, democracy and social orientation) and the determination of certain values, in particular fundamental rights.[17]

All these functions of constitutional law have already been projected onto the supranational level where the EU has taken over the many spheres previously retained for the nation state.[18]

In the scope of this study, we will not dive into this topic. In order to proceed, the relevant question is whether Article 50 TEU is compatible with the constitutional approach of the EU and its law or not.

3. Article 50 TEU and EU Constitutional Law

Currently, the interpretation of Article 50 TEU raises a wide array of doubts and questions,[19] which we have already partially addressed in an earlier book.[20] Therefore, we will refrain from conducting an extensive

[16] See, above all, Rainer Arnold, "European Constitutional Law", in Nadezda Siskova, *The Process of Constitutionalisation of the EU and Related Issues* (2008) 42 et seq. Rainer Arnold, "The Emergence of a European Constitutional Law", vol. 11.3 *Electronic Journal of Comparative Law*, (December 2007).

[17] Rainer Arnold, "European Constitutional Law", 46.

[18] Rainer Arnold, "The Emergence of a European Constitutional Law".

[19] For further reading see "Editorial Comments" *Common Market Law Review* (2016) 1491 et seq; Christophe Hillion, "Le retrait de l'Union européenne – une analyse juridique" *Revue trimestrielle de droit européen* (2016) 719 et seq; Paul Craig, "The Process: Brexit and the Anatomy of Article 50", in Federico Fabbrini (ed.), *The Law & Politics of Brexit* (2017) 49 et seq; Catherine Barnard, "Law and Brexit", *Oxford Review of Economic Policy* (2017) S4 et seq; Dora Kostakopoulou, "Brexit, Voice and Loyalty: Reflections on Article 50 TEU", *European Law Review* (2016) 484 et seq; Tamara Capeta, "Brexit and the EU Constitutional Order: A three Act Tragedy" *Croatian Yearbook of European Law and Policy* (2016) 1 et seq.

[20] Ana Maria Guerra Martins, *Os desafios contemporâneos à ação externa da União Europeia – Lições de Direito Internacional Público II* (2018) 427 et seq.

and profound analysis of Article 50 TEU. In the present study, we are only interested in examining whether Article 50 TEU does fall within the category of EU constitutional law. In order to achieve this goal, it is important to investigate the background of Article 50 TEU.

3.1. The background of Article 50 TEU

3.1.1. The discussion on a Member State's withdrawal before the Treaty of Lisbon

The topic of the withdrawal of a Member State from the European Communities has been studied by EU law scholarship since the very beginning of the European integration process.

Whereas, for one doctrinal strand, withdrawing from the European Communities was similar to withdrawing from another international organization or from any international treaty,[21] for other strand, the former European Communities and the current European Union as well as their constitutive Treaties have characteristics that set them apart from all other international organizations and from all international treaties. Therefore, the Member States seeking to withdraw from the EU would face particular and relevant obstacles. This second strand argued that the unlimited duration of the Treaties, the absence of an explicit provision dealing with the withdrawal process, the autonomy of the European Communities and of European Union law, the legal nature of the Founding Treaties, the legal system created by the Treaties, and the rights that the Treaties conferred to citizens, which ought not be suddenly jeopardized by any Member State, constituted the main obstacles against Member States' withdrawal right. As such, this group of scholars concluded that the potential withdrawal of a Member State from the European Union would be unlawful.[22]

[21] Peter M. Huber, "Der Staatenverbund der Europäischen Union" in Jörn Ipsen et al. (dir.), *Verfassungsrecht im Wandel* (1995) 355.

[22] See Theodor Schilling, "Treaty and Constitution. A Comparative Analysis of an Uneasy Relationship" *Maastricht Journal of European and Comparative Law* (1996) 62; Ulrich Everling, "Zur Stellung der Mitgliedstaaten der Europäischen Union als "Herren der Verträge" in Ulrich Beyerlin et al., *Recht zwischen Umbruch und Bewahrung, Festschrift für Rudolf Bernhard*t (1995) 1175; Jean-Victor Louis, *L'ordre juridique communautaire*, 6th ed. (1993) 90; Michel Wael-

By contrast, the supporters of the exit's lawfulness counter argued that the International Law of the Treaties, namely the *clausula rebus sic stantibus*, ought to be applied to the EC Treaties.

Although this discussion is somewhat outdated, decades and decades of political and legal integration that have resulted in the interconnection and interaction of national and European Union laws, involving governments, undertakings and citizens, cannot be forgotten and erased overnight.[23] With or without Article 50 TEU, the withdrawal of a Member State from the EU should have always been negotiated with the European Union and with the remaining Member States. That means that, had this provision never been introduced into the TEU, the withdrawal would still have required negotiations, which would always have had a constitutional impact on the EU.

3.1.2. The introduction of a withdrawal clause in the TECE

The origins of Article 50 TEU go back to the Treaty Establishing a Constitution for Europe (TECE), which incorporated the right of withdrawal in its Article I-60.

As it is well known, the Convention on the Future of Europe sought to create a constitutional framework for the governance of the Union and to leave the international framework definitively behind.[24] Article I-60 of the TECE was introduced with the aim of compensating the opponents of the constitutional perspective of the Treaties.

The writing of that provision, as set out in the Convention on the Future of Europe, has significantly changed from the first to the last ver-

broeck, "Art 240", in *Commentaire Megret. Le droit de la CEE*, vol. 15 (1987) 564; Ulrich Everling, "Sind die EG-Mitgliedstaaten der Europäischen Gemeinschaft noch Herren der Verträge?", *Festschrift für Hermann Mosler* (1983) 183; J. A. Hill, "The European Economic Community: the Right of Member State Withdrawal", *Georgia Journal of International and Comparative Law* (1982) 355, maxime 357; Manfred Zuleeg, "Der Bestand der Europäischen Gemeinschaft", in *Das Europa der zweiten Generation, Gedächtnisschrift für Christoph Sasse* (1981) 62.

[23] See Ramses A. Wessel, "You Can Check Out Any Time you Like, But Can You Really Leave?", *International Organizations Law Review* (2016) 197.

[24] On the withdrawal within the scope of the TECE, see Jean-Victor Louis, "Union Membership: Accession, Suspension of Membership Rights and Unilateral Withdrawal. Some Reflections", in Ingolf Pernice/Jiri Zemanek (eds.) *A Constitution for Europe: The IGC, the Ratification Process and Beyond* (2005) 229 et seq.

sion[25], having each amendment added more complexity. This provision was incorporated into the Treaty of Lisbon without any relevant discussion.

From a purely theoretical point of view, Article 50 TEU cannot be considered as an element that contributes to enhance European constitutionalism. On the contrary, it should be regarded as a concession to intergovernmentalism. In fact, it is not common for a constitution to provide for the rupture of the entity that it is supposed to constitute[26].

Having said that, it is important to underline that, in spite of the intergovernmental essence of the provision, once triggered, the withdrawal of a Member State from the EU certainly has an impact on European constitutionalism.

In other words, the departure of a Member State from the EU necessarily impacts the abovementioned three levels of European constitutionalism (the constitutional law of the Member State that withdraws, the constitutional law of the remaining Member States, and the constitutional law of the EU).

The constitutional impact of Brexit on the United Kingdom has already been the subject of brilliant analyses. Therefore, we simply refer the reader to them.[27] Notwithstanding, given the high level of political and economic integration achieved by the European Union, the impact on the constitutional law of the State that leaves the EU will, at least, be similar

[25] V. Piet Eeckhout/Eleni Frantziou, "Brexit and Article 50 TEU: A Constitutionalist Reading", *UCL European Institute, Working Paper,* December 2016, 5-6; 12-13.

[26] To the extent of our knowledge, the sole constitution in the world that expressly rules on secession is the one of the Federal Democratic Republic of Ethiopia. Article 39 on the Rights of Nations, Nationalities, and Peoples reads:
"1. Every Nation, Nationality and People in Ethiopia has an unconditional right to self-determination, including the right to secession."

[27] See Paul Craig, "Miller, Structural Constitutional Review and the Limits of Prerogative Power" (April 19, 2017), *Oxford Legal Studies Research Paper* No. 32/2017. Available at SSRN: https://ssrn.com/abstract=2955011, published in *Public Law* (2017) 48-72; Michael Dougan, "Brexit: The relationship between the UK Parliament and the UK Government", in Michael Dougan (ed.), *The UK after Brexit – Legal and Policy Challenges* (2017) 15 et seq.; Jo Hunt, Devolution, in Michael Dougan (ed.), *The UK after Brexit – Legal and Policy Challenges* (2017) 35 et seq; Michel Dougan, The "Brexit" threat to the Northern Irish Border: Clarifying the Constitutional Framework, in Michael Dougan (ed.), *The UK after Brexit – Legal and Policy Challenges* (2017) 53 et seq; and the contribution of Professor Brewer-Carias in *ERPL/RDPE,* 2019 (forthcoming).

to the one of the accession to the Union. However, the former is more unpredictable, since the constitutions of Member States do not contain any provisions on this issue. By contrast, most part of the Member States' constitutions comprise a set of provisions on the participation of the State into the European Union, on the accession to the European Union, on the reception of European Union law into domestic law.[28] However, these provisions are useless – or almost useless – when it comes to withdrawing from the European Union.

The constitutional impact of the withdrawal of a Member State on the remaining Member States is not so obvious. Nevertheless, the withdrawal of a Member State may well provoke mutations in the content of the constitutions of the remaining Member States.

To provide some examples, the domestic constitutional provisions concerning the European citizenship, the European Union, the principle of supremacy of EU law – provided that they exist – will acquire another meaning. They no longer include the Member State that withdraws, which means that the territory of the Union is restricted, the scope of application of the Treaties is modified, European citizenship is reduced to the nationals of 27 Member States, and so on.

In our opinion, the impact of Brexit on the constitutional law of the remaining States deserves more attention than it has been dedicated to this issue up to now. Due to space limitation, we need to proceed and focus on the impact of the withdrawal of the UK on EU Constitutional Law.

3.2. Impact of Brexit on the constitutional law of the EU

3.2.1. The rhetoric of sovereignty and democracy

Constitutionally speaking, Brexit was based on the rhetoric of state sovereignty and democracy. "Taking back control" over laws, borders, democracy, and money means nothing but "taking back control" over the most significant issues of the state sovereignty and its constitutional system. Putting this decision in the hands of the people through the referendum

[28] On the impact of European integration onto the constitutions of the Member States see, above all, Stefan Griller *et al* (eds), *National Constitutions and EU Integration* (2019) to be published. This book comprises a chapter on Portugal from the Author of the current study.

apparently legitimates Brexit according to the purest standards of state's constitutionalism. And this was the UK narrative before and after the referendum of 23 June 2016.

Notwithstanding, the rhetoric of sovereignty and democracy does not take many factors into account. Firstly, the effects of the withdrawal of a Member State are not restricted to the Member State that leaves the EU, but they are also felt in the other Member States. That means the sovereignty of the remaining Member States is also threatened. Secondly, it is true that the referendum is one means to express the will of the people, but it is not the sole legitimate tool in the context of the exercise of democracy. To put it bluntly, sometimes it is not the most accurate one, especially when nobody seriously considered the consequences of a negative result. Many scholars, including in the UK, criticized the political decision of launching a referendum on the exit of the EU. For instance, Jo Shaw drew attention to the particularities of the UK as a Union state and to the fact that some voices were not heard in the referendum vote and that those voices were also neglected during the debate that preceded the referendum[29] .

Moreover, the rhetoric of sovereignty and democracy relating to the Member States of the EU has to be rethought.

In the perspective of the remaining Member States, the withdrawal may be conceived as an "authoritarian" decision, since their citizens will lose certain rights – for instance, the ones inherent to EU citizenship – without having been consulted.[30]

In addition, the old notion of sovereignty, conceived by *Jean Bodin*[31] in the sixteenth century, is no longer valuable. The idea of sovereignty was – as many other ideas – a product of a certain time. As it is well known, it arose in a very particular environment and enjoyed certain unrepeatable circumstances. The survival of the State depended on the elimination of all other powers. Both dimensions of sovereignty – internal and external

[29] V. Jo Shaw, "The quintessentially democratic act? Democracy, political community and citizenship in and after the UK's referendum of June 2016" *Journal of European Integration* (2017) 12.

[30] For those who reject the constitutional approach of the EU, this may be regarded as a confirmation of their thesis – that the sovereignty of the State prevails. However, in our opinion, this is a rather limited perspective.

[31] J. Bodin, *De Republica* (1576).

– were born and developed within the scope of the State,[32] whose affirmation, as a political entity, required a strong internal and external authority.

The State as an institution needed to maintain a supreme governing authority over a defined territory, which is to be differentiated both from its constituent people and its office holders. The sovereignty was, in the internal perspective, the absolute and indivisible authority of the ruling power.[33] This theory was meant to serve a practical political purpose.[34]

The external dimension of the sovereignty, which includes the capacity of acting within the international community on an equal footing with other States, arose later in the nineteenth century.

Currently, the notion of sovereignty is obsolete or, at the very least, needs to be adapted to the new challenges of the world. The European integration process and global governance have proved that the State is not the only "master" of sovereignty. Sovereignty exists beyond the State[35]. Ideas, such as "pooled sovereignty", "shared sovereignty"[36], or "divided sovereignty" have been theorized by EU law scholarship since the very beginning of the European integration process. In other words, the change of circumstances has modified the meaning of sovereignty and has dragged the State's sovereignty to a less important place.

[32] On the concept of sovereignty and its evolution see Daniel Philpott, "Ideas and Evolution of Sovereignty", Sohail H. Hashimi (ed.), *State Sovereignty: Change and Persistence in International Relations* (1997) 15 et seq; Bruno de Witte, "Sovereignty and European Integration: the Weight of Legal Tradition", *Maastricht Journal of European and Comparative Law* (1995) 145 et seq; Joseph A. Camilleri/Jim Falk, *The End of Sovereignty? The Politics of a Schrinking and Fragmenting World* (1992) 11-68; R. P. Anand, *Sovereignty Equality of States in International Law,* Recueil des Cours de l'Académie de Droit International, t. 197 (1986) II 17-46.

[33] Martin Loughlin, "The erosion of sovereignty", *Netherlands Journal of Legal Philosophy* (2016) 58.

[34] Tina Oršolič Dalessio, "The issue of sovereignty in an ever closer union", *Cypriot Yearbook of European Law and Politics* (2014) 69.

[35] See, above all, Neil MaCcormick, "Beyond the Sovereign State", *Modern Law Review* (1993) 1-18

[36] Stefan Oeter, "Souveränität und Legitimation staatlicher Herrschaft im europäischen Mehrebenesystem", in Astrid Epiney *et al, Direkte Demokratie und Europäische Union. Démocratie directe et Union européenne* (1998) 29 et seq; *Idem,* «Souveränität und Demokratie als Probleme in der "Verfassungsentwicklung" der Europäischen Union», *Zeitschrift für ausländisches and öffenliches Recht und Völkerrecht* (1995) 666 et seq.

The withdrawal of a Member State from the Union is neither a pure expression of the sovereignty of the leaving State nor of all Member States. Firstly, in its origins, Article 50 TUE itself is an expression of a common exercise of individual national sovereignties of the EU Member States. Secondly, unless the Member State leaves without any agreement, the outcome of the negotiations on the basis of Article 50 TEU is far from being an expression of the sovereignty of the States. According to Article 50 TEU, the withdrawal agreement must be concluded on behalf of the Union by the Council, acting through a qualified majority that represents at least 72% of the members of the Council representing the participating Member States, comprising at least 65 % of the population of these States, after obtaining the consent of the European Parliament (Articles 50 (2) TEU, 218 (3) and 238 (3) (b) TFEU). That means the adoption of the withdrawal agreement by the Council, acting through a qualified majority, is completely beyond any conceptualization based on sovereignty, unless we accept that the EU is also a sovereign entity, which, in our opinion, is rather disputable. As such, the withdrawal agreement is concluded between the EU (not by the Member States) and the exiting's Member State.

To sum up, the narrative of sovereignty and democracy is not the most accurate to explain the Brexit process within the framework of the EU.

3.2.2. Inevitable changes in EU constitutional law as a result of Brexit

Irrespective of the legitimacy of Brexit, it is rather difficult to predict all consequences of the departure of a Member State within the framework of EU constitutional law.

One can easily anticipate certain inevitable changes irrespective of whether there is an agreement between both parties in accordance with Article 50 TEU or not. In the latter case, the impact is even expected to be more significant.

For the time being, it is impossible to make any prognosis concerning this issue. On 15 January 2019, the House of Commons rejected the Draft Agreement on the Withdrawal of the United Kingdom of Great Britain and Northern Ireland from the European Union and the European Atomic Energy Community, as agreed between the negotiating parties on 14 November 2018. Therefore, the risk of a disorganized and no-deal Brexit has never been higher, since 29 March 2019 is the deadline for the conclusion of the negotiations.

In order to understand the impact of Brexit within the scope of EU constitutional law, one has also to take into consideration the role that the UK has been playing in the EU since its accession.

The impact of Brexit would definitely be more significant if the UK was one of the engines of the integration process. On the contrary, the UK has never been an enthusiast of the "constitutionalization" of the EU – the UK was always an outsider or a partial outsider when it comes to the most significant EU constitutional developments. The UK opted out from the European Monetary Union, and from the euro, and partially opted out from the Area of Freedom, Security and Justice. Consequently, the UK has not taken part in the most important decisions of the last decade, which concerned the public debt, the euro, and the migration crisis.

Furthermore, the UK has always pushed back against the advances that could represent a deepening of integration. Even in crucial constitutional matters, such as the Charter of Fundamental Rights of the EU, and the security and defence policy, the UK always had a foot in and another one out.

Immediately before Brexit, while some Member States sought to save the EU from the abysm, the United Kingdom was only concerned about the negotiation of an agreement with the Union that would give it an even more special status within the Union.[37]

Having said that, one should not underestimate the constitutional impact of the UK withdrawal on the EU.

The departure of the UK from the Union will inevitably modify not only substantially, but also formally the constitution of the EU. The territorial scope of the Union, the institutional framework, and the EU objectives and policies will undoubtedly undergo significant changes. Other issues, such as the protection of fundamental rights, will apparently be less affected.

[37] See the Annex to the Conclusions of the European Council meeting of 18 and 19 February 2016 available at https://data.consilium.europa.eu/doc/document/ST-1-2016-INIT/en/pdf.

3.2.2.1. Constitutional impact of Brexit on the territorial clause

In relation to the territorial scope of the Treaties, which is set out in Article 52 TEU and Article 355 TFEU, both provisions will change after Brexit, once the United Kingdom is out of the EU.

Contrary to other provisions, Articles 52 TEU and 355 TFEU should be amended throughout the procedure of revision enshrined in Article 48 TEU. An eventual agreement concluded on the basis on Article 50 TEU is not sufficient to amend them, since that agreement is concluded between the EU and the exiting Member States and not between the Member States. Any international agreement concluded by the Union cannot modify the Founding Treaties. A source of EU primary law may only be modified by another source with the same value, unless the Treaties state otherwise, which is not the case.[38]

This is not similar to the accession of a Member State, because in this case the agreement is concluded between the Member States of the EU and the State acceding to the EU.

In short, Brexit will implicitly impact the Union's territory, which is one of the most relevant constitutional issues.

3.2.2.2. Constitutional Impact of Brexit on the EU's Institutional Framework

Another evident EU constitutional impact of the Brexit relates to the institutional system of the EU. It is obvious that the departure of a Member State will prompt formal modifications in most part of the institutions, organs and agencies, since the composition of all of them is, to some extent, based on a state criterion. Even in the EP, which is directly elected by the EU citizens, the state criterion plays a significant role.

More important than this are the substantial modifications. As it is well known, the bargain that occurs within the scope of the decision-making procedures is based on the preferences and interests of the Member States. The loss of one of them will necessarily determine that the inputs of that Member State are definitively lost and, as a consequence, the balance of powers within the EU institutions, organs and agencies will change.

[38] Federico Fabbrini, "Brexit and the EU Constitutional Reform", in Federico Fabbrini (ed.), *The Law & Politics of Brexit* (2017) 270.

Each Member State gives a different contribution to the common decision.[39]

Therefore, the withdrawal of a Member State will prompt new adjustments and new negotiating tactics. When the departing State is one of the biggest Member States, the impact on the institutional framework of the EU will be even more significant.

That means the withdrawal of the UK from the EU will entail profound institutional changes.

Starting with the EP, the decision of the European Council on the allocation of seats in the EP does not require the use of the revision procedure provided in Article 48 TEU. However, substantially, this decision has a quasi-constitutional value because it deals with crucial aspects of the functioning of the EU and, procedurally speaking, its approval is subject to a special legislative procedure rather similar to the revision procedure – it requires Member States' unanimity, EP involvement, and ratification by each Member State according to its respective constitutional rules. That means that the modification of this decision will compel Member States to engage in broad and complex bargaining.[40]

By contrast, the EU treaties provisions concerning the Commission, the European Council, the Council, and the Court of Justice may be applied to a Union of twenty-seven. That does not mean that these institutions will not suffer the impact of the departure of the UK. Differently, the Brexit negotiations have already led to some changes in the Union's institutional balance, such as the rules of the presidency of the Council. In addition, the European Commission regained the leading role in the Brexit's negotiations under the guidelines and the supervision of the European Council and its president. By contrast with former cases, the unity of the remaining Member States has been asserted since the very beginning of the negotiations under the political leadership of President Donald Tusk.

The rejection of the negotiation strategy of Theresa May, who demanded parallel discussions regarding the withdrawal and trade, illustrates the leadership of the Union in the Brexit's process. According to the

[39] See Uwe Puetter, "Brexit and EU Institutional Balance – How Member States and Institutions Adapt Decision-Making", in Federico Fabbrini (ed.), *The Law & Politics of Brexit* (2017) 250.

[40] Federico Fabbrini, "Brexit and the EU Constitutional Reform" 270.

President of the European Council, the negotiations should be informed by the following principles: minimization of disruption caused by UK withdrawal; securing agreement on the rights of EU citizens living in the UK; ensuring that the UK honors its financial commitments; and avoiding a hard border between Northern Ireland and Ireland. "These four issues are all part of the first phase of the negotiations. Once, and only once, we have achieved sufficient progress on the withdrawal, can we discuss the framework for our future relationship. Starting parallel talks on all issues at the same time, as suggested by some in the UK, will not happen."[41]

The EU's 27 leaders unanimously adopted the phased strategy in the European Council meeting of 29 April 2017.

From our point of view, this decision has a constitutional component and may well be regarded as a constitutional moment. Instead of contributing to divide Member States, Brexit aggregated them around a negotiating strategy that was proposed and supported by the European institutions.

Furthermore, voting in the Council will need to adapt to the departure of the UK. The procedural rules in the Council will suffer the impact of Brexit, as deliberations are based on a double majority (number of States and percentage of the population). The withdrawal of one of the most populous Member States will have consequences in the bargaining and in the balance of powers between the remaining Member States.

Finally, the European External Action Service (EEAS) and certain EU agencies, such as Europol, will lose important resources after the departure of the UK. In fact, the UK has been one of the major architects of Europol and has always played a very active role in its development and leadership.[42]

[41] Remarks by President Donald Tusk on the next steps following the UK notification, available at https://www.consilium.europa.eu/en/press/press-releases/2017/03/31/tusk-remarks--meeting-muscat-malta/

[42] On the impact of Brexit on the Europol see James Black et al, *Defence and Security after Brexit – Understanding the possible implications of the UK's Decision to leave the EU – Compendium Report* (Rand Europe, Cambridge, 2017) 121 et seq.; Deirdre Curtin, "Brexit and the EU Area of Freedom, Security and Justice – Bespoke Bits and Pieces", in Federico Fabbrini (ed.), *The Law & Politics of Brexit* 190.

3.2.2.3. Constitutional Impact of Brexit on the EU's objectives and policies

The impact of the departure of a Member State on the objectives of the Union, and on the EU's competences depends on the weight of the withdrawing Member State. Formally, everything may remain intact, but, substantially, there will be actual changes.

The prosecution of the aims of the Union always will be affected, because each Member State has its political priorities and interests and seeks to defend them inside the European Union. That means, for instance, that the departure of a Member State that usually supports environmental-friendly policies will certainly weaken this area. The departure of a Member State that usually opposes the enlargement of the Union's aims will certainly permit an extension of those aims.

Having said that, it is important to underline that prior to Brexit, the EU has already witnessed a prolonged period of disengagement of the UK with specific EU policies.[43] Therefore, the impact of Brexit will be lower than if the UK was one of the leaders of the integration process and will also depend on the degree of influence of the UK in a given policy.

When the UK does not participate in a certain EU policy, such as the monetary policy and the EMU, the impact of Brexit will be less important than in fields in which the UK has assumed a certain degree of leadership.[44] It is important to highlight that while, in general terms, there is no leadership of the UK in the integration process, there are, however, certain fields in which the UK plays a rather important role. This is the case of trade policy, external relations, and the creation and functioning of Europol. At least in these areas, the withdrawal of the UK will impact the EU's constitutional law.

In our opinion, the impact of Brexit will be much broader than this. Above all, the EU will lose a counterweight to the Paris-Berlin axis. Secondly, those expecting that Brexit will disentangle the Union from its major dilemmas and problems forget that said issues remain within the Union and need to be urgently solved. Thirdly, the withdrawal of the UK will

[43] Uwe Puetter, "Brexit and EU Institutional Balance" 249

[44] Uwe Puetter, "Brexit and EU Institutional Balance" 250 et seq.

cause a huge impact on budgetary matters, since the UK is a significant contributor to the EU budget. However, the constitutional impact, due to the financial framework structure of the Union, which is not fully in accordance with the principles of constitutionalism, will be less significant. Fourthly, although the UK is not the main supporter of the EU's Common Foreign and Security Policy (CFSP) and of the Common Security and Defense Policy (CSDP), these policies will hugely suffer the impact of Brexit, taking into account that the UK is the Member State that main financial contributor to security and defense and is also a Permanent Member of the UN Security Council.[45] According to Whitman, "... for the EU the loss of UK's diplomatic and military resources will diminish the collective capabilities at the disposal of EU foreign and defence policies".[46]

Conversely, other policies, including the social and employment policy, the health policy, and the consumer policy will lose one of its major opponents, which may catalyze further integration in these domains. A similar reasoning is applicable to the policy on fundamental rights. However, this issue merits an autonomous analysis in light of its constitutional relevance, which will be undertaken in the following subchapter.

Finally, it seems evident that the withdrawal of a Member State will necessarily entail changes to the Founding Treaties. That does not mean that the revision procedure of Article 48 TEU has to be triggered. Certain changes may be included in the withdrawal agreement itself – provided that it exists. Nevertheless, a reform of the Treaties according to Article 48 TEU is almost inevitable.

[45] On the impact of Brexit on the CFSP see Ramses A. Wessel/Adam Łazowski, "Legal Consequences of 'Brexit' for the Role of the EU and the UK in Global Affairs", Paper presented at the EUSA Conference, Panel 7A The Consequences of Brexit on Europe's role: Reinvigoration or Atrophy, Miami, 4-6 May 2017, available at file:///C:/Users/Ana%20Martins/Downloads/Wessel%20and%20Lazowski%20-%20Legal%20Consequences%20of%20Brexit%20-%20EUSA%20Miami%202017%20-%20Panel%207A.pdf; James Black *et al, Defence and Security after Brexit – Understanding the possible implications of the UK's decision to leave the EU – Compedium Report,* (2017) 25 et seq.

[46] Richard G. Whitman, "The UK and EU Foreign, Security and Defence Policy After Brexit: Integrated, Associated or Detached?", *National Institute Economic Review* 238 (2016) 44

From our viewpoint, the EU's competences will not change as a direct consequence of the withdrawal of a Member State. However, depending on the withdrawing Member State, it might be easier or more difficult to exercise some of said competences,[47] as well as to modify the Treaty in conformity with Article 48 TEU.

3.2.2.4. Constitutional Impact of Brexit on the EU Fundamental Rights and EU Citizenship

The risk that Brexit poses to the EU's constitutional law regarding fundamental rights and EU citizenship should not be underestimated.

From the perspective of the EU, the protection of fundamental rights belongs to the hard core of its constitutional law. Therefore, any attack to the *acquis* in this field shall be prevented.

This impact is not restricted to citizens of the Union or to citizens of the withdrawing Member State – on the contrary, it is much wider. As stated by Piet Eeckhout and Eleni Frantziou, "the withdrawal of a Member State from the European Union creates significant possibilities of regression in terms of fundamental rights, and of a panoply of other rights of persons and companies".[48]

It is possible to prevent the loss of EU citizenship rights[49] through the conclusion of an agreement between the withdrawing State and the EU in accordance with Article 50 TEU,[50] but there are certain fundamental

[47] The authors of the Clingendael Report argue that EU defence might well be one of the fields where the exit of the UK may be benefic. See Anne Bakker/Margriet Drent/Dick Zandee, *European Defence: how to engage the UK after Brexit?* (July 2017) 8.

[48] Piet Eeckhout/Eleni Frantziou, "Brexit and Article 50 TEU: A Constitutionalist Reading", *UCL European Institute Working Paper* (December 2016) 19.

[49] On the consequences of Brexit to the EU citizenship see Guayasén Marrero González," 'BREXIT' – Consequences for Citizenship of the Union and Residence Rights", 23 *Maastricht Journal of European and Comparative law* 5 (2016) 796-811; Oliver Garner, "After Brexit: Protecting European Citizens and Citizenship From Fragmentation", *EUI Working Paper LAW* (2016/22).

[50] The Draft Agreement on the withdrawal of the United Kingdom of Great Britain and Northern Ireland from the European Union and the European Atomic Energy Community, as agreed at negotiators' level on 14 November 2018, includes rules on the citizens' rights, but as this draft agreement was rejected by the House of Commons, it does not make any sense to elaborate on them in this study.

rights that are somewhat difficult to maintain, such as the right to access the Court of Justice of the European Union – either directly or through national courts by means of a reference in the context of a preliminary ruling –, as well as the fundamental rights acknowledged by the Charter, which are not part of the ECHR.[51]

The withdrawal of the UK means that the individual rights enshrined in the Treaties, including citizens' rights, and the right to an equal salary between men and women, the rights contained in the Charter of Fundamental Rights, including the economic and social rights, and the general principles of the EU, will not apply to the UK after 29 March 2019. Therefore, irrespective of the failure to conclude a general deal, it is absolutely necessary to reach an agreement on this issue in order to prevent an abrupt downgrading of EU citizens' rights.

However, the leaving of the UK also means that the Charter will be applied to other Member States without the constraints contained in Protocol No. 30 concerning the application of the Charter to the UK. If – as we argued in an earlier book[52] – this Protocol should be assessed as an obstacle to EU constitutionalism, the withdrawal of the UK may contribute to remove this obstacle.

Furthermore, the UK was one of the major opponents to the inclusion of economic and social rights in the Charter.[53] Consequently, the withdrawal of the UK may well allow a more flexible interpretation of those rights, contributing to minimize the difference between rights and principles (civil and political rights and social and economic rights).

Concerning the definition of EU citizenship, the UK has always opposed the residency criterion as a basis for obtaining EU citizenship, having remained always faithful to the criterion of nationality of a Member State. It is conceivable that the leaving of the UK may prompt certain changes in this domain.

With regard to the EU citizenship rights, the UK has always opposed the enlargement of that set of rights. The withdrawal of the UK may contribute to the extension of the citizens' rights.

[51] For instance, the most part of social rights.

[52] See Ana Maria Guerra Martins, *Manual de Direito da União Europeia* 2nd ed. (2017) 276.

[53] See Ana Maria Guerra Martins, "A Carta dos Direitos Fundamentais da União Europeia e os direitos sociais" *Direito e Justiça* (2001) 189-230.

Apart from the fundamental rights and the EU citizens' rights, the third-country nationals' rights may well suffer a positive impact of the UK's withdrawal, since this Member State has always had a rather restrictive approach to EU immigrants' rights.

The protection of fundamental rights also plays an important role in the EU's external relations (Article 21 TEU).[54] The EU and its Member States are bound by the fundamental rights enshrined in the Treaties and in the Charter when they act in an international environment. The EU has a human rights agenda that governs the agreements between the EU and third States.[55]

Taking into account that the UK plays an important role in the field of international relations and international diplomacy, after its exit, the EU will face more difficulties in imposing this agenda.

Having said that, we do not share the view that the leave of the UK does necessarily undermine the protection of fundamental rights in the EU. In our opinion, if there were no other Member States that traditionally create additional difficulties to the respect of the EU fundamental rights, such as Poland and Hungary, and other Member States where populism and nationalism have been increasing over the last years, such as Italy, the EU constitutional law relating to this area could even evolve after Brexit.

A final word to note that, depending on the existence of a withdrawal agreement – and it would be even worse without an agreement, as many

[54] On the role of fundamental rights within the scope of external relations, see Ana Maria Guerra Martins, *Os desafios contemporâneos à ação externa da União Europeia* 379 et seq.; Vivian Kube, "The European Union's External Human Rights Commitment: What is the Legal Value of Article 21 TEU?", *EUI Working Papers Law* 2016/10.

[55] On the human rights agenda of the EU see Jan Wouters/Marta Hermez, "EU Guidelines on Human Rights as a Foreign Policy Instrument: An Assessment", in Sara Poli (ed.), *Protecting Human Rights in the European Union's External Relations* (Cleer Papers 2016/5) 63 et seq; Samantha Velluti, "The Promotion and Integration of Human Rights in EU External Trade Relations", in Sara Poli (ed.), *Protecting Human Rights in the European Union's External Relations* (Cleer Papers 2016/5) 53 et seq.; Lorand Bartels, "A Model Human Rights Clause for the EU's International Trade Agreements", *German Institute for Human Rights* (2014); Francesca Martines, "Human Rights Clause in EU Agreements", in Sara Poli (ed.), *Protecting Human Rights in the European Union's External Relations* (Cleer Papers 2016/5) 37 et seq.

scholars[56] and institutions[57] have been stressing –, the protection of fundamental rights in the UK may well entail a retrocession. This topic is not, however, within the scope of the present study.

4. Can Brexit enhance the constitutional nature of EU Law?

After the referendum in the UK, one of the major fears in the EU arena was a potential domino effect.[58] In other words, Brexit could lead to the disintegration of the Union, since other Member States might want to follow the UK's example in a near future.

At that time, the increase in voting intentions in anti-European, populist, xenophobic and nationalist political parties in Austria, in the Netherlands, in France, and in Germany constituted a real threat. However, none of these political parties won the elections. As a result, "the fall of Europe" was not confirmed.

On the contrary, it seemed then that the Union had been strengthened by the election of Macron in France[59] and by the unity of the remaining Member States and European institutions throughout the Brexit negotiations, which was crucial for the constitutional future of the Union.

Some thought then that the final outcome of these negotiations would dictate the future of the Union. If the deal that the UK obtained was rather favorable for the UK, other Member States could be tempted to follow the same exit route.[60] If, in contrast, the UK obtained a deal as a "rule-taker"

[56] Colm O'Cinneide, "Brexit and human rights", Brexit: The International Legal Implications, Paper No. 16, February, 2018; Tobias Lock, "Human Rights Law in the UK After Brexit", *Edinburg School of Law Research Paper No. 2017/17*; Francie N. Berger, "Brexit and Human Rights: Implications for the Laws and People of the United Kingdom", in Jennifer A. Hillman/Gary Horlick (ed.), *Legal Implications of Brexit – Implications of the United Kingdom's Decision to withdraw from the European Union* (2017) 176 et seq.

[57] Caoilfhionn Gallagher QC/Angela Patrick/Katie O'Byrne, *Report on Human Rights Implications of UK Withdrawal From The EU – An Independent Legal Opinion Commissioned by The European United Left/Nordic Green Left* (Gue/Ngl), Group of The European Parliament, 2 March 2018.

[58] See Marlene Wind, "Brexit and Euroscepticism – Will "Leaving Europe" be Emulated Elsewhere?", in Federico Fabbrini (ed.), *The Law & Politics of Brexit* (2017) 221 et seq.

[59] Marlene Wind, "Brexit and Euroscepticism...", 223.

[60] See Marlene Wind, "Brexit and Euroscepticism...", 224-225.

without the "rule-making power", the temptation of other Member States to leave the Union would decrease significantly.[61]

In addition, the shock that Brexit has provoked could well, instead of causing a domino effect, turn into a reinvigoration of the EU project. Due to Brexit, different EU players – institutions, Member States, and individuals – became aware of the precariousness of the European integration project and, consequently, have more easily accepted the idea that the survival of the Union depends on the improvement and deepening of the Treaties.

Currently, for the first time in the history of the European integration process, everyone is aware that the threat of disintegration needs to be taken seriously. Therefore, the reform of the Treaties is on the table.

Moreover, it is conceivable that without the veto of the UK, it will be easier to modify the Treaties and to adopt secondary law on matters that still require unanimity. The bargaining that characterizes the negotiation of decision within the EU will certainly be easier when it comes to moving towards deeper integration. The most reluctant Member States become weaker, since they lose a rather powerful ally.

The recent developments in the domain of permanent structured cooperation and the creation of the European Defence Fund may well be a consequence of the Brexit effect in the defense policy.

However, having said this, one has also to admit that the future of the EU has never been so threatened. After two years of negotiations, there is no deal, the withdrawal of the UK risks to be disorganized, the current political situation in some remaining Member States, such as Italy, Hungary, and Poland, but also in France and Germany, cause major concerns. Some of these governments are rather anti-EU, and the ones that are not risk to lose political power in the next elections. For the first time in the history of the EU, the composition of the EP, which will come out of the next elections in May, risks to be mostly anti-EU.

In the event that all these dark scenarios are confirmed in the near future, not only Brexit, but all these factors will impact the constitutional nature of EU law. For the time being, it is impossible to predict how these events will unfold.

[61] See Marlene Wind, "Brexit and Euroscepticism...", 224-225.

5. Some (un)conclusive remarks

At the end of this study, we can hardly extract some definitive conclusions because Brexit is not concluded yet.

However, it is possible to anticipate that it will impact the constitutional core of the EU.

The territorial scope of the Founding Treaties and of the Union will decrease; the institutional framework will not only formally but, above all, substantially change, the institutional balance will not remain similar.

The departure of the UK can facilitate the development of some EU competences, such as the area of freedom, security and justice, the social policy and the monetary and economic policies, but at the same time it will also contribute to diminishing the EU action in some areas, such as the CFSP and the CSDP.

The fundamental rights, and the third-country nationals' rights may well improve and the citizens' rights may well suffer a contradictory impact. On the one side, the departure of the UK will certainly provoke a loss of rights, but, on the other side, without the opposition of the UK the citizens' rights may well be extended.

Provided that the EU actors take some lessons from Brexit, it may also lead to a reform of the Treaties and the reinforcement of the EU political power.

However, taking into account the anti-EU feelings in many Member States, the effects of Brexit – if it actually happens – may be contradictory. It is necessary to wait and see the end of the game.

Abstract

In the present article, the author analyses the consequences of Brexit to the EU constitutional nature and to its founding Treaties. After noting that the point of departure of the article is the theory of constitutionalism beyond the State, as well as the assumption that the EU and EU law have a constitutional nature, the author proceeds to discuss whether Article 50 TEU fits into this constitutional approach. The article argues that, in spite of the intergovernmental essence of the provision, once triggered, the withdrawal of a Member State from the EU has a rather significant constitutional impact not only in the EU and its founding Treaties, but also in the constitutional law of the remaining Member States. After ruling out the rhetoric of sovereignty and democracy that prompted Brexit, the article discusses the impact of Brexit on the EU's territorial clause, institutional framework, objectives and policies, fundamental rights, and citizenship. Finally, the article assesses whether Brexit could become a reinforcement of European constitutionalism, concluding that this scenario is somewhat unlikely, taking into account the rise of populist and nationalist political parties and movements, which are clearly anti-European, in many Member States.

II
A Revisão dos Tratados e o Alargamento dos Poderes dos Órgãos da UE

a) Article 48[1]

1. The Treaties may be amended in accordance with an ordinary revision procedure. They may also be amended in accordance with simplified revision procedures.

2. The Government of any Member State, the European Parliament or the Commission may submit to the Council proposals for the amendment of the Treaties. These proposals may, inter alia, serve either to increase or to reduce the competences conferred on the Union in theTreaties. These proposals shall be submitted to the European Council by the Council and the national Parliaments shall be notified.

3. If the European Council, after consulting the European Parliament and the Commission, adopts by a simple majority a decision in favour of examining the proposed amendments, the President of the European Council shall convene a Convention composed of representatives of the national Parliaments, of the Heads of State or Government of the Member States, of the European Parliament and of the Commission. The European Central Bank shall also be consulted in the case of institutional changes in the monetary area. The Convention shall examine the proposals for amendments and shall adopt by consensus a recommendation to a conference of representatives of the governments of the Member States as provided for in paragraph 4.

[1] O presente texto está publicado em Manuel Porto/Gonçalo Anastácio (coord.), *Treaty of Lisbon – Article by Article – Commentary on the European Union Treaties* Coimbra, Almedina, 2018, p. 180-187.

The European Council may decide by a simple majority, after obtaining the consent of the European Parliament, not to convene a Convention should this not be justified by the extent of the proposed amendments. In the latter case, the European Council shall define the terms of reference for a conference of representatives of the governments of the Member States.

4. A conference of representatives of the governments of the Member States shall be convened by the President of the Council for the purpose of determining by common accord the amendments to be made to the Treaties.

The amendments shall enter into force after being ratified by all the Member States in accordance with their respective constitutional requirements.

5. If, two years after the signature of a treaty amending the Treaties, four fifths of the Member States have ratified it and one or more Member States have encountered difficulties in proceeding with ratification, the matter shall be referred to the European Council.

6. The Government of any Member State, the European Parliament or the Commission may submit to the European Council proposals for revising all or part of the provisions of Part Three of the Treaty on the Functioning of the European Union relating to the internal policies and action of the Union.

The European Council may adopt a decision amending all or part of the provisions of Part Three of the Treaty on the Functioning of the European Union. The European Council shall act by unanimity after consulting the European Parliament and the Commission, and the European Central Bank in the case of institutional changes in the monetary area. That decision shall not enter into force until it is approved by the Member States in accordance with their respective constitutional requirements.

The decision referred to in the second subparagraph shall not increase the competences conferred on the Union in the Treaties.

7. Where the Treaty on the Functioning of the European Union or Title V of this Treaty provides for the Council to act by unanimity in a given area or case, the European Council may adopt a decision authorising the Council to act by a qualified majority in that area or in that case. This subparagraph shall not apply to decisions with military implications or those in the area of defence.

Where the Treaty on the Functioning of the European Union provides for legislative acts to be adopted by the Council in accordance with a special legislative procedure, the European Council may adopt a decision allowing for the adoption of such acts in accordance with the ordinary legislative procedure.

Any initiative taken by the European Council on the basis of the first or the second subparagraph shall be notified to the national Parliaments. If a national

Parliament makes known its opposition within six months of the date of such notification, the decision referred to in the first or the second subparagraph shall not be adopted. In the absence of opposition, the European Council may adopt the decision.

For the adoption of the decisions referred to in the first and second subparagraphs, the European Council shall act by unanimity after obtaining the consent of the European Parliament, which shall be given by a majority of its component members.

Origin

The initial version of the Treaties contained rules on revision procedures – Articles 96 ECSC Treaty, 236 EC Treaty and 204 Euratom Treaty. Those provisions were withdrawn by the Amsterdam Treaty, and replaced by Article 48 EUT. Article IV-7 of the Draft of the Constitutional Treaty, resulting from the Convention on the Future of Europe, as well as Articles IV-443 to IV-445 of the Treaty Establishing a Constitution for Europe (TECE) had, however, provided the primary source of inspiration for the current Article 48 EU Treaty.

Main related articles

Article 31 (3) EUT and Articles 25 (2), 81 (3), 82 (2) (d), 83 (3), 86 (4), 92 (2), 107 (2) (c), 153(2), 192 (2) 300, 312 (2), 331(1) (2), 353 TFEU.

Jurisprudence

Rulings by the European Court of Justice of 23/2/88 *United Kingdom c. Council*, 68/86, 1988, 855 et seq.; of 8/4/76, *Defrenne II*, 43/75, 1976, 455 et seq.; of 3/2/76, *Mangera*, 59/75, 1976, 1 et seq; of 31/3/71, *AETR*, 22/70, 1971, 263 et seq. Opinions given by the Court of Justice of 28/3/1996, 2/94, 1996, I-1759 et seq; of 10/4/92, 1/92, 1992, I-2821 et seq; of 14/12/91, *1/91*,1991, I-6079 et seq.

Doctrine

AAVV, *Les procédures de révision des traités communautaires: du droit international au droit communautaire*, Brussels, Bruylant, 2003; Bartole, S., "A proposito della revisione del trattato che istittuisce la costituzione dell' Unione Europea", *Dir. Pub.*, 2003, 771-785; Benz, A., "Amendment Procedure and the Future of the Convention". In Ingolf Pernice/Eugeni Tanchev (eds.), *Ceci n'est pas une Constitution – Constitutionalism without Constitution?*, Baden-Baden, Nomos, 2009, 190-202; Bieber, R., "Les limites materielles et formelles à la révision des traités etablissant la Communauté européenne". *RMCUE*, 1993, 343-350; Campins Eritja, M., "La revisione del Tratado de la Union Europea". *GJ*, Oct., 1995, 7-80; Closa, C., 'Between a Rock and a Hard Place: the Future of EU Treaty Revisions', *European Policy Analysis*, 2014, 1 et seq.; Craig, P., *The Lisbon Treaty – Law, Politics and Treaty Reform*, Oxford, Oxford Univ. Press, 2010, 443-448; Cruz Vilaça, J. L./Piçarra, N., "Y a-t-il des limites materielles à la révision des traités instituant les CE? ". *CDE*, 1993, 3-37; De Witte, B., "Entry into Force and Revision". In De Witte, B. (Ed.), *Ten Reflections on the Constitutional Treaty for Europe*, E. book, Robert Schuman Centre for Advanced Studies and European University Institut, San Domenico di Fiesole, 2003, 213-225; De Witte, B., "European Treaty Revision: a case of multilevel constitutionalism". In Pernice, I./Zemanek, J. (ed.), Op. Cit., 2005, 59-76; De Witte, B., "Rules of Change in International Law: How Special is the European Community?", *NYIL*, 1994, 299-333; Dehousse, R., "Au-delà du Plan B: comment reformer les clauses de révision des traités?". In Giuliano Amato/Herve Bribosia/Bruno de Witte (eds.), *Genèse et Destinée de la Constitution Européenne*, Brussels, Bruylant, 2007, 939-955; Déliège-Sequaris, M., Révision des traités européens en dehors des procédures prévues. *CDE*, 539-552; Louis, J.-V., "Quelques considérations sur la révision des traités instituant les Communautés", *CDE*, 1980, 553-558; Everling, U., "Sind die Mitgliedstaaten der Europäischen Gemeinschaft noch Herren der Verträge?", in *Festschrift fur Hermann Mosler*, Berlin, Springer, 1983, 173-191; Guerra Martins, A. M., *A natureza juridica da revisão do Tratado da União Europeia*, Lisbon, Lex, 2000, 425-618; Guerra Martins, A. M., "O modelo de revisão na Constituição Europeia: em busca de uma terceira via?", in *Estudos em Honra de Ruy de Albuquerque*, Coimbra, Coimbra Editora, 2006, 61-86; Idem, "Amendment of the Constitution – Procedural and Political Questions", in Pernice, I./Zemanek, J. (ed.), *A Constitution for Europe: The IGC, the Ratification Process and Beyond*, Baden-Baden, Nomos, 2005, 199--210; Idem, "As Convenções de Filadélfia e de Bruxelas – convergências e divergências do processo de formação das Constituições americana e europeia", in Miranda, J. *et al.* (org.), *Estudos em Memoria do Professor Doutor Antonio Marques dos Santos*, vol. II, Coimbra, Almedina, 2005, 13-30; Koenig, C./Pechstein, M., "EU-Vertragsanderungen". *EuR*, 1998, 130-150; Louis, J.-V., "La révision des traités et l'Union européenne", in *Hommage a Georges Goriely*, Brussels, 1989, 193-203; Mangas Martin, A., "La dinamica de las revisiones de los tratados y los deficits estructurales de la Union Europea: reflexiones generales criticas", in *Estudios in homenaje al Professor M. Diez Velasco*, Madrid, 1993, 1055-1066; Pfersmann, O., "The New Revision of the Old Constitution", in Weiler/Eisgruber (eds.), *Altneuland: The EU Constitution in a Contextual Perspective*, Jean Monnet Working Paper 5/04, 2004, (http://centers.law.nyu.edu/jeanmonnet/papers/04/040501-10.pdf); Piris, J.-C., *The Lisbon Treaty – A Legal and Political Analysis*, Cambridge, Cambridge Univ. Press, 2010, 104-109; Lucia Serena Rossi, 'A New Revision of the EU Treaties after Lisbon?'. In L.S. Rossi and F. Casolari (eds.), *The EU after Lisbon – Amending or Copying with the Existing treaties?*, Springer, 2014, 3 et seq.; Ziller, J., "The Law and Politics of the Ratifi cation of the Lisbon Treaty", In Griller, S./Ziller, J. *The Lisbon Treaty, EU Constitutionalism without a Constitutional Treaty?*, Viena, Springer, 2008, 309-335.

The general revision procedure has been provided by the Treaties, since their very first version, and it was considered mandatory by the CJEU (e.g. *Defrenne*, cit.). The wording of the general revision clause has remained unmodified until the Treaty of Lisbon. It included three phases: a transnational one, an international one and a domestic one.

At the procedure of revision's launching the transnational level of decision played a rather important role. The Commission had the right of initiative, which used to be shared with the Member State Governments. If the Council, after having consulted the EP and the Commission, gave its assent to the IGC meeting, this would be convened by the President of the Council. The previous Article 48 EUT also provided that the ECB Council would be consulted in the event of institutional amendments related to the monetary field. In practical terms, and without being expressly foreseen by the treaties, the European Council had always taken a relevant role within the revision procedure. It convoked the IGC, it established the main issues of negotiation, and it reached the political consensus at the end of the negotiations.

The IGC began the international phase, which was mainly dominated by the Member States, represented at the highest level. The eventual modifications to be introduced into the Treaties' content and structure were negotiated, discussed and approved in that forum. In general, every IGC benefited from the collaboration of working groups nominated by the Governments, with the exception of the IGC 2003 (and the IGC 2007), in which a new method was trialed – a convention of governments, national parliaments and EP representatives – whilst still maintaining the ultimate responsibility of the Member States, who would make decisions in consensus.

Following the set and the signature of the new text, it would start a domestic phase, in which each Member State ratified the modifications according to its constitutional requirements.

This procedure has been conceived for a Community of six Member States, in which the requirement for double unanimity (at the international and the domestic level) seemed to be a manifestation of cohesion between them. The successive enlargements of the EU showed that the inherent rigidity of such a procedure could jeopardize the success of the future revisions of the Treaty (as it was clearly evidenced during the negotiations of the Treaty of Nice). The risk of blockage, the lack of transparency and efficiency, and the democratic legitimacy deficit of such a procedure (Dehousse, 2007, 941) rendered its modification mandatory. One of the most innovative proposals in this area came from the Commission.

During the Convention on the Future of Europe, the Commission introduced the so-called Penelope Draft, in which, on the one hand, it suggested that the revision of the Treaties should be performed by a majoritarian decision, and on the other hand, it accepted the right to withdrawal with the acquisition of a special status – respecting the *acquis* – by those who represented the minority.

That is to say in the so-called Penepole Draft the double unanimity would be removed. However, the Convention did not accept this change. Consequently, the TECE Draft had slightly modified the revision procedure (Article IV-7): the EP's power of initiative was extended; the national parliaments had to be notified of the draft's revisions; the European Council was given the power of decision on revision, on condition of a consultation with the EP and the Commission should give a favourable decision; and the President of the European Council was given the power to convoke a convention in order to analyse the drafts of amendments and to adopt, by consensus, a recommendation aimed at the IGC, except when envisioned modifications do not justify this. The unity of the procedure, as well as the requirement for the double unanimity of the Member States, was maintained, which means that legal nature of the revision procedure remained untouched.

Article IV-7 also established that, if two and a half years after the signature of a treaty amending the Treaty establishing a Constitution for Europe (this period was reduced to two years in the IGC 2004 (v. Article IV-443 (4)), and if four fifths of the Member States have ratified it and one or more States had encountered difficulties in proceeding with ratification, the matter shall be referred to European Council.

By contrast, the text emerging from the IGC 2004 – TECE – had rather modified the revision procedure through the inclusion of distinct standards in the Treaty, in accordance with the extension and importance of the amended provisions (Articles IV-443 to IV-445 TECE). Nevertheless, having combined the procedures established in three provisions into a single one – current Article 48 EUT – the Treaty of Lisbon maintained the distinction between the ordinary revision procedure ((2) to (5)) and the simplified revision procedures ((6) and (7).

The innovations introduced by the Treaty of Lisbon in Article 48 had apparently two aims: on the one hand, they try to respond to the criticism concerning the previous version of the provision and, on the other hand, they try to match the wording of the Treaty and the practice of the Union with regard to the revision of the Treaties. The ordinary revision procedure intends to introduce modifications in any part of the Treaties, which could have an effect of a global revision of the Treaties, whereas the simplified revision procedures only apply to the specific cases established within them. In other words, the latter applied to the modifications of part III of the TFEU, regarding the policies and internal actions of the Union ((6), and to the modifications of the decision procedure ((7).

The ordinary revision procedure operates in three steps (as it happened in the former Article 48 EUT): a transnational one, an international one, and a domestic one. In accordance with Article 48 (2) EUT, the initiative of the procedure of revision is shared between the governments of the Member States, the EP and the Commission, which can all submit revision proposals to the Council. The Council must then send them to the European Council and notify the national parliaments of them. The participation of the EP aims to overcome the democratic deficit of the former procedure. The notifications of the proposals of revision to the national parliaments intends not only increasing the transparency and democracy of the procedure, but also improving its efficiency, since the approval of the revision within the domestic level is generally a power of the national parliaments. Contrasting with the correspondent provisions of the TECE, Article 48 (2) TEU expressly mentions that revision proposals can either increase or diminish the powers attributed to the Union by the Treaties. It should be noted that nothing in the previous version of the Treaties imposed an increasing of powers of the Union, therefore this item must be viewed as an "obsessive insistence" (this expression is borrowed by Jacques Ziller) of the Member States in the affirmation of its own powers.

Article 48 (3) EUT establishes the intervention of the European Council in the ordinary revision procedure, which is, in fact, in accordance with the Union practice in this area. It is up to this institution, upon consultation with the EP and the Commission, to decide, by simple majority, on the pursuit of an analysis of these revision proposals. The ECB must also be consulted if the intended alterations concern institutional modifications within the monetary field. Having arrived at the conclusion that the revision must be implemented, one of two methods can be followed: the conventional one or the intergovernmental one. The first method implies that the President of the European Council convoked a convention composed by representatives of the national parliaments, Heads of State, or Governments of the Member States, of the EP, and of the Commission, in order to analyse the revision proposals and to adopt, by consensus, a recommendation addressed to the IGC. However, if the scope of the envisioned modification does not justify this, the conventional method will be not followed and the convention will not be called.

In this case, the European Council must decide, by simple majority, after approval from the EP.

The introduction of the conventional method, which was already tested at the time of the CFREU and the TECE negotiations, shall be seen as a path forward the "constitutionalisation" of the Union, insomuch as it aims to make the revision procedure more transparent and more democratic, as well as reducing the possibility of blockages (Benz, 2009, 193). However, this method will rarely be used, since it will be only applied to wide revisions or even the global revision of the Treaty. This scenario is not expected in the near future (Piris, 2010, 105).

Under the terms of Article 48 (4) EUT, the decision on the modifications to introduce into the Treaties continues to compete to the ICG, and the decision within it is achieved by mutual consent between the Member States. The amendments of the Treaty will only enter into force, after the ratification by the Member States, in accordance with their constitutional requirements. In other words, despite an increase of the EP's participation (at the level of the initiative, the hearing on the launching of the revision, the participation of the convention, and the approval of the lack of a convention) and of the national parliaments (especially at the level of the participation in the convention), the final word remains the responsibility of each Member State, in a double sense: the modifications are approved by consensus in an IGC and enter into force depending on the constitutional law of the States, which, generally, require parliamentary approval and the ratification of the Head of State, and additionally a referendum in some cases (v.g. Denmark and Irlande).

Retaking the Article IV-7 of the TECE Draft and Article 443 (4) TECE, Article 48 (5) EUT establishes that the European Council will analyse the matter if, after a period of two years after the signature of the treaty amending the Treaties, four fifths of the Member States have ratified it and one or more Member States have encountered difficulties proceeding with ratification. The meaning of that analysis and the consequences of it need be defined. Naturally, it is possible to foresee several scenarios but none of them should envisage the Treaty entering into force without the approval of the Member State or the Member States in difficulty (De Witte, 2005. 76).

Article 48 EUT also establishes two simplified revision procedures, whose common denominator is the idea that the convocation of a convention and/or an IGC are dispensable.

Article 48 (6) applies only to Part III TFEU, which is comprised by 24 titles (Articles 26 to 196 TFEU), including very important and different matters, such as the internal market, the four freedoms, the economic and monetary union, the area of freedom, security and justice, agriculture, fishing, the environment, social policy, employment policy, and the approximation of legislation. For this reason, it is no wonder that the authors of the Treaty of Lisbon have surrounded it with innumerable precautions (Craig, 2010, 447). First and foremost, the amendments to be made cannot increase the powers attributed to the EU through the Treaties.

Secondly, it is the European Council – the body dominated by the Member States – that decides on the amendments, deliberating by unanimity after consulting the EP and the Commission, as well as the ECB in case of institutional changes in the monetary area. Thirdly, there are the Member States that approve the amendments to be included in the Treaties, in accordance with their constitutional requirements.

This procedure differs from the ordinary one because it dismisses the convocation of the IGC and/or the Convention. However, it is similar to it in the essential issue of the need for double unanimity among the Member States.

Article 48 (7) contains a different revision mechanism. In practice, it concerns a genuine general *passarelle* clause, which can take two different forms.

On the one hand, the European Council may decide that in the areas or cases, where the TFEU and of Title V of the TEU currently require an unanimous decision of the Council, it will be authorized to decide by qualified majority, (cf., for instance, Articles 25 (2) (2) (d), 83 (3), 86 (4), 92 (2), 107 (2) (c) and 300 TFEU). The decisions with military implications and those in the area of defence are excluded from this procedure. On the other hand, the European Council can decide that, where the TFEU determines that the Council adopts a legislative act, in accordance with a special legislative procedure (cf., for instance, Articles 81 (3) (2), 153 (2) (b) (2); 192 (2); 333 (2) TFEU), the European Council can adopt a decision, authorizing the adoption of these acts under the terms of the ordinary legislative procedure. In both cases, the national parliaments are informed of the initiatives and may oppose to within six months. The opposition of one parliament is sufficient to prevent the adoption of the decision. If none of the national parliaments oppose, then the decision may be adopted by the European Council, by unanimity, having been approved by the EP, which decides by the majority of its members. Although the Member States approval, in accordance with their constitutional requirements, is not needed, the participation of national parliaments, as well as the participation of the EP, ensures the domestic and the transnational democratic legitimacy of the procedure.

In accordance with Article 353 TFEU, Article 48 (7) EUT is neither applicable to Articles 311 (3) (4) and 312 (2) TFEU – which concern budgetary matters – nor to Articles 352 and 354 TFEU, which concern the flexibility and suspension of rights resulting from the quality of the Union member, respectively.

b) Article 352[2]

1. If action by the Union should prove necessary, within the framework of the policies defined in the Treaties, to attain one of the objectives set out in the Treaties, and the Treaties have not provided the necessary powers, the Council, acting unanimously on a proposal from the Commission and after obtaining the consent of the European Parliament, shall adopt the appropriate measures. Where the measures in question are adopted by the Council in accordance with a special legislative procedure, it shall also act unanimously on a proposal from the Commission and after obtaining the consent of the European Parliament.

2. Using the procedure for monitoring the subsidiarity principle referred to in Article 5(3) of the Treaty on European Union, the Commission shall draw national Parliaments' attention to proposals based on this Article.

3. Measures based on this Article shall not entail harmonisation of Member States' laws or regulations in cases where the Treaties exclude such harmonisation.

4. This Article cannot serve as a basis for attaining objectives pertaining to the common foreign and security policy and any acts adopted pursuant to this Article shall respect the limits set out in Article 40, second paragraph, of the Treaty on European Union.

[2] O presente testo está publicado em Manuel Porto/Gonçalo Anastácio (coord.), *Treaty of Lisbon – Article by Article – Commentary on the European Union Treaties* Coimbra, Almedina, 2018, p. 1350-1353.

Origin

Article 95 (1) (2) ECSC Treaty, 203 EAEC Treaty, 235 EEC Treaty and I-18 TECE

Main related articles

Articles 3, 5 (3), 23 – 42 and 48 TEU, 353 TFEU.

Main related secondary legislation

Former Articles 235 EEC Treaty and 308 EC Treaty were the legal basis of more than five hundred regulations, directives and decisions (whether alone or in conjunction with other provisions of the Treaty). As an example, one can quote Council Directive 76/207/EEC of 9 February 1976 on the implementation of the principle of equal treatment for men and women as regards access to employment, vocational training, and working conditions (OJ L 39, 14.2.1976, p. 40-42); Council Directive 78/659/EEC of 18 July 1978 on the quality of fresh waters needing protection or improvement in order to support fish life (OJ L 222, 14.8.1978, p. 1-10), and Council Directive 79/581/EEC of 19 June 1979 on consumer protection in the indication of the prices on foodstuff s (OJ L 158, 26.6.1979, p. 19-21). Even some agencies were created on the legal basis of Article 308 EC Treaty, such as the European Union Agency for Fundamental Rights (Council Regulation (EC) 168/2007 of 15 February 2007 (OJ L 53, 22.2.2007, p. 1-14).

Jurisprudence

ECJ, Opinion 2/94 of 28/3/1996, 1996, I-1759 et seq; and Rulings of 9/10/2001, *Netherlands/EP and Council*, C-377/98, 2001, 7079 et seq; of 18/11/99, *Commission/Council*, C-209/98, 1999, I-8067 et seq; of 9/7/87, *Migration Policy*, 281, 283 to 285, 1987, 3203 et seq; of 26/3/87, *Commission/Council*, 45/86, 1987, 1493 et seq; of 12/7/73, *Massey-Ferguson*, 8/73, 1973, 897 et seq; of 31/3/71, *AETR*, 22/70, 1971, 263 et seq.

Doctrine

Bungenberg, M. (2000) "Dynamische Integration, Art 308 und die Forderung nach dem Kompetenzkatalog". *EuR*, 879-900; Lorenz, T./Puhs, W. (1998) "Eine Generalermachtigung im Wandel der Zeit: Art 235 EG-Vertrag". *Zeitschrift fur Gesetzgebung*, 142-154; Forester, S. (1996) "Art 235 EGV und das Subsidiaritatsprinzip des Art 3b Abs 2 EGV". *Osterreichische Juristen-Zeitung*, 281-291; Guerra Martins, A. M. (1995) *O art. 235º do Tratado da Comunidade Europeia – clausula de alargamento de competencias dos orgaos comunitarios*, Lisboa, Lex; Kock, H. F. (1988) "Die 'implied powers' der Europaischen Gemeinschaften als Anwendungsfall der 'implied powers' internationaler Organisationen uberhaupt". In *Liber Amicorum honouring Ignaz-Seidl Hohenveldern*, Colonia, Carl Heymanns Verlag, 279-299; Dorn, D.-W. (1986) *Art 235 EWGV – Prinzipien der Auslegung. Die Generalermachtigung zur Rechtsetzung im Verfassungssystem der Gemeinschaften*, Colonia, Engel Verlag; Raux, J. (1984) "Le recours à l'article 235 du traité CEE en vue de la conclusion des accords externes". In *Melanges offerts a Pierre-Henry Teitgen*, Paris, A. Pedone, 407-439; Kaiser, J. H. (1980) "Grenzen der EG-Zustandigkeit". *EuR*, 97-118; Olmi, G. (1979) "La place de l'article 235 CEE dans le système des attributions de compétence a la Communauté". In *Melanges Fernand Dehousse*, vol. 2, Paris, Fernand Nathan, 279-295; Everling, U. (1976) "Die allgemeine Ermächtigung der Europaischen Gemeinschaft zur Zielverwirklichung nach Art 235 EWG-Vertrag. *EuR*, 2-21; Tomuschat, C. (1976) "Die Rechtsetzungsbefugnisse der EWG in Generalermachtigungen insbesondere in Art 235 EWGV". *EuR*, 45-67; Lauwaars, R. H. (1976) "Art 235 als Grundlage fur die flankierenden Politiken im Rahmen der Wirtschafts- und Wahrungsunion". *EuR*, 100-129; Schwartz, I. E. (1976) "Le pouvoir normative de la Communauté, notamment en vertu de l'article 235 – une compétence exclusive ou parallèle". *RMC*, 280-290; Giardina, A. (1975) "The Rule of Law and Implied Powers in the European Communities". *IYIL*, 99-111; Lesguillons, H. (1974) "L'extension des compétences de la CEE par l'article 235 du traité de Rome". *AFDI*, 886-904; Peeters, G. (1973) "L'article 235 du Traité CEE et les relations exterieures de la CEE". *RMC*, 141-144; Marenco, G. (1970) "Les conditions d'application de l'article 235 du traité CEE". *RMC*, 147-157; Schumacher, D. (1970) "Die Ausfüllung von Kompetenzlucken im Verfassungsrecht der Europäischen Gemeinschaften". *AWD*, 539-545; Von Meibom, H. (1968) "Lückenfullung bei der Europäischen Gemeinschaftenvertragen – Zur Anwendung des Artikels 235 des EWG-Vertrages". *NJW*, 2165-2170.

The provision, which corresponds to the current Article 352 TFEU – Article 308 EC Treaty – remained unaltered until the entry into force of the Treaty of Lisbon, notwithstanding the criticism and the proposals of amendment. Article 308 EC Treaty was considered by the majoritarian doctrine to be a complimentary or a subsidiary legal basis for the adoption of measures by the Community institutions. It specifically intended to integrate omissions of the Treaty and to enlarge the powers of the EC institutions. The use of the provision depended on the cumulative verification of the following substantial requisites: i) the necessity of an action of the Community; ii) in order to attain one of the Community objectives; iii) within the framework of the functioning of the common market; iv) the absence of the necessary powers of action. Formally, the decision was adopted by a unanimous decision of the Council, on proposal from the Commission and with the consultation of the EP. Throughout the history of European integration, the old Articles 235 EEC Treaty and 308 EC Treaty had been the legal basis of several measures (regulations, directives, decisions and even international agreements) in various fields, such as the internal market, agriculture, social, environmental and monetary policies. The successive revisions of the Treaties had not changed the frequency of the application of this provision.

If we compare the current wording of Article 352 with the one of the old Article 308 EC Treaty, we can verify that some requisites remain in force: i) the need for an action of the Union; ii) in order to attain one of the objectives set out in the Treaties and iii) the Treaties have not provided the necessary powers.

One has to note that the question of assessing whether an action is necessary or not depends largely on the legislature's freedom of interpretation. Therefore, only in very few cases – which must involve a manifest error of appreciation – will be concluded that a certain action is not necessary. In other words, the assessment of the necessity of an action depends much more on political than judicial criteria. Taking into account the fact that the adoption of measures, in accordance with Article 352 TFEU, is subjected to the rule of unanimity within the Council, the need of an action of the Union exists – in practice – when all representatives of the Member States consider that it is necessary.

The requirement of the Union objectives draws on Article 3 TEU, covering several matters, such as the area of freedom, security and justice (AFSJ), the free movement of persons and the internal market. However, the objectives within the context of the common foreign and security policy (CFSP) are excluded and the limits of article 40 TEU (cf. Article 352 (4) TFEU) must be respected.

The requirement for the absence of necessary powers may perhaps be more difficult to fulfil after the entry into force of the Treaty of Lisbon, given the increase of legal basis for the adoption of Union acts. However, it is not sure that it will happen in the future, since the old Article 308 EC Treaty had remained in use as a legal basis of Union acts after the successive revisions.

Apart from these requirements, the Treaty of Lisbon amended Article 352 with the aim to adapt it to the innovations introduced in other parts of the Treaty: i) the current unitary structure of the Union (cf. Article 1 TEU) implied an extension of the scope of application of the provision to all matters of the Union, with the exception of certain areas of the CFSP (cf. Article 352 (4)); ii) in accordance with the majority doctrine, which supported the outdated nature of the wording related to the functioning of the common market, it was deleted; iii) the action of the Union must now be included within the framework of policies defined in the Treaties, which leads to the enlargement of the scope of application of the provision, given that it is no longer strictly linked to economic questions; iv) the measures adopted under the terms of Article 352 TFEU shall not entail harmonisation of Member States' laws or regulations, in cases where the Treaties exclude such harmonisation.

To sum up, on the one hand, the ambit of material application of the provision was enlarged, however, on the other hand, it was limited. The enlargement results from the unitary structure of the Union, which leads to the empowerment of the Council to adopt acts within the AFSJ's domain. However, the same possibility does not exist when it concerns CFSP' matters. The limitation of the ambit of material application of the provision is even more evident concerning the abovementioned exclusion of the harmonisation' measures of Member States' laws and regulations, in cases where the Treaties exclude such harmonization. This limitation is, notwithstanding, more theoretical than real, since in earlier versions of the Treaties these measures were also dismissed, if the Treaties excluded them.

As regards the formal requirements, the amendments of Article 352 TFEU were, in some cases, also imposed by the modifications inserted in other parts of the Treaties. Therefore, Article 352 (2) establishes that the Commission shall draw national parliaments' attention to proposals on this Article. That means the application of the procedure for monitoring the subsidiarity principle (cf. Article 5 (3) TEU). This constitutes a limitation of Council's powers, indeed. However, it contributes to a more democratic Union, due to the participation of the national parliaments.

The powers of the EP also became stronger: instead of a mere consultation, the acts based on this provision require the consent of the EP.

Finally, it should be noted that this Article cannot be subjected to a simplified procedure of revision (Article 353 TFEU).

c) Article 353[3]

Article 48(7) of the Treaty on European Union shall not apply to the following Articles:

- *Article 311, third and fourth paragraphs,*
- *Article 312(2), first subparagraph,*
- *Article 352, and*
- *Article 354.*

Origin

This provision is completely new.

Main related articles

Article 48 (7) TEU.

[3] O presente texto está publicado em Manuel Porto/Gonçalo Anastácio (coord.), *Treaty of Lisbon – Article by Article – Commentary on the European Union Treaties* Coimbra, Almedina, 2018, p. 1353-1354.

Doctrine

Cf. Bibliography of Article 48 TEU.

According to this provision, Articles 311, third and fourth paragraph and 312 (2) TFEU related to budgetary matters, as well as Article 352 TFEU concerning the flexibility clause, and Article 354 TFEU which covers the suspension of certain rights resulting from Union membership are excluded of the scope of application of the simplified revision procedure set out in Article 48 (7) TEU. That is to say, these provisions can only be modified in accordance with the ordinary revision procedure established in Article 48 (2) to (5) TEU) or regarding the simplified revision procedure set out in Article 48 (6) TEU. The *ratio* of this solution is certainly founded in the importance of these Articles, whose revision shall require the ratification of all Member States, in accordance with their constitutional requirements.

The systematic insertion of the provision is, however, opened to criticism. These exceptions must have been included in Article 48 (7) TEU, like the case of military matters.

III
Direito Institucional da União Europeia

A) Parlamento Europeu[1]

1. O modo de designação dos membros do PE

O PE é composto por representantes dos cidadãos da União e os seus membros são eleitos por sufrágio universal direto, livre e secreto, por um mandato de cinco anos (art. 14º, nºs 2 e 3, TUE). A base de legitimidade do PE advém, portanto, dos cidadãos da União.

2. O estatuto dos membros do PE

Segundo o art. 223º, nº 2, TFUE, o PE, por meio de regulamentos adotados, por iniciativa própria, de acordo com um procedimento legislativo especial, estabelecerá o estatuto e as condições gerais de exercício das funções dos seus membros, após parecer da Comissão e mediante aprovação do Conselho.

3. A composição do PE

O número de Deputados e a repartição dos representantes pelos Estados-Membros tem variado ao longo dos tempos. Atualmente, o art. 14º, nº 2, par. 1º, TUE estabelece que o número de Deputados não pode ser superior a setecentos e cinquenta, mais o Presidente e que a representação

[1] Este texto destina-se a ser publicado na Enciclopédia Luso-Brasileira de Direito Internacional, coordenada por Manuel de Almeida Ribeiro e Marcílio França.

dos cidadãos é degressivamente proporcional com um limiar mínimo de seis representantes por Estado-Membro e que a nenhum Estado-Membro podem ser atribuídos mais do que noventa e seis lugares.

A atribuição do número concreto de parlamentares a cada Estado--membro não consta do articulado dos Tratados, tendo sido remetida pelo art. 14º, nº 2, par. 2º, TUE para uma decisão unânime do Conselho Europeu, por iniciativa do PE e com a aprovação deste.

4. A organização e o funcionamento do PE

O PE tem um direito de auto-organização que decorre dos Tratados (art. 232º TFUE).

De acordo com o artigo 14º, nº 4, TUE, o PE elege de entre os seus membros o seu Presidente bem como a Mesa. O PE dispõe de comissões permanentes, tendo o art. 226º TFUE oficializado o recurso às comissões de inquérito temporárias.

Os Deputados podem organizar-se em grupos políticos. Atualmente existem oito grupos (Partido Popular Europeu (Democratas-Cristãos), Aliança Progressista dos Socialistas e Democratas no PE, Conservadores e Reformistas Europeus, Aliança dos Democratas e Liberais na Europa, Confederal da Esquerda Unitária Europeia/Esquerda Nórdica Verde, Verdes/Aliança Livre Europeia, Europa da Liberdade e da Democracia Direta e Europa das Nações e da Liberdade) e alguns Deputados não inscritos.

O art. 10º, nº 4, TUE reconhece o papel dos partidos políticos a nível europeu como fator de integração, dado que contribuem para a criação de uma consciência política europeia e para a expressão da vontade política dos cidadãos da União, permitindo o art. 224º TFUE a adoção, segundo o processo legislativo ordinário, de um estatuto dos partidos políticos ao nível europeu.

A duração da legislatura do PE é de cinco anos. O PE tem uma sessão anual que se reúne por direito próprio na segunda terça-feira do mês de março (art. 229º, par. 1º, TFUE) e pode reunir-se em sessão extraordinária, a pedido da maioria dos seus membros, do Conselho ou da Comissão (art. 229º, par. 2º, TFUE). Além disso, funciona em comissão.

A regra de votação no seio do Parlamento é a maioria dos votos expressos (art. 231º TFUE), exceto nos casos em que se prevê outra regra expressamente no Tratado, como, por exemplo, para efeitos da aprovação de uma moção de censura (art. 234º TFUE).

5. Os poderes do PE

Na versão originária dos Tratados, o PE dispunha de uma competência muito mais limitada, mas após a sua eleição por sufrágio direto e universal, em 1979, este órgão começou a reclamar cada vez mais poderes em consonância com a sua legitimidade democrática direta.

Atualmente, nos termos do art. 14º, nº 1, TUE, o PE exerce, juntamente com o Conselho, a função legislativa e a função orçamental. Além disso, o PE exerce funções de controlo político e funções consultivas em conformidade com as condições estabelecidas nos Tratados. Compete-lhe igualmente eleger o Presidente da Comissão.

Da leitura dos Tratados resulta, pois, que o Parlamento detém os seguintes poderes:

a) Legislativo – que exerce através da aprovação de atos legislativos segundo os procedimentos legislativos, ordinário (art. 289º, nº 1, TFUE) e especial (art. 289º, nº 2, TFUE).
b) Aprovação dos acordos de associação, do acordo de adesão da União Europeia à Convenção Europeia dos Direitos do Homem, dos acordos que criem um quadro institucional específico mediante a organização de processos de cooperação, dos acordos com consequências orçamentais significativas para a União, dos acordos que abranjam domínios aos quais seja aplicável o procedimento legislativo ordinário ou o procedimento legislativo especial, quando a aprovação do PE é obrigatória (art. 218º, nº 6, al. a), TFUE).
c) Orçamental – o PE detém um poder idêntico ao do Conselho (art. 314º TFUE).
d) Fiscalização política:
   1. Nos termos do artigo 230º TFUE, o PE ou os seus membros podem colocar, oralmente ou por escrito, questões à Comissão. O Conselho Europeu e o Conselho são igualmente ouvidos pelo PE.
   2. O PE tem competência para aprovar uma moção de censura à Comissão (art. 234º TFUE), por maioria de dois terços de votos expressos, que representem a maioria dos membros que o com-

põem. Se a moção de censura for aprovada, os membros da Comissão devem demitir-se coletivamente das suas funções e o Alto Representante da União para os Negócios Estrangeiros e a Política de Segurança deve igualmente demitir-se das funções que exerce na Comissão. A Comissão é, portanto, politicamente responsável perante o PE (art. 17º, nº 8, TUE). Não obstante a competência de aprovação de uma moção de censura à Comissão, a dupla maioria exigida para a aprovação da mesma tem impedido que, até à data, se tenha conseguido reunir o número de votos necessários para censurar a Comissão.

3. O PE detém ainda competência de controlo político através da possibilidade de constituir comissões de inquérito temporárias (art. 226º TFUE) e, por outro lado, da exigência de apresentação de relatórios e informações ao PE por parte de outros órgãos da União (cfr. entre outros, arts. 15º, nº 6, al. d), TUE; 25º, par. 1º; 121º, nºs 2 e 5; 126º, nº 11; 134º, nº 3; 175º, par. 2º; 190º; 228º, nº 1, par. 3º, TFUE)).
4. O PE pode proceder a debates de política geral e votar resoluções sobre quaisquer assuntos de atualidade.
5. O PE controla igualmente as atividades da Europol e da Eurojust (arts. 88º, nº 2, e 85º, nº 1, TFUE).

e) Designação de membros de outros órgãos – o PE participa na designação de membros de outras instituições, órgãos e organismos. Os casos mais relevantes são os da eleição do Presidente da Comissão (art. 17º, nº 7, par. 1º, TUE) e do Provedor de Justiça (art. 228º, nº 1, TFUE).

f) Participação no domínio da revisão dos Tratados, designadamente, no procedimento de revisão ordinário e nos procedimentos de revisão simplificados previstos no art. 48º TUE bem como na regulamentação da sua própria eleição (art. 223º TFUE).

Refira-se, por último, que o PE pode ainda, por maioria dos seus membros, solicitar à Comissão que lhe submeta as propostas adequadas sobre as questões que se lhe afigure requererem a elaboração de atos da União para efeitos de aplicação dos Tratados (art. 225º TFUE).

Bibliografia

CORBETT, Richard – "The Evolving Roles of the European Parliament and of National Parliaments", in Andrea BIONDI/Piet EECKHOUT/Stefanie RIPLEY, *EU Law After Lisbon*, Oxford, Oxford University Press, 2012, p. 248--261.

CORBETT, Richard/JACOBS, Francis/NEVILLE, Darren – *The European Parliament*, 9ª ed., Londres, Harper, 2016.

CRAIG, Paul – "The Role of the European Parliament under the Lisbon Treaty", *in* Stefan GRILLER/Jacques ZILLER, *The Lisbon Treaty – EU Constitutionalism without a Constitutional Treaty?*, Viena, Springer, 2008, p. 109-134.

CRAIG, Paul/DE BURCA, Grainne – *EU Law: Text, Cases and Materials*, 6ª ed., Oxford, Oxford University Press, 2015, p. 50-56.

DELCOURT, Christine – "Du Traité Constitutionnel au Traité de Lisbonne: Quelles évolutions pour les institutions parlementaires?", in E. BROSSET/C. CHEVALLIER-GOVERS/V. EDJAHARIAN/C. SCHNEIDER, *Le traité de Lisbonne – Reconfiguration ou déconstitutionnalisation de l'Union européenne?*, Bruxelas, Bruylant, 2009, p. 75-103.

DIALER, Doris/MAURER, Andreas/RICHTER, Margarethe – *Handbuch zum Europäischen Parlement*, Baden-Baden, Nomos, 2015.

GUERRA MARTINS, Ana Maria – *Manual de Direito da União Europeia*, 2.ª ed., Coimbra, Almedina, 2017, p. 399-407.

MOREIRA, Vital – "Anotação aos artigos 14º TUE e 223º a 227º TFUE", *in* Manuel LOPES PORTO/Gonçalo ANASTACIO (coord.), *Tratado de Lisboa – Anotado e comentado*, Coimbra, Almedina, 2012, p. 66-71 e 847-857.

B) Conselho Europeu[2]

1. A génese do Conselho Europeu

O Conselho Europeu é uma instituição da União Europeia que tem a sua origem nas Cimeiras de Chefes de Estado e Chefes de Governo, que ocorreram desde 1961. Tratava-se de conferências diplomáticas à margem das então Comunidades Europeias, nas quais se discutiam os assuntos relacionados com a cooperação política. Após a Cimeira da Haia de 1969, estas

[2] Este texto destina-se a ser publicado na Enciclopédia Luso-Brasileira de Direito Internacional, coordenada por Manuel de Almeida Ribeiro e Marcílio França.

conferências passaram a debruçar-se também sobre os assuntos comunitários.

A partir da Cimeira de Paris, de 9 e 10 de dezembro de 1974, os Chefes de Governo, preocupados em globalizar as atividades comunitárias e as que relevam da cooperação política, decidiram reunir-se, acompanhados dos Ministros dos Negócios Estrangeiros, três vezes por ano, e sempre que necessário, em Conselho das Comunidades e a título de cooperação política, acrescentando ainda que estas reuniões não afetavam de forma nenhuma as regras e os processos estabelecidos nos Tratados, nem as dos acordos de Luxemburgo e de Copenhaga, no que diz respeito à cooperação política.

Assim nasce o Conselho Europeu, o qual teve a sua origem imediata num ato informal dos Estados-Membros. O Conselho Europeu devia desempenhar uma dupla função. Por um lado, deveria ocupar-se dos assuntos comunitários e, por outro lado, deveria configurar-se como o órgão da cooperação política europeia.

Porém, só após o Ato Único Europeu (JOCE L 169, de 29/06/1987) se passou a prever nos Tratados, de modo expresso, a sua composição.

2. A composição e a organização do Conselho Europeu

Com o Tratado de Maastricht (JOCE C 191, de 29.07.1992) consagrou-se uma base jurídica específica para o Conselho Europeu que o transformou em instituição da União Europeia. Coube, no entanto, ao Tratado de Lisboa (JOUE C 306, de 17.12.2007) alcandorá-lo a instituição da União de pleno direito, fazendo assim convergir o Direito com os factos (art. 13º, nº 1, TUE).

O art. 10º, nº 2, TUE prevê que os Estados-Membros estão representados no Conselho Europeu pelo respetivo Chefe de Estado ou de Governo e o art. 15º, nº 2, TUE precisa esta composição, juntando-lhe o seu Presidente (o que é uma inovação do Tratado de Lisboa) bem como o Presidente da Comissão. O Alto Representante para os Negócios Estrangeiros e a Política de Segurança, criado pelo Tratado de Lisboa, participa igualmente nos trabalhos.

Nos termos do art. 15º, nº 3, TUE, quando a ordem do dia o exigir, os membros do Conselho Europeu podem fazer-se assistir por um ministro (que pode ser o Ministro dos Negócios Estrangeiros ou qualquer outro) e o Presidente da Comissão por um membro da Comissão. O Presidente do PE pode ser convidado para ser ouvido pelo Conselho Europeu (art. 235º, nº 2, TFUE).

Esta instituição reúne-se duas vezes por semestre, por convocação do seu Presidente, podendo, se a situação assim o exigir, ser convocadas reuniões extraordinárias (art. 15º, nº 3, TUE).

3. A presidência do Conselho Europeu

A mais recente inovação, no domínio do Conselho Europeu, foi introduzida pelo Tratado de Lisboa e consta do art. 15º, nº 5, TUE. O sistema das presidências rotativas semestrais, exercidas pelo Chefe de Estado ou de Governo do Estado-Membro a quem cabia a presidência do Conselho, foi substituído por um Presidente eleito pelo próprio Conselho Europeu por maioria qualificada, por um período de dois anos e meio, cujo mandato é renovável uma vez, podendo, em caso de impedimento ou de falta grave, o mesmo Conselho Europeu pôr termo ao seu mandato, de acordo com o mesmo procedimento.

As funções do Presidente do Conselho Europeu são enumeradas, pela primeira vez, nos Tratados. Nos termos do art. 15º, nº 6, TUE, o Presidente do Conselho Europeu preside aos trabalhos e dinamiza-os (al. a)), assegura a preparação e a continuidade dos trabalhos do Conselho Europeu, em cooperação com o Presidente da Comissão e com base nos trabalhos do Conselho dos Assuntos Gerais (al. b)), atua no sentido de facilitar a atuação e o consenso no âmbito do Conselho Europeu (al. c)) e apresenta um relatório ao Parlamento Europeu após cada uma das reuniões do Conselho Europeu (al. d)). O Presidente do Conselho Europeu assegura igualmente ao seu nível e nessa qualidade, a representação externa da União no âmbito da Política Externa e de Segurança Comum. Ora, esta função pode justapor-se às funções do Alto Representante para os Negócios Estrangeiros e a Política de Segurança, pelo que o preceito salvaguarda essa possibilidade.

4. O modo de funcionamento do Conselho Europeu

O Conselho Europeu decide por consenso, salvo disposição em contrário dos Tratados (art. 15º, nº 4, TUE). A maioria qualificada está prevista expressamente, entre outros, nos arts. 236º, al. a) e b), TFUE) e ainda em outros casos (designadamente, nos arts. 17º, nº 7, e 18º, nº 1, TUE).

O Conselho Europeu delibera ainda por maioria simples sobre as questões processuais e sobre a adoção do seu regulamento interno (art. 235º, nº 3, TFUE).

Quando o Conselho Europeu se pronuncia por votação, o seu Presidente e o Presidente da Comissão não votam (art. 235º, nº 1, par. 2º, TUE). A abstenção dos membros presentes ou representados não obsta à adoção das deliberações do Conselho Europeu que exijam a unanimidade (art. 235º, nº 1, par. 3º, TUE), a qual é, aliás, requerida em muitas situações (por exemplo, nos arts. 7º, nº 2, 14º, nº 2, 17º, nº 5, 22º, nº 1, 31º, nº 3, 42º, nº 2, TUE e 312º, nº 2, 354º e 355º, nº 6, TFUE).

5. A competência do Conselho Europeu

Como os Tratados inicialmente não previam o Conselho Europeu, também não lhe atribuíam quaisquer poderes. Após a sua criação a definição dos seus poderes foi objeto de alguma confusão com os poderes do Conselho de Ministros.

Hoje em dia, esta situação está totalmente ultrapassada. O art. 15º, nº 1, TUE, refere que o Conselho Europeu dá à União os impulsos necessários ao seu desenvolvimento e define as orientações e prioridades políticas gerais da União e não exerce a função legislativa. A exclusão da função legislativa não é, todavia, absoluta, na medida em que o Conselho Europeu pode ter de agir em vez do Conselho em certos casos (cfr. arts. 48º, 82º, nº 3, 83º, nº 3, 87º, nº 3, TFUE).

Bibliografia

CRAIG, Paul/DE BÚRCA, Graínne – *EU Law: Text, Cases and Materials,* 6ª ed., Oxford, Oxford University Press, 2015, p. 46-48.

EGERMONT, Frédéric – *The Changing Role of the European Council in the Institutional Framework of the European Union – Consequences for the European Integration Process,* Cambridge, Intersentia, 2012.

FORET, François (org.) – *The European Council and European Governance – The commanding heights of the EU,* Londres, Routledge, 2014.

GUERRA MARTINS, Ana Maria – *Manual de Direito da União Europeia*, 2.ª ed., Coimbra, Almedina, 2017, p. 407-410.

PUETER, Uwe – *The European Council and the Council – New Intergovernmentalism and Institutional Change*, Oxford, Oxford University Press, 2014.

TAULÈGNE, Béatrice – *Le conseil européen*, Paris, Puf, 1993.

WESSEL, Wolfgang – *The European Council*, Basingstoke, Palgrave Macmillan, 2016.

Parte II

A Pessoa Humana no Direito da União Europeia

IV
O princípio da dignidade da pessoa humana*

O princípio da dignidade da pessoa humana começou por se afirmar, nos direitos constitucionais dos Estados e no direito internacional dos direitos humanos, no âmbito da relação entre o indivíduo e o Estado, impondo a este último, na sua atuação, um dever de respeito, protecção e defesa. A dignidade da pessoa humana limita, contudo, todo o poder público, seja ele de natureza estadual ou não, pelo que não pode deixar de limitar o poder público da UE.

O princípio da dignidade da pessoa humana implica, no fundo, um dever geral e recíproco de respeito de cada um pelo outro e por todos, assim como um dever de respeito da sua própria dignidade.

A referência à dignidade da pessoa humana, no direito originário da UE, só se verificou com o TL. O direito derivado, porém, apelou à dignidade da pessoa humana, em ligação com a liberdade e com a igualdade de tratamento, muito mais cedo. Veja-se o caso, nos finais da década de 60, do considerando nº 5 do Regulamento (CEE) nº 1612/68, de 15 de Outubro de 1968, relativo à livre circulação dos trabalhadores na Comunidade (publicado no JOCE L 257, de 19/10/1968, p. 2 e seguintes (actualmente revogado pela Directiva nº 2004/38/CE, do Parlamento Europeu e do Conselho, de 29 de Abril de 2004, JOUE L 229, de 29/6/2004, p. 35 e seguintes).

Além disso, a ideia da dignidade pessoa humana enforma – ainda que implicitamente – a jurisprudência do Tribunal de Justiça, pelo menos,

* Este estudo está publicado em Ana Paula Brandão/Francisco Pereira Coutinho/Isabel Camisão/Joana Covelo de Abreu, *Enciclopédia da União Europeia*, Petrony, 2017, p. 308-310.

desde a década de 70. Assim, por exemplo, no acórdão de 8 de Abril de 1976, processo nº 43/75, *Defrenne II*, Rec. 1976, p. 455), a condenação das discriminações fundadas no sexo, tem subjacente a ideia da dignidade da mulher.

Na década de 80 aparecem referências à dignidade da mulher em resoluções, programas de acção, declarações comuns e comunicações dos órgãos comunitários, ou seja, no *soft law*.

Até ao TL, a protecção da dignidade da pessoa humana fazia parte do direito da UE igualmente pela via das tradições constitucionais comuns aos Estados-Membros e do direito internacional dos direitos humanos, enquanto princípio geral, tendo irradiado para todos os domínios do direito da UE.

Com a entrada em vigor do TL, a dignidade pessoa humana é reconhecida, no direito originário, essencialmente, no artigo 2º do TUE e no artigo 1º da CDFUE.

Assim, o artigo 2º do TUE indica que o primeiro valor em que se funda a União é, precisamente, o respeito pela dignidade humana. Só depois se enunciam a liberdade, a democracia, a igualdade, o Estado de Direito e o respeito pelos direitos humanos. Contrariamente ao que sucedia com o antigo artigo 6º, nº 1, TUE, o actual preceito do TUE vincula tanto o legislador e o administrador, como os tribunais da União e os tribunais nacionais. Ou seja, vincula tanto os órgãos da União como os dos Estados--Membros.

A base axiológica da União, incluindo a protecção da dignidade da pessoa humana vai influenciar, em primeiro lugar, a interpretação e a aplicação de qualquer disposição de ambos os Tratados – TUE e TFUE –, o que significa que o Tribunal de Justiça e os tribunais nacionais devem ter em conta os valores da União, quando interpretam e aplicam o seu Direito.

Em segundo lugar, os órgãos da União devem respeitar a dignidade da pessoa humana quando adoptam actos legislativos ou administrativos, e até nas suas práticas administrativas.

Em terceiro lugar, quer os candidatos a Estados-Membros quer os Estados-Membros devem respeitar a dignidade da pessoa humana. Nos termos do artigo 49º do TUE, a adesão à União de um novo Estado-Membro depende, antes de mais, do respeito dos valores referidos no artigo 2º TUE. De acordo com o artigo 7º TUE, a existência de um risco manifesto de violação grave dos valores referidos no artigo 2º pode levar à suspensão de certos direitos dos Estados-Membros em questão, incluindo o direito de voto do representante desse Estado-Membro no seio do Conselho.

Além disso, a CDFUE confere à dignidade da pessoa humana um lugar proeminente, uma vez que abre com ela o catálogo dos direitos fundamentais da União, o que significa que a dignidade da pessoa humana constitui o frontispício dos direitos fundamentais da União.

O título I relativo à dignidade é composto por cinco preceitos. O artigo 1º da Carta declara que a dignidade do ser humano é inviolável, o que, à partida indicia que se trata de um direito autónomo. Por outro lado, a dignidade da pessoa humana também deve ser vista como o fundamento dos restantes preceitos deste Título, fundando os direitos fundamentais mais elementares, como sejam o direito à vida, o direito à integridade física, a proibição da tortura e dos tratamentos ou penas desumanos ou degradantes e a proibição da escravatura e do trabalho forçado.

O direito da UE, incluindo a CDFUE, não define o conteúdo, a natureza e a função que a dignidade da pessoa humana desempenha no contexto do sistema de direitos fundamentais da UE e não existe na doutrina um consenso universal quanto a estes aspectos. Das anotações do *Praesidum* da Convenção sobre o Futuro da Europa, ao artigo 1º da CDFUE, as quais, nos termos do artigo 52º, nº 7, CDFUE, se destinam a orientar os órgãos jurisdicionais da União e dos Estados-Membros na interpretação da Carta, resulta que "*[a] dignidade do ser humano constitui não só um direito fundamental em si mesma, mas também a própria base dos direitos fundamentais.*

Apesar de o predomínio inicial dos objectivos económicos da integração europeia ter contribuído para ofuscar esta realidade, a verdade é que o respeito da dignidade da pessoa humana se traduz, em direito da UE, por um lado, num verdadeiro direito subjectivo e, por outro lado, no fundamento último dos outros direitos fundamentais.

O Tribunal de Justiça confirmou que o direito fundamental à dignidade da pessoa humana faz parte do direito da União, no seu acórdão de 9 de Outubro de 2001, no processo C-377/98, *Países Baixos contra o Parlamento Europeu e Conselho* (Colect. 2001, p. I-7079, nos pontos 70 a 77, cfr. Anotações do *Praesidium* ao artigo 1º da CDFUE).

Note-se, contudo, que o carácter de direito fundamental do respeito da dignidade pessoa humana não é pacífico, o que se compreende, tendo em conta que foi introduzido, na jurisprudência, pela via das tradições constitucionais comuns dos Estados-Membros. Ora, com excepção da Alemanha, em que, por razões históricas, parece existir algum consenso no sentido de o artigo 1º da *Grundgesetz* consagrar um direito fundamental ao respeito da dignidade da pessoa humana, em todos os outros Estados-Membros a questão é controversa.

Aliás, o Tribunal, mais do que a existência de um direito fundamental à dignidade da pessoa humana ou ao respeito da dignidade da pessoa humana, tem vindo a afirmar a existência de um princípio geral de direito de respeito da dignidade da pessoa humana. Fê-lo, nas conclusões do Advogado-geral Jacobs, no caso *Konstantinidis* (acórdão de 30/3/93, proc. C-168/91, Col. 1993, p. I-1191), bem como no caso *P. contra S.* (acórdão de 30/4/1998, proc. C-13/94, Col. 1998, p. I-2143) e no caso *Omega* (acórdão de 14/10/2004, proc. C-36/02, Col. 2004, p. I-9609).

Por outro lado, o princípio da dignidade da pessoa humana é o fundamento último de muitas normas dos Tratados, como, por exemplo, os artigos 18º e seguintes do TFUE, relativos à não discriminação e à cidadania da União, ou os artigos 67º e seguintes do TFUE sobre o espaço de liberdade, segurança e justiça, os quais devem ser interpretados e aplicados com base no valor da dignidade humana. E já era assim na versão anterior dos Tratados.

Além disso, "(...) *nenhum dos direitos consignados na (...) Carta poderá ser utilizado para atentar contra a dignidade de outrem e (...) a dignidade do ser humano faz parte da essência dos direitos fundamentais nela consignados. Não pode, pois, ser lesada, mesmo nos casos em que um determinado direito seja objecto de restrições*" (cfr. Anotações do *Praesidium* ao artigo 1º da CDFUE).

Daqui decorre que o respeito da dignidade da pessoa humana se deve considerar incorporado no conteúdo de todos os outros direitos consagrados na Carta, elevando-a a princípio interpretativo de todos eles.

Bibliografia

Ana Maria Guerra Martins, *Manual de Direito da União Europeia*, 2.ª ed., Almedina, Coimbra, 2017, p. 200 e seguintes.

Ana Maria Guerra Martins, "A protecção da dignidade humana no Tratado de Lisboa", *Estudos em homenagem ao Prof. Doutor José Joaquim Gomes Canotilho* (Fernando Alves Correia/Jónatas E. M. Machado/João Carlos Loureiro (org.)), vol. III, Coimbra Editora, Coimbra, 2012, p. 473-498.

Ana Maria Guerra Martins, *A igualdade e a não discriminação dos nacionais de Estados terceiros legalmente residentes na União Europeia – da origem na integração económica ao fundamento na dignidade do ser humano,* Almedina, Coimbra, 2010, p. 499 e seguintes.

Christopher McCrudden, "Human Dignity and Judicial Interpretation of Human Rights", *European Journal of International Law*, vol. 19, nº 4, 2008, p. 655-724.

V
A Cidadania da União Europeia 30 anos depois da adesão de Portugal à União Europeia[*]

1. Introdução

Trinta anos após a adesão de Portugal às então Comunidades Europeias[1], atualmente, União Europeia, é tempo de proceder a um primeiro balanço acerca do significado dessa adesão para a vida das portuguesas e dos portugueses. Na verdade, as consequências da adesão fazem-se sentir em todos os domínios. Desde logo, na facilidade com que atualmente circulam as mercadorias, as pessoas, os serviços e os capitais no espaço territorial da União Europeia, nas maiores exigências em matéria de direito do ambiente (o qual, em bom rigor, não existia antes da adesão), na celebração de contratos públicos (o qual é influenciado numa larga escala pelo direito da União Europeia), nas exigências de controlo da dívida e da despesa públicas (o que ainda recentemente impôs medidas de austeridade muito severas em Portugal[2]), na existência de uma moeda única, comum aos Estados-Membros da zona euro (entre os quais Portugal se inclui), na ausência progressiva de controlos de fronteiras e, para o que mais nos

[*] Este estudo encontra-se publicado em Eduardo Paz Ferreira (coord.), *União Europeia – reforma ou declínio*, Lisboa, Veja, 2016, p. 277-292.

[1] Portugal é membro da União Europeia desde 1 de Janeiro de 1986.

[2] No âmbito deste estudo não se vai tratar do impacto dessas medidas nos direitos de cidadania das portuguesas e dos portugueses e na proteção dos direitos fundamentais em geral. Este assunto já foi, em parte, objeto de um outro artigo por nós publicado. V. Ana Maria Guerra Martins, "Constitutional Judge, Social Rights and Public Debt Crisis – the Portuguese Constitutional Case Law", *MJ*, 2015, p. 678 e segs.

interessa neste estudo, na aquisição da qualidade de cidadão da União e na aquisição dos direitos que lhe são inerentes.

Provavelmente, nem todos terão consciência do profundo impacto do direito da União Europeia no seu dia-a-dia, mas a verdade é que todas as decisões políticas, sejam elas tomadas pelos Parlamentos nacionais, pelos Governos dos Estados-Membros ou por outras entidades públicas, são influenciadas pelo direito da União.

No âmbito deste estudo vamos debruçar-nos, tão-somente, sobre a forma como a cidadania da União afetou e afeta as portuguesas e os portugueses, onde quer que residam.

Assim, num primeiro momento, estudar-se-á, sucintamente, os antecedentes e a criação da cidadania da União pelo Tratado de Maastricht bem como o seu impacto na Constituição Portuguesa. Num segundo momento, referiremos os direitos e os deveres que as portuguesas e os portugueses adquiriram por força da criação da cidadania da União assim como as consequências de ser nacional de um Estado que não faz parte da União Europeia. Num terceiro momento, debruçar-nos-emos sobre a importância da jurisprudência do Tribunal de Justiça da União Europeia no domínio da cidadania da União e, por fim, analisaremos um acórdão do Tribunal Constitucional Português em que o impacto dessa jurisprudência é muito visível. Por último, apresentaremos algumas conclusões.

2. A cidadania da União Europeia – antecedentes, criação pelo Tratado de Maastricht e impacto na Constituição Portuguesa

2.1. Antecedentes

A introdução no Tratado de Maastricht das normas relativas à cidadania da União Europeia é posterior à adesão de Portugal às Comunidades Europeias, mas "*a ideia de uma cidadania da Comunidade e a retórica do "Povo Europeu" já [se encontrava] em circulação há muito tempo*"[3].

Já o relatório Tindemans, o projeto de Tratado Spinelli e o relatório apresentado pelo comité Adonino ao Conselho Europeu de Bruxelas, de

[3] Paul Craig/Gráinne de Búrca, *EU Law – Text, Cases and Materials*, 5ª ed., Oxford, 2011, p. 820.

29 e 30 de março de 1985, se referiam à Europa dos Cidadãos, elencando algumas medidas necessárias para a construir.

Não obstante, o Ato Único Europeu não integra qualquer norma relativa à cidadania europeia, pois, ao tempo, a Europa não estava preparada para encarar o desafio político que a cidadania representava[4].

2.2. A introdução da cidadania da União no Tratado de Maastricht

2.2.1. As dificuldades inerentes à natureza da União

O contexto de aprofundamento da dimensão política da integração europeia e de desenvolvimento da dimensão social que se viveu no Tratado de Maastricht levou à introdução das normas relativas à cidadania. Como bem nota Jo Shaw, "*se a União representa uma forma (emergente) de uma entidade política ['polity'], então tem de ter membros e estar relacionada com um 'povo'*"[5].

Porém, a aplicação do conceito de cidadania a uma entidade política, que se não enquadra na esfera da *estatalidade*, como é o caso da União Europeia, causa inúmeras dificuldades, a começar, desde logo, pela escolha do critério de atribuição da mesma. Embora se tivessem discutido outros critérios, como foi o caso da residência, o que acabou por ficar consagrado nos Tratados foi a nacionalidade dos Estados-Membros, o que implica uma certa subordinação da cidadania da União Europeia às leis de nacionalidade dos Estados-Membros[6].

Ora, sendo a atribuição da nacionalidade, na ótica do direito internacional, uma competência exclusiva dos Estados, fazendo mesmo parte do

[4] Sobre as origens da cidadania da União, ver Anastasia Iliopoulou, *Libre circulation et non-discrimination, élements du statut de citoyen de l'Union européenne*, Bruxelas, 2008, p. 10 e segs; Jean-François Akandji-Kombé, «L'émergence de la citoyenneté européenne. De Rome à Maastricht», *in* Stéphane Leclerc/Jean-françois Akandji-Kombé (ed.), *La Citoyenneté Européenne*, Bruxelas, 2006, p. 7 e segs; Marie José Garot, *La citoyenneté de l'Union europeénne*, Paris, 1999, p. 73 e segs; Mª Dolores Blázquez Peinado, «Los derechos de ciudadania y otros derechos reconocidos a los ciudadanos de la Union: de Maastricht a Amsterdam», *Rev. Der. Com. Eur.*, 1998, p. 263 e segs; Michelle C. Everson/Ulrich K. Preuss, *Concepts, Foundations, and Limits of European Citizenship*, Bremen, p. 14 e segs e 48 e segs.

[5] Jo Shaw, «The Interpretation of European Union Citizenship», *MLR*, 1998, p. 295.

[6] Inês Quadros, "A cidadania europeia e domínio reservado dos Estados – o Rei de Midas no Tribunal de Justiça?", *in* Sofia Oliveira Pais (coord.), *EU Citizenship – Challenges and Opportunities*, Porto, 2015, p. 241 e segs.

seu domínio reservado[7], tal não foi posto em causa pela consagração da cidadania da União, uma vez que os Estados-Membros mantêm intacta a sua competência para definir o modo como atribuem a nacionalidade[8]. Nas palavras de HANS ULRICH JESSURUN D'OLIVEIRA, "[*o*] *direito da nacionalidade pertence ao núcleo duro da identidade e da independência dos Estados como sujeitos de Direito Internacional*"[9].

O próprio Tribunal de Justiça, por exemplo, no caso *Kaur*[10], confirmou a competência estadual em matéria de atribuição da nacionalidade, embora tenha também acrescentado, no caso *Micheletti*[11], que o exercício desta competência deverá respeitar o direito comunitário[12]. A União não pode, portanto, ela própria, atribuir a cidadania com base em critérios independentes, como o *jus soli*, o *jus sanguinis* ou até a residência[13]. O conceito de cidadania da União, consagrado no Tratado de Maastricht, revela-se totalmente dependente dos direitos dos Estados-Membros, dado que a ligação entre a União Europeia e os seus cidadãos é indiretamente criada através da nacionalidade dos Estados-Membros[14].

O atual texto do artigo 20º, nº 1, do TFUE é, na sua essência, idêntico ao do antigo artigo 8º, nº 1, do TCE introduzido pelo Tratado de Maastricht. Com efeito, o artigo 20º, nº 1, do TFUE, estabelece que «*é cidadão da União qualquer pessoa que tenha a nacionalidade de um Estado-membro*». O Tratado de Amesterdão acrescentou que «*a cidadania da União é complementar da cida-*

[7] Ver Convenção relativa a certas questões sobre os conflitos das leis da nacionalidade (1930) e a Convenção Europeia sobre Nacionalidade (1997). Cfr. NGUYEN QUOC DINH/PATRICK DAILLIER/MATHIAS FORTEAU/ALAIN PELLET, *Droit International Public*, 8ª ed., Paris, 2009, p. 548.

[8] Neste sentido, HANS ULRICH JESSURUN D'OLIVEIRA, «Nationality and the European Union After Amsterdam», *in* DAVID O'KEEFFE/PATRICK TWOMEY (ed.), *Legal Issues of the Amsterdam Treaty*, Oxford, Hart, 2000, p. 395 e segs.

[9] HANS ULRICH JESSURUN D'OLIVEIRA, "Nationality and the European Union..., p. 411.

[10] Acórdão de 20/02/2001, *Kaur*, proc. C-192/99, Col. 2001, p. I-1237.

[11] Acórdão de 7/7/2002, *Micheletti*, Proc. C-369/90, Col. 1992, p. I- 4239, paras.10-11.

[12] Cfr. HELEN TONER, "Judicial Interpretation of European Union Citizenship – Transformation or Consolidation?", *MJ*, 2000, p. 170 e segs.

[13] Ver LUIS MARÍA DÍEZ PICAZO, «Cidadania Europea», in *Constitutionalismo de la Unión Europea*, Madrid, 2002, p. 52.

[14] Ver CYNTHIA JEAN, «La citoyenneté européenne: signification et perspetives dans le cadre du traité d'Amsterdam», *REI*, 1997, p. 739.

dania nacional e não a substitui» e o Tratado de Lisboa substituiu a expressão *"é complementar"* por *"acresce"*.

A cidadania da União é, pois, uma cidadania de sobreposição (*«citoyenneté de superposition»*)[15]. A cidadania da União *"não é um estado independente, uma vez que está ligada a todas as pessoas que têm a nacionalidade de um dos Estados-Membros – por outras palavras, é parasitária das definições de nacionalidade determinadas ao nível nacional"*[16]. Daqui decorre que cada Estado pode ter as suas diferentes regras de nacionalidade e de cidadania, o que conduz à desigualdade das condições de acesso[17], condicionando a atribuição da cidadania da União[18] e, consequentemente, os direitos das pessoas.

No entanto, importa salientar que a simples consagração da cidadania da União nos Tratados representa uma alteração de paradigma no que diz respeito à conceção do estatuto da pessoa no ordenamento jurídico comunitário[19], sendo mais um passo na afirmação de uma identidade europeia[20]. O indivíduo deixa de ser visto como um mero agente económico ou o beneficiário da integração europeia para passar a ser um elemento essencial da construção europeia[21]. Nas palavras de ANASTASIA ILIOPOU-

[15] VLAD CONSTANTINESCO, «La Citoyenneté de l'Union: une "vraie" citoyenneté?», *in* LUCIA SERENA ROSSI, *Vers une nouvelle architecture de l'Union Européenne – Le projet de Traité-constitution*, Bruxelas, 2004, p. 205.

[16] JO SHAW, «The Interpretation...», p. 298.

[17] Neste sentido, MARIE-JOSÉ GAROT, "A New Basis for European Citizenship: Residence?", *in* MASSIMO LA TORRE (ed.), *European Citizenship – An Institutional Challenge*, Haia, 1998, p. 233.

[18] Ver CYNTHIA JEAN, «La citoyenneté européenne...», p. 740.

[19] Neste sentido, J. LIÑAN NOGUERAS, "De la ciudadania europea a la Ciudadania de la Union", *GJ*, 1992, p. 65.

[20] Sobre a relação entre a cidadania e a identidade europeia, ver ANDREAS FOLLESDAL, "A Common European Identity for European Citizenship?", *German Law Journal*, 2014, p. 765 e segs.; FRANCISCO BALAGUER, "European Identity, Citizenship and the Model of Integration", *in* ALESSANDRA SILVEIRA *et al.*, *Citizenship and Solidarity in the European Union*, Bruxelas, 2013, p. 219 e segs; ELSPETH GUILD, *The Legal Elements of European Identity – EU Citizenship and Migration Law*, Haia, 2004, p. 13 e segs; N. W. BARBER, "Citizenship, Nationalism and the European Union", *ELR*, 2002, p. 242 e segs; SERGIO BARTOLE, "La cittadinanza e l'identità europea", *Annuario 1999, La costituzione europea, Atti del XIV Convegno Annuale, Perugia*, Milão, 1999, p. 445 e segs; CONSTANTIN A. STEPHANOU, «Identité et citoyenneté européennes», *RMC*, 1991, p. 30 e segs.

[21] Neste sentido, ROBERT KOVAR, «Le droit du citoyen de l'Union Européenne de circuler et de séjourner librement sur le territoire des Etats Membres», *in Mélanges en hommage au Doyen*

LOU, *"a cidadania visa colocar o indivíduo no centro do edifício europeu e afirmar a dimensão humana e social deste"*[22].

Além disso, a inclusão da cidadania no Tratado de Maastricht implicou a aceitação de um pressuposto, qual seja o de que os Europeus partilham alguns valores e comungam de uma herança cultural comum. Por outras palavras, o Tratado pressupõe que, quando comparados com outros povos, os Europeus têm algo em comum[23]. A cidadania da União contribui, portanto, ela própria, para a formação de uma identidade comum europeia[24].

Em suma, desde a entrada em vigor do Tratado de Maastricht, todos os nacionais dos Estados-Membros, incluindo, naturalmente, as portuguesas e os portugueses, passaram a ter duas cidadanias – a dos seus próprios Estados e a da União. Apesar disso, não têm duas nacionalidades. Com efeito, há cidadãos da União, mas não há quaisquer nacionais da União. A nacionalidade continua totalmente ligada aos Estados-Membros, pelo que a diferença entre cidadania e nacionalidade voltou a adquirir relevância[25].

2.2.2. As consequências da utilização do critério da nacionalidade na atribuição da cidadania da União

A doutrina tem criticado bastante esta solução[26], tendo alguns pugnado pela separação da cidadania da União dos direitos dos Estados-Membros bem como pela substituição do critério da nacionalidade pelo da residên-

Gérard COHEN-JONATHAN, vol. II, Bruxelas, 2004, p. 1049; ULRICH K. PREUSS, "Two Challenges to European Citizenship", *in* RICHARD BELLAMY e. a., *Constitutionalism in Transformation, European and Theoretical Perspectives*, Oxford, 1996, p. 122 e segs.

[22] ANASTASIA ILIOPOULOU, *Libre circulation...*, p. 15.

[23] Ver ANA MARIA GUERRA MARTINS, «Les valeurs communes et la place de la Charte en Europe», *ERPL/REDP*, 2002, p. 130 e segs.

[24] Cfr. ANA MARIA GUERRA MARTINS, "A cidadania da União Europeia – Definição, conteúdo e contributo para a constitucionalização da União Europeia", *in Estudos em Homenagem ao Professor Doutor PAULO DE PITTA E CUNHA*, p. 9 e segs; Idem, "Citizenship in the European Union – Conditions of Citizenship", *ERPL/REDP*, 2007, p. 83 e segs.

[25] ELSPETH GUILD, *The Legal Elements of European Identity...*, p. 37.

[26] Para um estudo mais aprofundado do debate académico em torno da cidadania da União, v. DIMITRY KOCHENOV, "The Present and the Future of EU Citizenship – A Bird's Eye View of the Legal Debate", *Jean Monnet Working Paper 02/12*.

cia[27]. Este critério teria a dupla vantagem de ser autónomo, de não ser algo de novo, uma vez que já é usado no direito da União a outros propósitos, e de não alterar a competência dos Estados-Membros em matéria de nacionalidade[28]. Além disso, permitiria a inclusão de aproximadamente 13 milhões de nacionais de Estados terceiros legalmente residentes na União.

A dependência da cidadania relativamente à nacionalidade dos Estados-Membros poderia eventualmente ter uma consequência negativa para os indivíduos, a saber, a perda da nacionalidade de um Estado-Membro implicaria a perda da cidadania da União e dos direitos que lhe são inerentes[29], o que levou alguma doutrina, desde o início, a sustentar que o indivíduo deveria poder conservar a qualidade de cidadão da União para poder continuar a exercer certos direitos, designadamente, o direito de livre circulação, o que configuraria uma solução mais conforme com a lógica da União de proteção do indivíduo[30]. O Tribunal de Justiça acabou

[27] Neste sentido, SAMANTHA BESSON/ANDRÉ UTZINGER, "Introduction: Future Challenges of European Citizenship – Facing a Wide-Open Pandora's Box", *ELJ*, 2007, p. 581; DORA KOSTAKOPOULOU, "European Union Citizenship: Writing the Future", *ELJ*, 2007, p. 644; JEAN-YVES CARLIER, "Les enjeux de la citoyenneté européenne", *in* STÉPHANE LECLERC/ JEAN-FRANÇOIS AKANDJI-KOMBÉ (ed.) *La Citoyenneté Européenne*, Bruxelas, 2006, p. 44; DORA KOSTAKOPOULOU, "Ideas, Norms and European Citizenship: Explaining Institutional Change", *MLR*, 2005, p. 243; Mª CONCEPCIÓN PÉREZ VILLALOBOS, "La cultura de los derechos fundamentales en Europa. Los derechos de los imigrantes extracomunitarios y el nuevo concepto de ciudadanía", *in Derecho Constitucional y Cultura, Estudios en Homenaje a PETER HÄBERLE*, Madrid, 2004, p. 706 e 709 e segs; BLANCA VILÁ COSTA, "The Quest for a Consistent Set of Rules Governing the Status of non-Community Nationals", *in* PHILIP ALSTON, *The EU and Human Rights*, Oxford, 1999, p. 441; MARIE-JOSÉ GAROT, "A New Basis for European Citizenship...", p. 229 e 233 e segs; ALVARO CASTRO OLIVEIRA, "The Position of Resident Third-Country Nationals: is it too early to grant them Union Citizenship?", *in* MASSIMO LA TORRE (ed.), *European Citizenship...*, p. 196; RUT RUBIO MARÍN, "Equal Citizenship and the Difference that Residence Makes", *in* MASSIMO LA TORRE (ed.), *European Citizenship...*, p. 206 e segs; ANDREW EVANS, "Union Citizenship and the Constitutionalization of Equality in EU Law", *in* MASSIMO LA TORRE (ed.), *European Citizenship...*, p. 291.

[28] Neste sentido, ANASTASIA ILIOPOULOU, *Libre circulation...*, p. 28.

[29] Neste sentido, ALVARO CASTRO OLIVEIRA, "The Position of Resident Third-Country...", p. 186.

[30] Neste sentido, ANASTASIA ILIOPOULOU, *Libre circulation...*, p. 25; STEPHEN HALL, «Loss of Union Citizenship in Breach of Fundamental Rights", *ELR*, 1996, p. 129.

por aceitar esta tese, entre outros, no caso *Rottmann*[31], de que falaremos adiante.

2.2.3. Os limites dos poderes dos Estados em sede de atribuição da nacionalidade

Numa perspetiva antropocêntrica, a cidadania não deve ser considerada um limite aos direitos e deveres do indivíduo, mas antes aos deveres e aos poderes do Estado nacional[32].

O mecanismo do reconhecimento da nacionalidade dos outros Estados não é desconhecido do direito internacional[33], mas no direito da União Europeia, ao contrário do que sucede naquele[34], o Estado-membro da União não pode recusar o reconhecimento da nacionalidade de uma pessoa a quem outro Estado-Membro reconhece a qualidade de seu nacional[35]. Além disso, também não pode fazer depender esse reconhecimento de quaisquer outras condições, além da nacionalidade, tais como a residência no Estado-Membro, o que significa que "*os Estados-Membros devem incondicionalmente aceitar a cidadania da União conferida por outro Estado-Membro*"[36] e, desse modo, condicionar o gozo e o exercício dos direitos consagrados no direito da União Europeia. De facto, a cidadania da União "*introduziu uma restrição importante ao poder do Estado retirar a nacionalidade aos indivíduos; uma vez que também esses indivíduos são cidadãos da União*" [...] "*Tais medidas devem conformar-se com os standards de direitos humanos protegidos pelo Tribunal de Justiça*"[37].

Um dos casos mais impressivos, neste domínio, é o caso *Chen*[38], no qual o Tribunal admitiu o direito de uma criança (filha de pais chineses), nascida num Estado-membro da União Europeia – que atribui a nacio-

[31] Ac. de 02/03 2010, *Rottmann*, Proc. C-135/08, ECLI:EU:C:2010:104.

[32] Mª Concepción Pérez Villalobos, "La cultura de los derechos fundamentales...", p. 711.

[33] Cfr., por todos, Nguyen Quoc Dinh/Patrick Daillier/Mathias Forteau/Alain Pellet, *Droit International...*, p. 548.

[34] Cfr. Acórdão de 6 de abril de 1955, *Liechtenstein v. Guatemala (Nottebohm)*, ICJ Rep. 1955, p. 23.

[35] Koen Lenaerts/Piet Van Nuffel, *Constitutional Law of the European Union*, 2ª ed., Londres, 2005, p. 545.

[36] Acórdão de 7/7/2002, *Micheletti*, cit., paras.10-11.

[37] Stephen Hall, "Loss of Union Citizenship...", p. 129.

[38] Acórdão de 19/10/2004, *Chen*, proc. C-200/02, Col. 2004, p. I-9925.

nalidade a todos aqueles que nascem no seu território – o direito de residência num outro Estado-Membro da União na sua qualidade de cidadã da União. Esse direito de residência foi igualmente reconhecido à mãe da criança, cidadã chinesa, pois só assim se consegue assegurar o efeito útil do direito da criança[39]. Esta jurisprudência vai ser mais tarde confirmada no caso *Alokpa*[40].

Como veremos, a jurisprudência do Tribunal de Justiça nem sempre evoluiu no sentido do aprofundamento dos direitos de cidadania e da consequente limitação dos poderes dos Estados-Membros.

Em suma, ao aceitarem a cidadania da União, os Estados-Membros aceitam também um certo grau de reconhecimento recíproco, incondicional e mútuo, no que diz respeito às regras de nacionalidade. Porém, as soluções adotadas pelas diferentes leis de nacionalidade são bastante divergentes, o que acaba por conduzir ao tratamento diferenciado de indivíduos que se encontram em situações idênticas, sem que se verifique qualquer justificação além da nacionalidade.

2.2.4. Nota crítica

Uma entidade política, como a União Europeia, cuja base axiológica é, segundo o Tratado da União Europeia, o respeito pela dignidade humana, pela liberdade, pela democracia, pela igualdade, pelo Estado de direito e pelo respeito dos direitos humanos (artigo 2º do TUE), não pode compactuar com este estado de coisas.

Aliás, a cidadania só pode operar num ambiente democrático com respeito pelos direitos fundamentais e pelos princípios da igualdade e da não discriminação[41]. A criação da cidadania europeia deve ser encarada como um instrumento de legitimidade democrática[42] e como uma forma

[39] Sobre o caso *Chen*, ver Bjorn Kunoy, "A Union of National Citizens: the Origins of the Courts Lack of *Avant-Gardisme* in the *Chen* Case", *CMLR*, 2006, p. 179 e segs.

[40] Ac. de 10/10/2013, *Alokpa*, proc. C-86/12, ECLI:EU:C:2013:645.

[41] Vlad Constantinesco, «La Citoyenneté de l'Union...», p. 213.

[42] Cynthia Jean, «La citoyenneté européenne...», p. 741. No mesmo sentido, N. W. Barber, "Citizenship...", p. 246; Dora Kostakopoulou, "Ideas, Norms and European Citizenship: Explaining Institutional Change", *MLR*, 2005, p. 233.

de aumentar o sentimento de pertença à União e de adesão a um projeto comum[43].

Como melhor veremos adiante, o Tribunal de Justiça, na tentativa de minorar estes efeitos negativos, considerou que todo o cidadão da União tem direito a um tratamento igual ao exercer direitos que lhe advêm do direito comunitário (atualmente, do direito da União Europeia), especialmente, no exercício das liberdades garantidas pelo TCE (hoje TFUE). A desigualdade de tratamento tem de ser justificada sempre com base em razões objetivas, independentes da nacionalidade das pessoas em causa, e tem de ser proporcionada ao objetivo legitimamente prosseguido[44].

2.3. O impacto da cidadania da União na Constituição Portuguesa

Como já tivemos oportunidade de afirmar e desenvolver noutros lugares[45], a interdependência, a interação e a influência mútua entre o direito da União Europeia e os direitos constitucionais nacionais é, hoje em dia, uma realidade indesmentível, a qual se expressa, do ponto de vista teórico, através, entre outras, das teses do constitucionalismo multinível[46] ou do pluralismo constitucional[47]. Não sendo este o local próprio para desenvol-

[43] Anastasia Iliopoulou, *Libre circulation...*, p. 17.

[44] Acórdão de 11/7/2002, *D'Hoop*, proc. C-224/98, Col. 2002, p. I-6191, paras 27-41; Acórdão de 2/10/2002, *Garcia Avello*, proc. C-148/02, Col. 2002, para. 31. Para um comentário do caso *D'Hoop*, cfr. Anastasia Iliopoulou/Helen Toner, "A New Approach to Discrimination against Free Movers? D'Hoop v Office National de l'Emploi", *ELR*, 2003, p. 389 e segs.

[45] V., por todos, Ana Maria Guerra Martins, *Manual de Direito da União Europeia*, Coimbra, Almedina, 2012, p. 35 e segs.

[46] Sobre o constitucionalismo multinível, cfr., por todos, Ingolf Pernice, "Multilevel Constitutionalism in the European Union", *ELR*, 2002, p. 511-529; Idem, "Multilevel Constitutionalism and the Treaty of Amsterdam: European Constitution-Making Revisited?", *CMLR*, 1999, p. 707 e segs; Idem, "The Treaty of Lisbon: Multilevel constitutionalism in action", *The Columbia Journal of European Law*, 2009, p. 372; Idem "Multilevel Constitutionalism and the Crisis of Democracy in Europe", *EuConst*, 2015, p. 547 e segs.

[47] Para um estudo aprofundado do constitucionalismo plural, v. todos os contributos em Matej Avbelj/Jan Komárek, *Constitutional Pluralism in the European Union and Beyond*, Oxford, 2012 e ainda J.H.H. Weiler, "Prologue: global and pluralist constitutionalism – some doubts", in Gráinne de Búrca/J.H.H. Weiler, *The Worlds of European Constitutionalism*, Cambridge, 2012, p. 8 e segs; Daniel Halberstam, "Local, global and plural constitutionalism: Europe meets the world", in Gráinne de Búrca/J.H.H. Weiler, *The Worlds of European*

ver este tema, não podemos deixar de referir que uma das manifestações mais evidentes do constitucionalismo multinível consiste na necessidade de adaptação das ordens jurídicas internas ao direito da União Europeia com o intuito de se conformar com aquele direito e, deste modo, evitar, posteriormente, conflitos de normas. Questão que, aliás, constitui a principal preocupação do constitucionalismo plural.

Assim sendo, a introdução das normas de cidadania da União no Tratado de Maastricht implicou revisões constitucionais em vários Estados-Membros, entre os quais se conta Portugal. Com efeito, a revisão constitucional de 1992[48] alterou, entre outras disposições, o artigo 15º da Constituição relativo a estrangeiros e apátridas. Além de a epígrafe do preceito ter passado a mencionar os cidadãos europeus, foi aditado um nº 5 com o seguinte texto:

> "*A lei pode atribuir, em condições de reciprocidade, aos cidadãos dos Estados-Membros residentes em Portugal, o direito de elegerem e serem eleitos Deputados ao Parlamento Europeu*".

Esta alteração teve, apenas e tão-somente, em vista conformar a Constituição Portuguesa ao então Tratado da Comunidade Europeia.

3. Os direitos (e deveres) das portuguesas e dos portugueses inerentes à cidadania da União

3.1. As bases jurídicas dos direitos de cidadania da União

Uma vez definida a titularidade da cidadania da União, há que esclarecer quais os direitos lhe estão associados. Ora, tendo em conta a quantidade de emigrantes que Portugal tem espalhados pelos Estados-Membros da União Europeia esta não é, para nós, uma matéria irrelevante.

Constitutionalism, p. 150 e segs; NICO KRISCH, "The case for pluralism in postnational law", in GRÁINNE DE BÚRCA/J.H.H. WEILER, *The Worlds of European Constitutionalism*, p. 203 e segs; MIGUEL POIARES MADURO, *A Constituição Plural – Constitucionalismo e União Europeia*, Cascais, 2006, p. 15 e segs.

[48] Lei Constitucional nº 1/92, de 25 de novembro, publicada no DR, I Série A, nº 273, de 25/11/1992.

O estatuto do cidadão da União tem, após o Tratado de Lisboa[49], uma dupla base no direito originário – o TFUE e a CDFUE[50].

Nos termos do artigo 20º, nº 2, do TFUE, os cidadãos gozam dos direitos e estão sujeitos aos deveres previstos no Tratado. Entre esses direitos contam-se os que estão mencionados na Parte II do Tratado relativa à cidadania – artigos 21º a 24º do TFUE –, mas também outros, como é o caso do direito a não ser discriminado em razão da nacionalidade nas

[49] Sobre a cidadania da União no Tratado de Lisboa, cfr. NIAM NIC SHUIBHNE, "EU Citizenship after Lisbon", in DIAMOND ASHIAGBOR/NICOLA COUNTOURIS/IOANNIS LIANOS, *The European Union after the Treaty of Lisbon*, Cambridge, 2012, p. 136 e segs; PAUL CRAIG/GRAÍNNE DE BÚRCA, *EU Law...*, p. 819 e segs; DAMIAN CHALMERS/GARETH DAVIES/GIORGIO MONTI, *European Union Law*, 4ª ed., Cambridge, 2011, p. 439 e segs; JO SHAW, «Citizenship: Contrasting Dynamics at the Interface of Integration and Constitutionalism», *in* PAUL CRAIG/ /GRAÍNNE DE BÚRCA, *The Evolution of EU Law*, 2ª ed., Oxford, 2011, p. 575 e segs; JO SHAW, «The constitutional development of citizenship in the EU context: with or without the Treaty of Lisbon», INGOLF PERNICE/EVGENI TANCHEV (eds.), *Ceci n'est pas une Constitution – Constitutionalisation without a Constitution?*, Baden-Baden, 2009, p. 104 e segs; MARIA JOSÉ RANGEL DE MESQUITA, «Cidadania Europeia e legitimação democrática após o Tratado de Lisboa», *in Cadernos o Direito*, 2010, p. 149 e segs; ANNETTE SCHRAUWEN, "European Union Citizenship in the Treaty of Lisbon: Any Change at all", *MJ*, 2008, p. 55 e segs.

[50] Sobre os direitos de cidadania consagrados na Carta, cfr. ROSTANE MEHDI, «Article II-99», *in* LAURENCE BURGORGUE-LARSEN *et al.*, *Traité établissant une Constitution pour l'Europe – Commentaire article par article, Parte II – La Charte des droits fondamentaux de l'Union*, tomo II, Bruxelas, 2005, p. 505 e segs; MICHEL VERPEAUX, «Article II-100», *in* LAURENCE BURGORGUE-LARSEN *et al.*, *Traité établissant une Constitution pour l'Europe...*, tomo II, p. 514 e segs; DENYS SIMON, «Article II-101», *in* LAURENCE BURGORGUE-LARSEN *et al.*, *Traité établissant une Constitution pour l'Europe...*, tomo II, p. 525 e segs; JACQUES ZILLER, «Article II-102», *in* LAURENCE BURGORGUE-LARSEN *et al.*, *Traité établissant une Constitution pour l'Europe...*, tomo II, p. 538 e segs; CLAUDE BLUMANN, «Article II-103», *in* LAURENCE BURGORGUE-LARSEN *et al.*, *Traité établissant une Constitution pour l'Europe...*, tomo II, p. 551 e segs; HUGUES PORTELLI, «Article II-104», *in* LAURENCE BURGORGUE-LARSEN *et al.*, *Traité établissant une Constitution pour l'Europe...*, tomo II, p. 567 e segs; JEAN-PAUL JACQUÉ, «Article II-105», *in* LAURENCE BURGORGUE-LARSEN *et al.*, *Traité établissant une Constitution pour l'Europe...*, tomo II, p. 573 e segs; FLORENCE POIRAT, «Article II-106», *in* LAURENCE BURGORGUE-LARSEN *et al.*, *Traité établissant une Constitution pour l'Europe...*, tomo II, p. 578 e segs; SIEGFRIED MAGIERA, «Kapitel V, Bürgerrechte», *in* JÜRGEN MEYER (org.), *Kommentar zur Charta der Grundrechte der Europäischen Union*, Baden-Baden, 2003, p. 433 e segs; MARC FALLON, "Les droits fondamentaux liés à la citoyenneté de l'Union Européenne, sous les regards croisés du traité C.E. et de la Charte", *in* YVES CARLIER/OLIVIER DE SCHUTTER (dir.), *La Charte des droits fondamentaux de l'Union européenne – son apport à la protection des droits de l'Homme en Europe*, Bruxelas, 2002, p. 149 e segs; DENYS SIMON, «Les droits du citoyen de l'Union», *RUDH*, 2000, p. 22 e segs.

matérias do âmbito de aplicação do Tratado que está previsto no artigo 18º TFUE.

Por sua vez, a CDFUE prevê os direitos de cidadania, no seu Título V, nos artigos 39º a 46º. Note-se que nem sempre a redação e a sistematização dos preceitos constantes da Carta coincidem com as do TFUE. A Carta autonomiza, por exemplo, o direito a uma boa administração, enquanto o TFUE não procede de modo idêntico. O artigo 45º da Carta menciona expressamente os nacionais de Estados terceiros que residem legalmente no território de um dos Estados-Membros no domínio da liberdade de circulação e permanência, ao contrário do que sucede no TFUE.

Sublinhe-se, todavia, que, com exceção desta última, as divergências apontadas são mais aparentes do que reais, justificando-se, essencialmente, por duas razões: i) a negociação da Carta foi independente e anterior à negociação da revisão dos Tratados e ii) a Carta constitui um texto autónomo, cujo âmbito de aplicação é mais restrito.

3.2. Os direitos decorrentes da cidadania da União

Os direitos de cidadania podem ser agrupados em função dos seus destinatários. Com efeito, não obstante a cidadania ser, em princípio, excludente dos nacionais de terceiros Estados, tem-se assistido a um movimento de extensão dos beneficiários dos direitos de cidadania, que aponta no sentido de uma tendência de generalização da proteção jurídica[51].

Assim, podemos distinguir os direitos de cidadania da União[52] que estão reservados aos cidadãos da União e que incluem os direitos de participação política, ou seja, o direito de participar, ativa e passivamente, nas eleições europeias e municipais (artigo 22º do TFUE e artigos 39º

[51] Neste sentido, VLAD CONSTANTINESCO, «La Citoyenneté de l'Union...», p. 207.

[52] Sobre os direitos de cidadania da União, ver, entre muitos outros, MARIA JOSÉ RANGEL DE MESQUITA, "As facetas da cidadania na integração europeia", *in* SOFIA OLIVEIRA PAIS (coord.), *EU Citizenship...*, p. 193 e segs.; ANA MARIA GUERRA MARTINS, "A cidadania da União Europeia...", p. 9 e segs; Idem, "Citizenship in the European Union...", p. 83 e segs; STÉPHANE LECLERC, "Les droits du citoyen européen", *in* STÉPHANE LECLERC/JEAN-FRANÇOIS AKANDJI-KOMBÉ (ed.), *La Citoyenneté...*, p. 51 e segs; CATHERINE WIHTOL DE WENDEN, "Les Fondements de la Citoyenneté Européenne", *in* STÉPHANE LECLERC/JEAN-FRANÇOIS AKANDJI-KOMBÉ (ed.), *La Citoyenneté Européenne...*, p. 24 e segs; MAXIMO LA TORRE, «Citizenship: a European...», p. 131 e segs.

e 40º da Carta) e o direito à proteção diplomática (artigo 23º do TFUE e artigo 46º da Carta) dos direitos de cidadania se encontram ligados à residência, isto é, um conjunto de direitos que são atribuídos a qualquer pessoa, desde que resida num dos Estados-Membros da União. De entre estes últimos, contam-se o direito de queixa ao Provedor de Justiça (artigo 24º, par. 3º, do TFUE e artigo 43º da Carta), o direito de petição ao Parlamento Europeu (artigo 24º, par. 3º, do TFUE e artigo 44º da Carta), o direito de acesso aos documentos do Parlamento Europeu, do Conselho e da Comissão (artigo 15º, nº 3, do TFUE e artigo 42º da Carta). Por fim, devem mencionar-se os direitos de cidadania que são atribuídos a qualquer pessoa, independentemente de serem ou não cidadãos da União, dos quais se destacam o direito a uma boa administração (artigo 41º da Carta) e o direito a dirigir-se, por escrito, às instituições da União em qualquer das línguas dos Tratados e a receber uma resposta nessa mesma língua.

Note-se ainda que o direito de livre circulação depende da residência, mas o conteúdo do direito varia consoante se trate de nacionais dos Estados-Membros ou de nacionais de terceiros Estados, sendo que dentro destes últimos existem diferentes regimes. Assim, os primeiros gozam do direito de livre circulação e residência, o qual é extensivo às suas famílias, em conexão com a livre circulação de pessoas e serviços (artigo 21º, nº 1, do TFUE e artigo 45º, nº 1, da Carta)[53], enquanto os segundos estão sujeitos a condições muito mais restritas previstas no direito da União Europeia (artigo 45º, nº 2, da Carta).

Nos termos do artigo 25º do TFUE, é possível reforçar o atual quadro de direitos e/ou aditar novos direitos, sem necessidade de revisão dos Tratados pelos processos previstos no artigo 48º do TUE. Até ao momento este mecanismo ainda não foi usado.

São estes, pois, os direitos de cidadania que as portuguesas e os portugueses gozam pelo facto de Portugal pertencer à União Europeia.

[53] Sobre o direito de livre circulação dos cidadãos da União, cfr. CHRISTINE KADDOUS, "Droits de L'Homme et Libertés de Circulation: Complémentarité ou Contradiction?", *in Mélanges en hommage à Georges Vandersanden*, Bruxelas, 2008, p. 563 e segs.; JAN ZIEKOW, "Die Freizügigkeit des Unionsbürgers", *in* OLIVER DÖRR (dir.), *Ein Rechtsleher in Berlin, Symposium für* ALBRECHT RANDELZHOFER, Berlim, 2004, p. 102 e segs.

3.3. Apreciação crítica do estatuto de cidadão da União

O estatuto do cidadão da União, tal como está consagrado no Tratado, tem sido, contudo, alvo de várias críticas, devido ao seu caráter incompleto ou condicionado.

No que diz respeito ao exercício dos direitos, a cidadania da União difere profundamente da cidadania estadual, uma vez que o exercício da maioria dos direitos depende da condição de o nacional se deslocar do Estado de que é nacional para outro Estado-Membro e de aí passar a residir. Esta exigência, na prática, pode conduzir a situações paradoxais, em que um nacional de um Estado-Membro que nunca saiu do território do Estado de que é nacional e um cidadão de um Estado terceiro que já nasceu num Estado-Membro da União do qual também nunca saiu, por força de acordos celebrados entre o seu Estado de origem e a União pode gozar de um direito à não discriminação em função da nacionalidade, no que diz respeito à livre circulação de trabalhadores, enquanto o nacional do Estado-membro – porque não circulou – não goza.

Finalmente, deve sublinhar-se que o estatuto de cidadão da União não comporta qualquer dever, sendo composto, única e exclusivamente, por direitos. Neste aspeto, a cidadania da União também contrasta com a cidadania estadual, a qual abrange alguns deveres, como, por exemplo, o dever de pagar impostos. Aliás, a ausência de deveres dos cidadãos da União é bem reveladora da fraqueza dos laços da ligação entre o cidadão e a União.

Além disso, algumas das normas referentes à cidadania da União (ver, por exemplo, artigo 22º, nºs 1 e 2, do TFUE) admitem derrogações, com base na invocação de motivos bastante genéricos ("*sempre que problemas específicos de um Estado o justifiquem*"). Por outro lado, a implementação das normas relativas à cidadania exige, nalguns casos, a unanimidade no Conselho, o que demonstra bem as dificuldades que os Estados-Membros enfrentam na cedência de soberania neste domínio.

3.4. A faceta excludente da cidadania da União

Importa realçar que, além da faceta de inclusão ou *includente*, que acabámos de estudar, a cidadania da União tem igualmente uma faceta de exclusão ou *excludente*, a qual afasta os estrangeiros, nacionais de países terceiros, e os apátridas, total ou parcialmente, dos direitos que lhe estão associados, incluindo o direito à não discriminação[54]. A cidadania da União diferencia "nós" e "eles".

Isto significa que se Portugal não tivesse aderido às Comunidades, as portuguesas e os portugueses, residentes num Estado-Membro da União Europeia, teriam o estatuto de nacional de um país terceiro, o qual nem sequer se encontra definido no Tratado, sendo apenas definido no direito derivado[55]. Acresce que esse estatuto é muito diversificado[56]. No fundo, é nacional de um país terceiro quem não for nacional de um Estado-Membro.

Se abstrairmos dos imigrantes ilegais ou irregulares que fazem parte de um contingente – cujo número, pela própria natureza das coisas, é extremamente difícil de determinar – dentro dos nacionais de Estados terceiros legalmente residentes na União, atendendo aos direitos que lhes são atribuídos, o seu estatuto é gradativo, isto é, admitem-se níveis diferentes de direitos para nacionais de terceiros Estados, consoante a ligação que o Estado de que são nacionais tem com a União ou então consoante os laços, designadamente, familiares que os próprios indivíduos têm com a União.

Ora, seria, pois, ao abrigo desse estatuto, o qual não depende inteiramente da própria pessoa, mas de um conjunto de fatores que não domina, que o conjunto de portuguesas e de portugueses que reside em Estados-Membros da União Europeia ou que neles pretende residir, que para

[54] Ver Catherine Barnard, "Article 13: Through the Looking Glass of Union Citizenship", *in* David O'Keeffe/Patrick Twomey (ed.), *Legal Issues of the Amsterdam Treaty*, Oxford, 2000, p. 379.

[55] O direito derivado já definiu o que entende por nacional de país terceiro como a "*pessoa que não seja um cidadão da União na aceção do nº 1 do artigo 17º do Tratado*". Ver, por exemplo, artigo 2º, al. a), da diretiva nº 2003/109/CE do Conselho, de 25 de Novembro de 2003, relativa ao estatuto dos nacionais de países terceiros residentes de longa duração (JOUE L 16, de 23/1/2004, p. 44 e segs.); artigo 2º, al. a), da diretiva nº 2004/114/CE do Conselho, de 13 de Dezembro de 2004, relativa às condições de admissão de nacionais de países terceiros para efeitos de estudos, de intercâmbio de estudantes, de formação não remunerada ou de voluntariado (JOUE L 375, de 23/12/2004, p. 12 e segs.), e artigo 2º, al. a), da diretiva nº 2005/71/CE, de 12 de Outubro de 2005, relativa a um procedimento específico de admissão de nacionais de países terceiros para efeitos de investigação científica (JOUE L 289, de 3/11/2005, p. 15 e segs.).

[56] Jean-François Akandji-Kombé, «Le droit des étrangers...», p. 360.

eles se desloca ou pretende deslocar, que neles estuda ou pretende estudar, que neles exerce a profissão de investigador ou pretende exercer, se encontrariam. Diga-se, em abono da verdade, que esse estatuto, mesmo nos casos ditos "privilegiados"[57], é sempre menos protetor do que o estatuto de cidadão da União.

4. A jurisprudência do Tribunal de Justiça da União Europeia no domínio da cidadania

4.1. Uma jurisprudência casuística e ambivalente

Chegados a este ponto, importa chamar a atenção para o facto que, além do direito originário e do direito derivado (o qual, por falta de espaço, não pode ser objeto de análise neste estudo), a construção pretoriana do Tribunal de Justiça muito tem contribuído para delinear os contornos do estatuto de cidadão da União, como, aliás, sucede em todos os outros domínios do direito da União Europeia[58].

Com efeito, ancorando a cidadania as suas raízes na ideia de liberdade e de igualdade, o Tribunal, após uma primeira fase (1993-1997), por alguns apelidada de *"judicialmente minimalista"*[59], em que limitou os direitos de cidadania em função do exercício da liberdade de circulação, numa segunda fase (que se iniciou em 1998), o Tribunal explorou a vertente constitucional da cidadania da União, colocando o acento tónico na ligação entre ela e a igualdade de tratamento (e a não discriminação) em função da nacionalidade, o que levou ao alargamento do âmbito de aplicação das normas relativas à cidadania. Operou-se, portanto, uma mudança de paradigma.

[57] Na impossibilidade de estudar, nesta sede, o estatuto dos nacionais de terceiros Estados legalmente residentes num Estado-Membro da União Europeia, cfr. ANA MARIA GUERRA MARTINS, *A igualdade e a não discriminação dos nacionais de Estados terceiros legalmente residentes na União Europeia – Da origem na integração económica ao fundamento na dignidade do ser humano*, Coimbra, 2010, p. 287 e segs.

[58] Sobre a evolução da jurisprudência do TJ em matéria de cidadania da União, ver, por todos, GERARD-RENÉ DE GROOT/NGO CHUN LUK, "Twenty Years of CJEU Jurisprudence on Citizenship", *German Law Journal*, 2014, p. 821 e segs.

[59] DORA KOSTAKOPOULOU, "Ideas, Norms and European Citizenship...", p. 233.

Para exemplificar o que acaba de se afirmar, podemos mencionar as decisões *Martinez Sala*[60], *Bickel-Franz*[61], *Grzelczyk*[62] e, mais tarde, as decisões *Chen* e *Alokpa*, acima mencionadas.

Porém, importa notar que esta mudança de paradigma não foi definitiva, dado que o TJ procedeu, noutros casos, a interpretações das normas relativas à cidadania da União, constantes tanto do direito originário como do direito derivado, bem mais restritivas, como sucedeu, por exemplo, nas decisões *Wijsenbeek*[63], *Kaba I*[64] e *Kaba II*[65]. Aliás, estas interpretações mais restritivas também não constituíram a última palavra do Tribunal, neste domínio, dado que apenas um ano e meio após o último acórdão *Kaba*, o Tribunal retomou a sua jurisprudência anterior, nas decisões *Trojani*[66], *Schempp*[67], *Tas-Hagen Tas*[68], *Morgan*[69] e *Schwarz and Gootjes-Schwarz*[70].

Esta aparente instabilidade da jurisprudência do Tribunal deve-se, essencialmente, ao casuísmo com que o Tribunal encara a cidadania da União. Como defende Koen Lenaerts, não se verificam grandes saltos na fundamentação das decisões, mas antes a construção de uma jurisprudência com base numa técnica argumentativa e segundo o método progressivo – "*stone by stone*"[71].

Mais recentemente, nos casos *Rottmann*[72] e *Ruiz Zambrano*[73], o Tribunal de Justiça aceitou que, ainda que não se verifique o exercício da liberdade de circulação, o artigo 20º do TFUE se opõe a uma medida nacional ainda que não prive formalmente o indivíduo dos direitos inerentes ao estatuto de cidadão da União, mas, na prática, produz os mesmos efeitos, uma vez

[60] Ac. de 12/5/98, *Martinez Sala*, proc. C-85/96. Col. 1998, p. I-2691.

[61] Ac. de 24/11/98, *Bickel and Franz*, proc. C-274/96, Col. 1998, p. I-7637.

[62] Ac. de 20/9/2001, *Grzelczyk*, proc. C-184/99, Col. 2001, p. I–6193.

[63] Ac. de 21/9/99, *Wijsenbeek*, proc. C-378/97, Col. 1997, p. I-6207.

[64] Ac. de 11/4/2000, *Kaba I*, proc. C-356/98, Col. 2000, p. I-2623.

[65] Ac. de 6/3/2003, *Kaba II*, proc. C-460/00, Col. 2003, p. I-2219.

[66] Ac. de 7/9/2004, *Trojani*, proc. C-456/02, Col. 2004, p. I-7573.

[67] Ac. de 12/07/2005, proc. C-403/03, Col. 2005, p. I-6421.

[68] Ac. de 26/10/2006, proc. C-192/05, Col. 2006, p. I-10451.

[69] Ac. de 23/10/2007, proc. C-11/06, Col. 2007, p. I-9161.

[70] Ac. de 11/9/2007, proc. C-76/05, Col. 2007, p. I-6849.

[71] Koen Lenaerts, "EU Citizenship and the European Court of Justice's '*stone-by-stone*' approach', *International Comparative Jurisprudence*, 2015, p. 1.

[72] Ac. cit.

[73] Ac. de 08/03/2011, *Ruiz Zambrano*, proc. C-34/09, ECLI:EU:C:2011:124.

que priva os cidadãos do gozo efetivo do essencial dos direitos conferidos pelo estatuto de cidadão da União.

O Tribunal não esclareceu, no entanto, três questões essenciais: Como interagem os artigos 20º e 21º TFUE sem o elemento do exercício da liberdade de circulação? Quando é que uma medida nacional leva à privação de direitos de cidadania? Se e em que medida os direitos fundamentais devem ser tidos em conta para determinar a privação dos direitos de cidadania? A resposta a estas questões vai ser dada posteriormente, nos casos *McCarthy*[74] e *Dereci*[75]. No primeiro caso, o Tribunal interpreta restritivamente a noção de medida nacional capaz de produzir um efeito de privação de direitos, tendo, no segundo caso, continuado esta visão restritiva, ao considerar que só há privação dos direitos de cidadania quando o nacional de um Estado-Membro tiver de abandonar o território da União e não apenas o território do Estado-Membro em causa. Por outro lado, o Tribunal considerou que os direitos não devem ser tidos em conta quando se avalia a questão prévia de saber se há ou não privação dos direitos[76]. Posteriormente, nos casos *Iida*[77] e *Ymeraga*[78], o Tribunal reafirmou esta jurisprudência[79].

Mas é no que diz respeito à matéria dos subsídios sociais, pensões não contributivas, subsídios de subsistência e subsídios de residência que o Tribunal, após ter demonstrado alguma abertura, por exemplo, nos casos *Collins*[80] e *Brey*[81], tem desenvolvido uma jurisprudência ainda mais restri-

[74] Ac. de 05/05/2011, *McCarthy*, Proc. C-439/09, ECLI:EU:C:2011:277.

[75] Ac. de 15/11/2011, *Dereci e o.*, Proc. C-256/11, ECLI:EU:C:2011:734.

[76] Para um estudo crítico destes três acórdãos do Tribunal de Justiça, cfr., entre outros, Dimitry Kochenov/Richard Plender, "EU Citizenship: From an Incipient Form to an Incipient Substance? The Discovery of the Treaty Text", *ELR*, 2012, p. 369 e segs; Panos Stasinopoulos, "EU Citizenship as a Battle of the Concepts: *Travailleur* v *Citoyen*", *European Journal of Legal Studies*, 2011, p. 74-103.

[77] Ac. de 08/11/2012, *Iida*, Proc. C-40/11, ECLI:EU:C:2012:691.

[78] Ac. de 08/05/2013, *Ymeraga*, Proc. C-87/12, ECLI:EU:C:2013:291.

[79] Uma análise contextualizada desta jurisprudência pode ver-se em Koen Lenaerts, "EU Citizenship...", p. 1-10.

[80] Ac. de 23/3/2004, *Collins*, proc. C-138/02, Col. 2004, p. I-2703.

[81] Ac. de 19/09/2013, *Brey*, proc. C-140/12, ECLI:EU:C:2013:565.

tiva, por exemplo, nos casos *Dano*[82], *Alimanovic*[83] *e Garcia Nieto*[84], a qual não pode deixar de ser associada à crise económica e financeira que assola a Europa desde 2008[85].

Em conclusão, a jurisprudência do TJ no domínio da cidadania da União, devido ao seu caráter muito casuístico conduz a uma certa incerteza e insegurança. O Tribunal atém-se muito às circunstâncias do caso, o que torna, por vezes, difícil antecipar as normas e os princípios aplicáveis num determinado caso. Tal é agravado pelo facto de o Tribunal se basear em normas não escritas, como a de que uma medida nacional não deve "*privar os cidadãos do gozo efetivo do essencial dos direitos conferidos pelo seu estatuto de cidadão da União*" ou a garantia de "*direitos derivados de um cidadão da União*" aos nacionais de Estados terceiros.

4.2. O impacto da jurisprudência do Tribunal de Justiça da União Europeia no Tribunal Constitucional Português – estudo de caso

Esta jurisprudência tem, naturalmente, impacto em Portugal. Não será demais afirmar que os tribunais nacionais são os tribunais comuns de direito da União Europeia[86].

No âmbito deste estudo não é possível fazer uma avaliação desse impacto nas decisões de todos os tribunais portugueses, pelo que vamos apenas mencionar um caso em que o Tribunal Constitucional Português até chegou a equacionar a hipótese de suscitar uma questão prejudicial ao Tribunal de Justiça – o Acórdão nº 141/2015, de 3 de março de 2015[87]. Discutiu-se a questão de saber se, para apreciar a constitucionalidade de uma norma nacional que previa um ano de residência legal em Portugal para os cidadãos da União Europeia poderem requer o rendimento social de inserção (um benefício social), era necessário suscitar uma questão

[82] Ac. de 11/11/2014, *Dano,* proc. C-333-13, EU:C:2014:2358.

[83] Ac. de 15/09/2014, *Alimanovic,* proc. C-67/14, ECLI:EU:C:2015:597.

[84] Ac. de 25/02/2016, *Garcia Nieto,* C-299/14, ECLI: EU:C:2016:114.

[85] V. Sofia Oliveira Pais, "Current Challenges: Freedom of Movement and Access of Economically Inactive Union Citizens to Social Benefits", *in* Sofia Oliveira Pais (coord.), *EU Citizenship...,* p. 21 e segs.

[86] Para maiores desenvolvimentos, v. Ana Maria Guerra Martins, *Manual de Direito da União Europeia,* p. 539 e segs.

[87] Acessível em http://www.tribunalconstitucional.pt/tc/acordaos/20150145.

prejudicial ao Tribunal de Justiça, na medida em que o direito de livre circulação e de residência dentro do território português por parte dos cidadãos da União e das suas famílias poderia ser posto em causa.

Porém, tendo em conta a Diretiva 2004/38/CE e a Jurisprudência do Tribunal de Justiça, ao tempo, o caso *Dano*, acima citado, o Tribunal Constitucional considerou que não havia dúvida de que o direito da União Europeia tolerava o regime jurídico nacional em causa[88], pelo que não suscitou qualquer questão prejudicial ao Tribunal de Justiça.

5. Síntese conclusiva

No presente estudo procurou-se avaliar em que medida os direitos de cidadania das portuguesas e dos portugueses se modificaram num sentido expansivo ou restritivo, por força da adesão de Portugal à União Europeia, tendo-se chegado às seguintes conclusões:

a) Todas e todos aqueles que tiverem nacionalidade portuguesa são cidadãos da União, pelo que dispõem de uma dupla cidadania;
b) Essa cidadania não se baseia na nacionalidade da entidade que a atribui, mas sim na nacionalidade do Estado-Membro, no caso, Portugal;
c) A cidadania da União confere determinados direitos às pessoas, designadamente, o direito de livre circulação e permanência no território dos Estados-Membros, o direito de eleger e ser eleito nas eleições para o PE bem como nas eleições municipais do Estado-Membro da residência, nas mesmas condições que os nacionais desse Estado, o direito de proteção diplomática e consular, no território de Estados terceiros, por parte das autoridades diplomáticas e consulares de qualquer Estado-Membro, direitos esses de que as portuguesas e os portugueses passaram a usufruir;
d) Porém, note-se que, para se atingir a plenitude dos direitos de cidadania, ainda se exige, em muitos casos, a prévia circulação do cidadão da União do território do seu para outro Estado-Membro. Além disso, especialmente quando estão em causa benefícios sociais, continua a exigir-se a chamada "condição de recursos", o que significa

[88] Posteriormente, outros acórdãos do TJUE, citados no nº anterior, parecem ter corroborado a posição do Tribunal Constitucional Português.

que a cidadania da União ainda não se emancipou totalmente do mercado interno;

e) Apesar de todas as limitações que o estatuto de cidadão da União comporta, ele é bastante mais favorável do que o mais privilegiado estatuto de nacional de Estado terceiro;

f) É certo que se tem vindo a reclamar a progressiva equiparação entre os direitos dos cidadãos da União e os direitos dos nacionais de Estados terceiros legalmente residentes na União, mas a verdade é que se verificam atualmente entraves muito fortes a essa equiparação, como sejam o terrorismo, os movimentos de refugiados e a crise económica e financeira, pelo que os cidadãos da União, entre os quais se incluem as portuguesas e os portugueses, gozam de um estatuto privilegiado no espaço territorial da União Europeia;

g) O futuro da cidadania da União passa, sem dúvida, pela maior interação com a Carta dos Direitos Fundamentais e com a proteção dos direitos fundamentais em geral, o que até, ao momento, ainda não se consumou inteiramente.

VI
As decisões do TJUE nos casos *Achbita e Bougnaoui* A não discriminação em função da religião no emprego

Abstract

On 14 March 2017 the Court of Justice of the European Union issued two judgements – *Achbita* and *Bougnaoui* – related to discrimination on the grounds of religion and belief under Directive 2000/78/EC. In both cases the Court deemed that the ban of the use of the Islamic headscarf at work by the employer should not be assessed as a direct discrimination against those two women. While in *Achbita* the Court added that even if it could be envisaged as an indirect discrimination, the ban could be justified by the policy of neutrality of the enterprise. By contrast, in *Bougnaoui*, the Court rejected that the wish of customers not to have services provided by an employee wearing an headscarf is not a genuine and determining occupational requirement. Therefore, the discrimination was not justified. The purpose of this article is to critically analyze those decisions.

Palavras-chave

Liberdade religiosa; uso do véu islâmico; discriminação direta, indireta e múltipla, princípio da proporcionalidade e liberdade de empresa.

1. Introdução

O texto que agora se publica surge na sequência da intervenção oral proferida na conferência sobre *Liberdade religiosa e vivência em sociedade plural*

– a propósito dos acórdãos do TJUE nos processos C-157/15 e C-188/15, organizada em conjunto pela Comissão da Liberdade Religiosa e pelo Centro de Investigação de Direito Público do Instituto de Ciências Jurídico-Políticas (Faculdade de Direito da Universidade de Lisboa), em Setembro de 2017.

De então para cá estas decisões foram objeto de muitos comentários, de um modo geral, bastante críticos, por parte da doutrina, tanto na blogoesfera[1] como nos meios mais tradicionais, incluindo revistas da especialidade[2] e *working papers*[3], pelo que não podemos deixar de levar em conta todo este manancial de informação e reflexão.

[1] Schona Jolli considera uma vergonha que o Tribunal tenha perdido a primeira oportunidade de proferir uma decisão sólida sobre discriminação em função da religião no trabalho. "It needed perspective, proportionality and a judicial underlining of support for religious minorities across Europe, many of whom have found themselves on the frontline of unwelcome attention in political and social debates on migration, identity and integration. It needed to find a way to balance the individual's rights against that of an employer, where any clash arose, and to provide reasoned guidance for how those interests could be weighed against each other in law."
Para esta Autora, o tribunal não fez nenhuma das duas coisas.
Schona Jolli, "Achbita & Bougnaoui: A strange kind of equality", in https://www.cloisters.com/blogs/achbita-bougnaoui-a-strange-kind-of-equality.
Para outras visões muito críticas, ver, entre muitos outros, Monique Steijns, *"Achbita and Bougnaoui: raising more questions than answers", in* https://eutopialaw.com/2017/03/18/achbita-and-bougnaoui-raising-more-questions-than-answers/; Adina Portaru, *"CJEU Cases C-157/15 Achbita and C-188/15 Bougnaoui – Does 'neutrality' trump religious freedom?"*, 24 March, 2017, https://voelkerrechtsblog.org/cjeu-cases-c-15715-achbita-and-c-18815-bougnaoui/; Gareth Davies, *"Achbita V G4s: Religious Equality Squeezed Between Profit and Prejudice"*, https://europeanlawblog.eu/2017/04/06/achbita-v-g4s-religious-equality-squeezed-between-profit-and-prejudice/; Sara Benedi Lahuerta, **"**Wearing the veil at work: Achbita and Bougnaoui – Can a duty to reasonable accommodation be derived from the EU concept of indirect discrimination?**"**, in http://eulawanalysis.blogspot.com/2016/03/wearing-veil-at-work-achbita-and.html.

[2] V., entre outros, Joseph Weiler, "Je Suis Achbita!", *European Journal of International Law*, 2017, p. 989-1018; Erica Howard, «Islamic Headscarves and the CJEU: *Achbita* and *Bougnaoui*», *MJ*, 2017, p. 348-366; José Rafael Marín Aís, "Freedom of Religion in the Workplace v. Freedom to Conduct a Business, the Islamic Veil before the Court of Justice: *Ms. Samira Achbita* Case", *European papers*, 2018, p. 409-417.

[3] V, por exemplo, Dagmar Schiek, "On uses, mis-uses and non-uses of intersectionality before the European Court of Justice (ECJ), *The ECJ rulings Parris (C-433/15, Achbita (C-157/15 and Bougnaoui (C-188/15) as a Bermuda Triangle?*", *CETLS online Paper Series*, Volume 7 (3), 2018.

Ainda que a questão controvertida – saber se o uso do chamado véu islâmico por parte de mulheres muçulmanas no seu local de trabalho pode justificar o despedimento numa empresa privada – já tenha sido objeto de decisões por alguns tribunais nacionais – nem sempre de forma coincidente – assim como pelo Tribunal Europeu dos Direitos do Homem, o Tribunal de Justiça da União Europeia nunca se tinha pronunciado sobre o tema, pelo que a sua decisão era aguardada com muita expectativa. Talvez por isso, a deceção causada pelos casos *Achbita*[4] e *Bougnaoui*[5] tenha sido maior.

Antes de nos pronunciarmos sobre a fundamentação de cada uma das decisões, importa proceder a uma breve apresentação das mesmas, começando pela matéria de facto. Em seguida, exporemos quais as razões que motivaram a decisão do TJ em cada um dos casos. Só então estaremos em condições de proceder a uma apreciação crítica.

2. As decisões do TJUE

As decisões do TJUE proferidas, no âmbito dos processos nºs C-157/15 (*Achbita*) e C-188/15 (*Bougnaoui*), em 14/3/2017, surgem na sequência de dois reenvios prejudiciais (do Tribunal da Cassação Belga e do Tribunal da Cassação Francês, respetivamente), tendo sido antecedidas de conclusões de diferentes advogadas-gerais – Kokott[6] e Sharpston[7] – as quais propuseram soluções diversas.

2.1. Matéria de facto

A matéria de facto subjacente a cada uma das decisões é relativamente simples.

No processo nº C-157/15, a Senhora *Samira Achbita*, de confissão muçulmana, empregada, por tempo indeterminado, desde 12 de fevereiro de 2003, como rececionista da G4S, que é uma empresa privada que presta, designadamente, serviços de receção e acolhimento a clientes tanto do setor público como do setor privado, em abril de 2006, informou os seus

[4] Ac. de 14 de março de 2017, *Achbita*, proc. nº C 157/15, ECLI:EU:C:2017:203.

[5] Ac. de 14 de março, *Bougnaoui*, proc. nº C 185/15, ECLI:EU:C:2017:204.

[6] Conclusões de 31 de maio de 2016, ECLI:EU:C:2016:382.

[7] Conclusões de 13 de julho de 2016, ECLI:EU:C:2016:553.

superiores hierárquicos de que tencionava, a partir de então, usar o lenço islâmico durante as horas de trabalho.

Em resposta, a direção da G4S informou *S. Achbita* de que o uso de um lenço não seria tolerado, uma vez que o uso visível de sinais políticos, filosóficos ou religiosos era contrário à neutralidade seguida pela empresa. À data, existia na G4S uma regra não escrita por força da qual os trabalhadores não podiam usar no local de trabalho sinais visíveis das suas convicções políticas, filosóficas ou religiosas.

Em 12 de maio de 2006, após um período de ausência do trabalho por doença, S. Achbita comunicou ao seu empregador que retomaria o trabalho, em 15 de maio, e que iria usar o lenço islâmico.

Em 29 de maio de 2006, o conselho de empresa da G4S aprovou uma alteração do regulamento interno, que entrou em vigor em 13 de junho de 2006, nos termos da qual «é proibido aos trabalhadores usar, no local de trabalho, sinais visíveis das suas convicções políticas, filosóficas ou religiosas ou praticar qualquer ritual decorrente de tais convicções».

Em 12 de junho de 2006, *S. Achbita* foi despedida devido à sua intenção reiterada de, enquanto muçulmana, usar o lenço islâmico no seu local de trabalho. Foi-lhe paga uma indemnização por despedimento correspondente a três meses de salário e benefícios adquiridos nos termos do contrato de trabalho.

No processo nº C-188/15, a situação é um pouco diferente. A Senhora *Asma Bougnaoui* encontrou, em outubro de 2007, numa feira de estudantes, antes do seu recrutamento pela empresa privada Micropole, um representante da mesma, que a informou do facto de que usar um lenço islâmico poderia colocar problemas quando estivesse em contacto com os clientes dessa sociedade. Quando *A. Bougnaoui* se apresentou, em 4 de fevereiro de 2008, na Micropole para aí realizar o seu estágio de fim de estudos, usava uma simples bandana. Posteriormente, passou a usar um lenço islâmico no seu local de trabalho. No final desse estágio, a Micropole contratou-a, a partir de 15 de julho de 2008, nos termos de um contrato por tempo indeterminado, na qualidade de engenheira de projetos.

No âmbito das suas funções, efetuava deslocações profissionais aos clientes da empresa. Na sequência de uma dessas deslocações, o cliente informou a empresa de que o uso do véu, que efetivamente utiliza todos os dias, incomodou alguns dos seus colaboradores e pediu igualmente que 'não houvesse véu da próxima vez'.

Após ter sido convocada, em 15 de junho de 2009, para uma entrevista prévia a um eventual despedimento, *A. Bougnaoui* foi despedida por carta de 22 de junho de 2009, com o fundamento de que quando a empresa a contratou o assunto do uso do véu foi abordado de forma muito clara, tendo sido precisado pela empresa o respeito do princípio da liberdade de opinião e as convicções religiosas de cada um, mas que, uma vez que estaria em contacto, interna ou externamente, com os clientes da empresa, nem sempre poderia usar o véu.

Com base no princípio de necessária neutralidade da empresa foi pedido à trabalhadora que o observasse em relação aos clientes e que não usasse o véu, o que não foi aceite.

Em consequência, a trabalhadora foi despedida.

Ambas as trabalhadoras recorreram aos tribunais nacionais para fazer valer os seus direitos, tendo invocado o caráter discriminatório do despedimento.

Em ambos os casos os tribunais de primeira instância negaram provimento a essa parte do recurso, pelo que *S. Achbita* e *A. Bougnaoui* interpuseram recurso para os respetivos Tribunais de Cassação (Belga e Francês).

2.2. As questões prejudiciais colocadas pelos tribunais nacionais

A questão colocada, no caso *Achbita*, foi a seguinte:

> «Deve o artigo 2º, nº 2, alínea a), da Diretiva [2000/78] ser interpretado no sentido de que a proibição de uma trabalhadora muçulmana usar um lenço [islâmico] no local de trabalho não constitui uma discriminação direta quando a regra vigente nas instalações do empregador proíbe [a todos os trabalhadores o uso], no local de trabalho, [de] sinais exteriores de convicções políticas, filosóficas e religiosas?»

Já no caso *Bougnaoui*, o tribunal nacional formulou a questão da seguinte forma:

> "Devem as disposições do artigo 4º, nº 1, da [Diretiva 2000/78] ser interpretadas no sentido de que constitui um requisito profissional essencial e determinante, em razão da natureza da atividade profissional em causa ou das condições da sua execução, o desejo de um cliente de uma empresa de aconselhamento informático de que as prestações

de serviços informáticos deixem de ser asseguradas por uma assalariada daquela empresa, engenheira de projetos, que usa o [lenço] islâmico?»

Note-se que ambas as questões prejudiciais se reportam à diretiva 2000/78/CE[8] mas o seu conteúdo é diferente. Enquanto a primeira questão incide sobre a questão de saber se a proibição de uma trabalhadora muçulmana usar um lenço islâmico no local de trabalho constitui uma discriminação direta, no segundo caso o que está em causa é a interpretação da expressão "*requisito profissional essencial e determinante*" previsto no artigo 4º da mesma diretiva.

Antes de mais, importa notar que a riqueza das questões jurídicas que estavam em causa nestes dois processos contrasta com a pobreza da formulação das questões prejudiciais. Na verdade, tanto num processo como no outro, além da discriminação direta, invocada no caso *Achbita*, e da questão da interpretação do "requisito profissional essencial e determinante", convocada no caso *Bougnaoui*, o uso do véu islâmico no local de trabalho convoca questões de discriminação não só direta como indireta assim como não só em função da religião como também em função do género e até da origem étnica, o que teria dado azo a que os tribunais nacionais tivessem colocado questões atinentes não só à discriminação indireta como também tivessem provocado alguma discussão sobre a discriminação múltipla. Porém, não o fizeram.

Além disso, estando em causa um conflito entre a liberdade religiosa e a liberdade de empresa, seria natural que os tribunais nacionais tivessem suscitado questões prejudiciais em matéria de critérios de decisão de conflitos de direitos no âmbito do direito da União Europeia, o que também não fizeram.

É certo que, tendo em conta a jurisprudência do Tribunal de Justiça, no que diz respeito à delimitação dos seus próprios poderes, no domínio do processo das questões prejudiciais[9], este pode debruçar-se sobre questões

[8] Diretiva 2000/78/CE do Conselho, de 27 de Novembro de 2000 que estabelece um quadro geral de igualdade de tratamento no emprego e na atividade profissional, JOCE L 303/16, de 2/12/2000.

[9] V., entre muitos outros, acórdãos de 12/01/10, *Wolf*, proc. C-229/08, EU:C:2010:3, nº 35; de 13/09/11, *Prigge e o.*, proc. C-447/09, EU:C:2011:573, nº 66; de 13/11/14, *Vital Pérez*, proc. C-416/13, EU:C:2014:2371, nº 36; e de 15/11/16, *Salaberria Sorondo*, proc. C-258/15, EU:C:2016:873, nº 33.

que não tenham sido expressamente suscitadas pelos tribunais nacionais, mas que o Tribunal considere necessárias à boa decisão da causa por parte dos tribunais nacionais, como, aliás, fez no caso em apreço.

Dito isto, importa, todavia, notar que os tribunais nacionais, nestes dois casos, não colocaram as questões prejudiciais da forma mais adequada e deixaram de fora questões muito relevantes, pelo que lhes deve ser imputada alguma parte da responsabilidade pela forma como o Tribunal de Justiça abordou o problema.

2.3. A decisão do Tribunal de Justiça no caso *Achbita*

Começando pelo caso *Achbita*, o Tribunal começou por explicitar o que se deve entender por discriminação direta, para efeitos de aplicação da diretiva 2000/78/CE do Conselho, de 27 de novembro de 2000, bem como o que se deve considerar como religião, uma vez que a diretiva não a define.

O Tribunal recorta o conceito de religião por remissão para a Convenção Europeia dos Direitos do Homem (artigo 9º), para as tradições constitucionais comuns aos Estados-Membros, enquanto princípios gerais de direito e para a Carta dos Direitos Fundamentais da União Europeia (artigo 10º) e daí retira um conceito amplo de «religião» que abrange quer o *forum internum*, isto é, o facto de ter convicções, quer o *forum externum*, ou seja, a manifestação em público da fé religiosa, o qual se deve considerar relevante para efeitos de aplicação da diretiva acima mencionada.

O Tribunal de Justiça recorta, pois, o âmbito da liberdade de pensamento, de consciência e de religião em sentido idêntico ao TEDH:

a) o direito a ter convicções;
b) o direito de manifestar essas convicções;
c) o direito à objeção de consciência.

A liberdade de pensamento tem, pois, uma dupla dimensão, a saber:

- A dimensão individual – abrange o direito de ter opiniões e convicções;
- A dimensão social e política – abarca a liberdade de as manifestar.

Em seguida, o TJUE averigua se a regra interna da empresa constituía uma discriminação direta, tendo considerado que tal discriminação não existia porque abrangia todos os trabalhadores e todas as convicções religiosas ou outras.

Por fim, apesar de o tribunal nacional não ter levantado essa questão, o Tribunal, ao abrigo do princípio da cooperação judicial a que atrás se aludiu, averigua se se poderá chegar à conclusão de que a regra interna em causa no processo principal institui uma diferença de tratamento indiretamente baseada na religião ou nas convicções, na aceção do artigo 2º, nº 2, alínea b), da diretiva 2000/78.

O Tribunal considerou que a verificação de que a obrigação aparentemente neutra que a norma interna contém implica, de facto, uma desvantagem específica para as pessoas que seguem uma determinada religião ou determinadas convicções é da competência do órgão jurisdicional nacional, mas de acordo com o artigo 2º, nº 2, alínea b), i), da diretiva 2000/78, essa diferença de tratamento não constituirá discriminação indireta, se for objetivamente justificada por um objetivo legítimo e se os meios para a realização desse objetivo forem adequados e necessários.

Ora, para o Tribunal a vontade da empresa de manter uma política de neutralidade política, filosófica ou religiosa deve ser considerada um objetivo legítimo e deve considerar-se que consubstancia um meio adequado para garantir a boa aplicação dessa política de neutralidade assim como se limita ao estritamente necessário pois abrange apenas os trabalhadores que têm contacto visual com os clientes.

O TJUE concluiu que:

> *"O artigo 2º, nº 2, alínea a), da Diretiva 2000/78/CE do Conselho, de 27 de novembro de 2000, que estabelece um quadro geral de igualdade de tratamento no emprego e na atividade profissional, deve ser interpretado no sentido de que a proibição de usar um lenço islâmico, que decorre de uma regra interna de uma empresa privada que proíbe o uso visível de quaisquer sinais políticos, filosóficos ou religiosos no local de trabalho, não constitui uma discriminação direta em razão da religião ou das convicções, na aceção dessa diretiva.*
>
> *Em contrapartida, essa regra interna de uma empresa privada é suscetível de constituir uma discriminação indireta na aceção do artigo 2º, nº 2, alínea b), da Diretiva 2000/78 se se demonstrar que a obrigação, aparentemente neutra, que prevê implica, de facto, uma desvantagem específica para as pessoas que seguem uma determinada religião ou determinadas convicções, exceto se for objetivamente justificada por um objetivo legítimo, como a prossecução por parte do*

empregador, nas suas relações com os seus clientes, de uma política de neutralidade política, filosófica e religiosa, e se os meios para realizar esse objetivo forem adequados e necessários, o que cabe ao órgão jurisdicional de reenvio verificar.

2.4. A decisão do Tribunal no caso *Bougnaoui*

Como se disse, no caso *Bougnaoui*, a questão colocada pelo órgão jurisdicional nacional foi diferente, pelo que a fundamentação do Tribunal apenas coincidiu, em parte, com a do caso *Achbita* e a decisão também foi num sentido diverso.

Assim, o que estava em causa neste processo era a questão de saber se o artigo 4º, nº 1, da diretiva 2000/78 que considera não existir discriminação sempre que, em virtude da natureza da atividade profissional em causa ou do contexto da sua execução, a característica relacionada com qualquer dos motivos de discriminação constitua um requisito essencial e determinante para o exercício dessa atividade, na condição de o objetivo ser legítimo e o requisito proporcional deve ser interpretado no sentido de que a vontade de um empregador de ter em conta os desejos de um cliente de que as prestações de serviços do referido empregador deixem de ser asseguradas por uma trabalhadora que usa um lenço islâmico constitui um requisito profissional essencial e determinante na aceção dessa disposição.

O Tribunal, remetendo para jurisprudência anterior[10], reiterou que resulta do artigo 4º, nº 1, da diretiva 2000/78 que não é o motivo em que se baseia a diferença de tratamento, mas uma característica relacionada com esse motivo, que deve constituir um requisito profissional essencial e determinante.

Por outro lado, salientou que só em circunstâncias muito limitadas uma característica relacionada, designadamente, com a religião pode constituir um requisito profissional essencial e determinante e que a característica em causa só pode constituir um requisito desse tipo «*em virtude da natureza da atividade profissional em causa ou do contexto da sua execução*».

Ora, segundo o Tribunal o conceito de «*requisito essencial e determinante para o exercício dessa atividade*», na aceção do artigo 4º, nº 1, da diretiva 2000/78, remete para uma exigência objetiva imposta pela natureza ou pelas condições de exercício da atividade profissional, pelo que não pode

[10] Ver nota anterior.

abranger considerações subjetivas, como a vontade do empregador de ter em conta os desejos concretos do cliente.

O Tribunal concluiu:

"O artigo 4º, nº1, da Diretiva 2000/78/CE do Conselho, de 27 de novembro de 2000, que estabelece um quadro geral de igualdade de tratamento no emprego e na atividade profissional, deve ser interpretado no sentido de que a vontade de um empregador de ter em conta os desejos de um cliente de que as prestações de serviços do referido empregador deixem de ser asseguradas por uma trabalhadora que usa um lenço islâmico não pode ser considerada um requisito profissional essencial e determinante na aceção dessa disposição".

3. Apreciação crítica de ambas as decisões do TJUE

A definição precisa da questão jurídica subjacente às duas decisões é, do nosso ponto de vista, extremamente importante porque é ela que vai condicionar, em larga escala, a aceitação ou a rejeição da fundamentação das mesmas.

Em nosso entender, a questão colocada é a de saber se a proibição pelo empregador privado do uso do véu islâmico a uma trabalhadora do sexo feminino que professa uma determinada religião – no caso, o Islamismo – a qual implica o uso de sinais exteriores, designadamente através do vestuário, no espaço físico da empresa nas relações com os clientes, é lícita, de acordo com o direito da União Europeia, nomeadamente, de acordo com a diretiva 2000/78/CE.

Daqui decorre, em primeiro lugar, que se está no âmbito das relações privadas (ou de direito privado, se se preferir), pelo que a jurisprudência que já se debruçou sobre este assunto nas relações entre privados e entidades públicas não deve ser chamada à colação.

Em segundo lugar, de acordo com o Islamismo o uso do lenço ou véu islâmico só é requerido às mulheres, o que significa que, à partida, as mulheres islâmicas estão em desvantagem se comparadas com os homens que professam o mesmo credo.

Em terceiro lugar, a proibição apenas se aplicava às trabalhadoras que tinham contacto visual com os clientes das empresas, o que implica que estas mulheres estão em desvantagem se comparadas com outras mulheres igualmente islâmicas que, por hipótese, se encontram no *back office*.

3.1. O direito a não ser discriminada/o em função da religião

A primeira questão jurídica que estas decisões convocam é a da interpretação dos conceitos de discriminação *tout court* e de discriminação direta e indireta, no âmbito da diretiva 2000/78/CE.

Em ambos os casos, o TJUE dá por assente que não há discriminação direta porque todas as religiões que implicam manifestações exteriores no uso vestuário são tratadas de modo idêntico. O Tribunal parece, pois, aceitar uma noção meramente formal de não discriminação, com todas as fragilidades que essa noção encerra[11].

O conceito de discriminação raramente se define em termos gerais.[12] Por facilidade de exposição, partamos da definição apresentada por Xavier Bioy (importada de Valérie Doumeng). "*A (discriminação) pode definir-se como uma desigualdade de atribuição e de exercício de direitos, mais precisamente, uma distinção entre pessoas, colocadas em condições ou situações semelhantes, fundada sobre um critério proibido ou neutro, mas tendo um efeito discriminatório sobre um grupo de pessoas, sem que haja qualquer motivo legítimo ou justificação objetiva e razoável. Para haver discriminação devem estar cumulativamente reunidos dois elementos. O primeiro consiste numa distinção entre indivíduos, fundada num critério inaceitável. Esta distinção pode traduzir-se quer numa exclusão, quer numa preferência, discriminação positiva ou à rebours. Pode fundar-se num critério proibido – discriminação direta – ou num critério neutro – discriminação indireta*".[13]

A discriminação pressupõe, portanto, um tratamento diferenciado de situações idênticas sem justificação objetiva, razoável e proporcional.

Note-se que a diretiva 2000/78/CE contem uma definição de discriminação direta, no artigo 2º, nº 2, al. a), nos termos do qual "*sempre que, por qualquer dos motivos referidos no artigo 1º, uma pessoa seja objeto de um tratamento*

[11] Em anterior trabalho já tivemos ocasião de alertar para os perigos desta noção. V. Ana Maria Guerra Martins, *A igualdade e a não discriminação dos nacionais de Estados terceiros legalmente residentes na União Europeia – da origem na integração económica ao fundamento na dignidade do ser humano*, Coimbra, Almedina, 2010, p. 65 e segs.

[12] Xavier Bioy, «L'ambiguïté du concept de non-discrimination», *in* Frederic Sudre/ Hèléne Surrel, *Le droit à la non-discrimination au sens de la Convention européenne des droits de l'homme*, Bruxelas, Bruylant, 2008, p. 51 e 52.

[13] Xavier Bioy, «L'ambiguïté du concept ...», p. 51 e 52.

menos favorável do que aquele que é, tenha sido ou possa vir a ser dado a outra pessoa em situação comparável".

A discriminação direta ocorre, portanto, quando uma pessoa é tratada de forma menos favorável do que outra que se encontra nas mesmas condições e circunstâncias, apenas porque possui características particulares, como sejam a raça, o sexo, a religião, a orientação sexual ou outras.

Como as considerações sobre a raça, o sexo, a deficiência, a religião e a orientação sexual não podem ser critério relevante para tratar as pessoas diferentemente, o tratamento menos favorável, em função disso, constitui uma discriminação direta, que não pode ser objetivamente justificada, a menos que esteja expressamente prevista na legislação alguma derrogação[14-15].

Assim sendo, a aferição da existência, ou não, de discriminação depende, desde logo, do termo de comparação.

Se se compararem as manifestações exteriores das diversas religiões facilmente chegaremos à conclusão que nem todas implicam sinais exteriores, por exemplo, através do uso de vestuário, pelo que se o termo de comparação for entre pessoas que professem religiões, em que a sua prática implica necessariamente a sua exteriorização, através do uso de vestuário – por exemplo, o uso do véu islâmico pelas muçulmanas, o uso do quipá pelos homens que professam a religião judaica ou o uso do turbante

[14] Neste sentido, Marianne Gijzen, *Selected Issues in Equal Treatment Law: a Multi-Layered Comparison of European, English and Dutch Law*, Antuérpia, Intersentia, 2006, p. 53 e ss; Lisa Waddington/Aart Hendriks, "The Expanding Concept of Employment Discrimination in Europe – From Direct Effect and Indirect Discrimination to Reasonable Accommodation Discrimination", *The Int'l J. Comp. Lab. Law and Industrial Relations*, 2002, p. 407.

[15] Sobre a discriminação direta, ver Criseide Novi, "La parità di trattamento tra uomo e donna in materia di occupazione e condizioni di lavoro nel diritto comunitario: il felice connubio tra codificazione e innovazione", *Dir. Pubb. Comp. Eur.*, 2004, 1251 e ss; Michel Miné, "Les concepts de discrimination directe et indirecte", *ERA*, 3/2003, p. 34 e 35; Anna Christensen, "Structural Aspects of Anti-Discriminatory Legislation and Processes of Normative Change", *in* Ann Numhauser-Henning, *Legal Perspectives on Equal Treatment and Non-Discrimination*, Haia, Kluwer, 2001, p. 39 e ss; Evelyn Ellis, "Gender Discrimination Law in the European Community", *in* Janet Dine/Bob Watt (ed.), *Discrimination Law, Concepts, Limitations and Justifications*, Londres/Nova Iorque, 1996, p. 16 e ss; Evelyn Ellis, "The Definition of Discrimination in European Community Sex Equality Law", *ELR*, 1994, p. 565 e ss.

pelos siques – então poderá não haver tratamento discriminatório, pois todos e todas são tratadas da mesma forma.

Mas se a comparação se fizer entre todas as convicções religiosas, políticas e filosóficas – as que impliquem e as que não impliquem manifestações exteriores no uso de vestuário – então, as primeiras serão certamente objeto de discriminação.

Como sabemos, há religiões que, pelo simples facto de se professarem, implicam o uso de certos sinais exteriores, designadamente, vestuário, enquanto outras não. Não é só no caso das mulheres que professam a religião islâmica que isso sucede. O mesmo se verifica, por exemplo, com a religião judaica, em que os homens usam o *quipá* ou com os siques, em que homens e mulheres usam turbante. Já a religião católica, por exemplo, não requer necessariamente o uso de vestuário ou sinais exteriores, embora a cruz seja um símbolo católico. Há até religiões que não incentivam o uso de sinais exteriores, como é o caso da religião protestante.

Assim, a primeira crítica que se pode fazer aos acórdãos em apreço é que o Tribunal deveria ter sido mais convincente na rejeição da existência de discriminação direta, até porque as advogadas-gerais tinham apresentado conclusões divergentes a este propósito. Enquanto KOKOTT negou a existência de discriminação direta, com base, entre outros, no argumento de que não é possível aplicar o entendimento amplo de discriminação direta adotado pelo Tribunal quando estão em causa particularidades físicas inseparáveis da pessoa ou características pessoais, como é o caso do sexo, idade ou orientação sexual, ao caso em apreço, porque nele estão em causa comportamentos baseados numa decisão ou convicção pessoal, SHARPSTON considerou que não é possível chegar a outra conclusão que não seja a de que o despedimento de *Bougnaoui* se deveu a uma discriminação direta.

Como se vê a questão da existência, ou não, de discriminação direta não é pacífica.

Pela nossa parte, não nos parece que a definição de discriminação direta possa variar – como sustenta a advogada-geral KOKOTT – em função da categoria suspeita que está em causa. O critério de aferição da discriminação direta não é o facto de se tratar de uma particularidade física inseparável da pessoa ou de uma característica pessoal, pois para muitas pessoas a discriminação com base na religião é tão, ou até mais ultrajante, humilhante e difícil de suportar do que a discriminação em função da cor da pele ou do género[16]. O Tribunal deveria, pois, ter aplicado o conceito amplo de discriminação direta que usa, por exemplo, para aferir se existe discriminação em função do sexo[17].

Não tendo sido essa a sua conclusão, o TJ – ainda que tal não lhe tenha sido suscitado pelos tribunais nacionais – prosseguiu na averiguação da existência de discriminação indireta.

Ora, a diretiva 2000/78/CE define a discriminação indireta do seguinte modo:

> *"(...) sempre que uma disposição, critério ou prática aparentemente neutra seja suscetível de colocar numa situação de desvantagem pessoas com uma determinada religião ou convicções, com uma determinada deficiência, pessoas de uma determinada classe etária ou pessoas com uma determinada orientação sexual, comparativamente com outras pessoas, a não ser que:*
>
> *i) essa disposição, critério ou prática sejam objetivamente justificados por um objetivo legítimo e que os meios utilizados para o alcançar sejam adequados e necessários (...),"*

A discriminação indireta pressupõe, portanto, que estejam reunidos os seguintes requisitos:

a) a existência de uma disposição, critério ou prática;
b) aparentemente neutros;
c) que "*seja susceptível de colocar (...) pessoas*";
d) "*com uma determinada religião ou convicções*";
e) "numa situação de desvantagem";
f) "comparativamente com outras pessoas".

Em suma, haverá discriminação indireta quando uma medida aparentemente neutra tiver um impacto desfavorável, desproporcionado num determinado grupo de pessoas.

[16] Neste sentido, JOSEPH WEILER, "Je Suis Achbita!", *European Journal of International Law*, 2017, p. 1001 e 1002.

[17] Neste sentido, ERICA HOWARD, «Islamic Headscarves and the CJEU: *Achbita* and *Bougnaoui*», *MJ*, 2017, p. 354.

O Tribunal, seguindo a advogada-geral KOKOTT, admitiu a possibilidade de existência de discriminação indireta nos dois casos, ainda que tenha remetido a verificação da mesma para o tribunal nacional.

Independentemente de se estar, ou não, de acordo com esta qualificação, parece-nos igualmente criticável que tenha sido remetida para o tribunal nacional a verificação da existência de uma desvantagem específica para as pessoas que seguem determinada religião, quando noutras situações, designadamente, de discriminação indireta em função do sexo, o Tribunal, ainda que não tenha ele próprio feito essa verificação, deu, frequentemente, diretrizes precisas quanto ao modo como deve ponderar o princípio da não discriminação e os outros interesses em causa[18].

3.2. O silêncio do TJ quanto à discriminação múltipla

Antes de avançar, importa discutir ainda um tema que está subjacente a estas duas decisões mas que foi totalmente ignorado pelo TJ, isto é, a existência ou não de discriminação múltipla.

Há muito que a doutrina tem vindo a alertar para a interação entre a discriminação em função do género e da religião e até em função da origem étnica no emprego quando as mulheres muçulmanas são impedidas de concorrer ou permanecer num determinado emprego devido ao uso do véu islâmico.

Nos dois casos em apreço estavam em causa duas mulheres cujo nome indicava claramente a sua ascendência árabe e que foram despedidas por se recusarem a trabalhar sem o lenço islâmico[19]. Ora, perante este quadro é no mínimo estranho que nem as advogadas-gerais nem o Tribunal tenham dedicado uma única palavra à discriminação múltipla, sendo certo que esta se define precisamente como aquela que resultar da discriminação em função de dois ou mais fatores suspeitos. Ou seja, o tratamento diferenciado de que uma determinada pessoa ou um determinado grupo são alvo pode ter fundamento em várias categorias suspeitas simultaneamente.

[18] Neste sentido, MARIANNE GIJZEN, *Selected Issues...*, p. 87; STEVE ANDERMAN, "Constitutional Law...", p. 107.

[19] V. DAGMAR SCHIEK, "On uses, mis-uses and non-uses of intersectionality before the European Court of Justice (ECJ), *The ECJ rulings Parris (C-433/15, Achbita (C-157/15 and Bougnaoui (C-188/15) as a Bermuda Triangle?*", *CETLS online Paper Series*, Volume 7 (3), 2018.

Com efeito, todos os seres humanos têm um género, uma cor de pele, uma orientação sexual, idade, convicções, pelo que a discriminação pode basear-se em mais do que um *critério suspeito* ao mesmo tempo. A situação mais comum é a discriminação de género interagir com outros fundamentos. As mulheres pertencentes a uma minoria étnica, as mulheres idosas, as mulheres negras e as mulheres deficientes fazem parte dos grupos mais desfavorecidos em muitos Estados-Membros[20].

A discriminação racial, por exemplo, está, frequentemente, relacionada com a discriminação com base na pertença a uma determinada minoria religiosa, étnica ou linguística. Outras vezes a discriminação religiosa mascara a discriminação racial[21].

Nos casos de discriminação múltipla verifica-se uma combinação de fatores com uma "*invisível interação de fundamentos*"[22], que é particularmente desvantajosa e prejudicial para as pessoas que dela são alvo.

Apesar de a diretiva 2000/78 não definir a discriminação múltipla, reconhece-a no seu considerando nº 3, pelo que o TJ deveria ter-se pronunciado sobre esta questão. Se o tivesse feito, muito provavelmente teria chegado à conclusão que existia discriminação múltipla naqueles dois casos.

3.3. A eventual justificação da medida e o princípio da proporcionalidade

Não se tendo o Tribunal pronunciado sobre a discriminação múltipla, mas tendo, de certo modo, admitido que poderia verificar-se a discriminação

[20] Neste sentido, Sandra Fredman, "Double Trouble: Multiple Discrimination and EU Law", *EADLR*, nº 2, 2005, p. 13-18.

[21] As fronteiras entre a raça e a religião nem sempre são fáceis de traçar. Pelo contrário, estas duas *categorias suspeitas* confundem-se, essencialmente, por duas razões: a) o grupo étnico define-se por uma identidade religiosa; b) os membros de uma determinada religião pertencem maioritariamente ao mesmo grupo racial ou étnico. Cfr. Lucy Vickers, *Religion et convictions: discrimination dans l'emploi – Le droit de l'Union européenne*, Luxemburgo, Office de pubblications officielles des Communautés européennes, 2006, disponível no sítio http://ec.europa.eu/employment_social/fundamental_rights/index...., p. 34.

[22] Neste sentido, Dagmar Schiek, "From European Union Non-discrimination Law towards Multidimensional Equality Law for Europe", *in* Dagmar Schiek/Victoria Chege, *European Union Non-discrimination Law – Comparative Perspectives on Multidimensional Equality Law*, Londres, Routledge-Cavendish, 2008, p. 13.

indireta, deve sublinhar-se que a medida aparentemente neutra só poderá ser mantida se tiver uma justificação objetiva e razoável[23] e se os meios utilizados para alcançar o objetivo forem os adequados e necessários. Ou seja, a medida só é lícita, do ponto de vista do direito da União Europeia, se respeitar o princípio da proporcionalidade.

Também aqui a fundamentação do Tribunal é criticável, pois, no caso *Achbita*, aceitou, quase sem discussão que a prossecução por parte do empregador, nas suas relações com os seus clientes, de uma política de neutralidade política, filosófica e religiosa, é justificação suficiente. Ora, o Tribunal foi bastante mais exigente noutras situações, como, por exemplo, quando estavam em causa outras categorias suspeitas, designadamente o género.

Assim, nos termos do caso *Bilka Kaufhaus*[24], a discriminação só pode estar justificada se preencher três critérios: os meios escolhidos devem corresponder a uma real necessidade; devem ser apropriados para atingir os fins visados e devem ser necessários para atingir os fins, o que inclui a ponderação de meios alternativos, menos discriminatórios para atingir o fim visado. Ou seja, a restrição dos direitos fundamentais só poderá estar justificada se respeitar o princípio da proporcionalidade.

A verificação do princípio da proporcionalidade compreende, portanto, três testes: o da adequação, o da necessidade e o da proporcionalidade *stricto sensu*. O primeiro teste refere-se à relação entre o meio e o fim, ou seja, os meios empregues pela medida devem ser adequados – nomeadamente razoáveis – para atingir os seus objetivos. O segundo teste impõe a ponderação do peso dos diferentes interesses em conflito. O Tribunal deve avaliar as consequências adversas que uma determinada medida tem num direito digno de proteção e determinar se essas consequências estão justificadas tendo em conta a importância do objetivo prosseguido, designadamente, se não há outras medidas menos restritivas. Em terceiro lugar, mesmo que a medida passe estes dois testes e ainda que não haja meios menos restritivos, ela não respeitará a proporcionalidade se tiver um efeito excessivo sobre os cidadãos por ela abrangidos[25].

[23] Neste sentido, Olivier De Schutter, «Prouver la discrimination», *ERA*, 3/2003, p. 46.

[24] Ac. de 13/05/86, proc. 170/84, ECLI:EU:C:1986:204.

[25] Neste sentido, Takis Tridimas, *The General Principles of EU Law*, 2ª ed., Oxford, Oxford Univ. Press, 2006, p. 139.

O que claramente significa que os interesses dos indivíduos devem ser pesados. Ora, não há razão para não aplicar os mesmos critérios a todas as categorias suspeitas. A religião, como fundamento de discriminação, não deve ser tratada de modo diferente.

Assim sendo, no caso *Achbita*, o Tribunal parece ter dado uma relevância excessiva ao princípio da neutralidade em detrimento da liberdade religiosa. Senão vejamos.

O Tribunal aceitou, em primeiro lugar, que o fim de projetar uma imagem de neutralidade da empresa era legítimo e que a proibição do uso do véu islâmico era adequada para atingir o fim em causa. Ou seja, o TJUE considerou que o primeiro teste da proporcionalidade estava preenchido.

Em segundo lugar, o Tribunal remeteu a ponderação da necessidade da medida para o tribunal nacional, considerando que se a proibição de usar sinais visíveis de exteriorização de uma religião apenas se reportasse aos trabalhadores que tinham contacto com o público a proibição passaria o teste da necessidade pois seria estritamente necessária.

Em terceiro lugar, o Tribunal deveria ter averiguado se a medida não era excessiva, tendo em conta os direitos em conflito. Para isso deveria ter ponderado o conflito de direitos com base nos bens jurídicos e nos valores que estavam em causa.

Ora, foi precisamente este o ponto que suscitou mais críticas da doutrina, chegando mesmo Joseph Weiler a deixar um espaço em branco, no seu comentário ao caso *Achbita*, para ilustrar o que o Tribunal disse sobre esta questão[26].

Em nosso entender, esta crítica estende-se ao caso *Bougnaoui*, pois, apesar de o Tribunal ter concluído de modo diferente, com base no artigo 4º, nº 1, da diretiva 2000/78/CE, relativamente à justificação da discriminação indireta foi ainda mais lacónico do que no caso *Achbita*.

Recorde-se que, no caso *Bougnaoui*, a questão colocada referia-se ao artigo 4º, nº 1, da diretiva 2000/78, pelo que o Tribunal se preocupou, essencialmente, em averiguar se a vontade de um empregador de ter em conta os desejos de um cliente de que as prestações dos serviços do empregador deixem de ser asseguradas por uma trabalhadora que usa véu islâmico pode ser considerada um requisito essencial e determinante para o exercício da atividade em causa.

[26] Joseph Weiler, "Je Suis Achbita!", *European Journal of International Law*, 2017, p. 997.

O TJ andou bem, neste caso, ao considerar que se trata de uma exigência objetiva que não deve abranger considerações subjetivas, como as que estão em causa no caso *Bougnaoui*.

Tendo em conta que, no essencial, concordamos com a decisão no caso *Bougnaoui*, retomemos o caso *Achbita* com o intuito de analisar a ponderação dos direitos em confronto efetuada pelo TJ.

3.4. A ponderação dos direitos em confronto: a liberdade religiosa e a liberdade de empresa

Como dissemos, o TJUE falhou, sobretudo, na ponderação da liberdade religiosa do indivíduo e da liberdade de empresa.

Note-se, contudo, que a liberdade religiosa prevista no artigo 9º CEDH e no artigo 10º da CDFUE pode ser restringida com fundamento na liberdade da empresa também ela prevista na CDFUE (artigo 16º). Não há direitos absolutos, o que significa que a liberdade religiosa pode ser objeto de restrições como qualquer outro direito fundamental. Deve igualmente sublinhar-se que quando há conflitos de direitos, as restrições de um direito devem ser ponderadas em função do outro direito que está em causa.

Ora, no caso *Achbita*, o TJUE não parece ter procedido a uma ponderação adequada da liberdade religiosa e da liberdade de empresa. O Tribunal deu claramente preferência a esta última, levando ao esvaziamento de um dos direitos em causa – a liberdade religiosa. Com efeito, para uma mulher islâmica não há alternativa ao uso do lenço na cabeça. Ou seja, na solução do conflito entre estes dois direitos não se verificou uma tentativa consistente de concordância prática, ao contrário do que fez o TEDH, por exemplo, no caso *Eweida*[27], o qual expressamente procurou um equilíbrio justo entre os dois direitos.

O TEDH ponderou a importância do direito a manifestar a liberdade religiosa numa sociedade democrática que deve ser tolerante e basear-se no pluralismo e na diversidade.

Antes de avançar, devem sublinhar-se dois pontos:

[27] Ac. de 15/1/2013, *Eweida e outros c. Reino Unido*, queixas nºs 48420/10, 59842/10, 51671/10 e 36516/10.

a) Uma adequada procura de equilíbrio entre direitos não conduz necessariamente à aceitação pelo empregador do uso de sinais exteriores, designadamente, no vestuário, no local de trabalho por parte dos trabalhadores, com fundamento na liberdade religiosa. Pode chegar-se à conclusão que a restrição à liberdade religiosa se justifica.
b) A jurisprudência do TEDH, apesar de proceder a uma apreciação mais exigente do princípio da proporcionalidade, concluiu, frequentemente, no sentido da licitude da restrição à liberdade religiosa. Aliás, fê-lo sempre que esteve em causa o uso de símbolos religiosos islâmicos, como veremos no *item* seguinte.

3.5. Os limites do diálogo dos juízes do Luxemburgo com os de Estrasburgo

Como já tivemos ocasião de evidenciar em anteriores trabalhos[28], o diálogo judicial, ainda que informal, pode ser muito relevante no domínio dos direitos fundamentais. Assim sendo, os juízes do Luxemburgo terão a ganhar se levarem em conta a jurisprudência de um tribunal especializado em direitos humanos, como é o caso do TEDH, o que não significa, necessariamente, seguir a jurisprudência alheia.

Dito isto, importa notar que, ao contrário do que, numa primeira leitura possa parecer, o TJUE, no caso *Achbita* (e também no caso *Bougnaoui*), não decidiu em contradição com a jurisprudência do TEDH, desde logo, porque nenhum dos casos decididos no TEDH se pode equiparar aos casos que correram no TJUE.

[28] Ver Ana Maria Guerra Martins, "Tribunais Constitucionais, Tribunais Europeus e Direitos Fundamentais – Do monólogo cauteloso ao diálogo construtivo", *Estudos em homenagem ao Conselheiro Presidente Moura Ramos*, vol. I, Coimbra, Almedina, 2016, p. 599-635; Idem, "O Diálogo entre as Jurisdições Constitucionais e as Jurisdições Europeias em matéria de Direitos Fundamentais", in Fausto de Santos Morais/José Carlos Kraemer Bortoloti, *A Jurisdição Constitucional e os desafios à concretização dos direitos fundamentais*, Rio de Janeiro, Editora Lumen Juris, 2016, p. 47-92; Ana Maria Guerra Martins/Miguel Prata Roque, "A tutela multinível dos direitos fundamentais", *Revista do Esmape*, vol. 19, nº 40, 2014, p. 35-70; Idem, "Judicial Dialogue in a Multilevel Constitutional Network – the Role of the Portuguese Constitutional Court", in M. Andenas/D. Fairgrieve, *Courts and Comparative Law*, Oxford, OUP, 2015, p. 300-328.

É certo que, no caso *Eweida*, acima citado, o TEDH considerou que a liberdade de empresa não podia justificar o afastamento da liberdade de religião, mas a verdade é que naquele caso os sinais exteriores de manifestação de uma determinada religião que estavam em causa eram completamente diferentes. Enquanto o símbolo religioso que estava em causa, no caso *Eweida*, era, segundo a própria decisão do TEDH, discreto, o mesmo não se pode dizer do uso de um lenço na cabeça. Trata-se de um símbolo muito mais visível. Só isso é suficiente para não se poder fazer qualquer transposição de um caso para o outro.

Além disso, ao contrário do que sucede no direito da União Europeia, a liberdade de empresa não é para a CEDH uma das suas bases de sustentação. Já no direito da União Europeia, a liberdade de empresa é um dos direitos mais relevantes. Não se pode esquecer que a União nasceu sob o signo da construção do mercado único. Pelo contrário, para a CEDH a liberdade religiosa é uma das bases de qualquer sociedade democrática e pluralista. Ou seja, o peso de um e de outro direito em cada uma das ordens jurídicas é diferente.

Mas a razão decisiva por que a jurisprudência *Achbita* e *Bougnaoui* não contradiz a jurisprudência do TEDH em matéria de liberdade religiosa prende-se com dois outros aspetos. Por um lado, a jurisprudência do TEDH sobre o uso de símbolos religiosos islâmicos, como é o caso da burka, do niqab e do véu islâmico referiu-se às relações entre privados e entidades públicas, o que não é o caso nos acórdãos do TJUE em apreço. Por outro lado, ainda que assim não fosse, o TEDH admitiu, de um modo geral, em todos os casos, em que se pronunciou sobre o uso de símbolos religiosos islâmicos no emprego que a restrição era legítima, pois visava prosseguir outros fins, como, por exemplo, o secularismo, a igualdade da mulher ou o princípio da neutralidade do Estado, era adequada, necessária e não excessiva.

Assim, no caso *Sahin*[29], estava em causa a proibição do uso do véu islâmico na universidade de Istambul. O TEDH aceitou que a interferência na liberdade religiosa estava justificada com base no secularismo e na igual-

[29] Ac. de 10/11/2005 (Grande Chambre), *Leyla Sahin c. Turquia*, queixa nº 44774/98.

dade da mulher invocados pelo Estado e que o princípio da proporcionalidade era respeitado[30].

No caso *Ebrahimian c. França*[31] estava em causa a não renovação de um contrato de trabalho como assistente social a uma trabalhadora que usava o véu islâmico. Tal como no caso anterior, o TEDH embora considerasse que havia interferência na liberdade de manifestar a sua religião, admitiu que o princípio da neutralidade dos serviços públicos era um fim legítimo que justificava a restrição e que se verificava a observação do princípio da proporcionalidade.

No caso *S.A.S. c. França*[32] e, mais recentemente, no caso *Belcacemi e Oussar contra a Béligica*[33] estava em causa o uso de véu islâmico integral em espaços públicos, pelo que as conclusões do TEDH também não são transponíveis para os casos *Achbita* e *Bougnaoui*.

Em suma, por muito desejável que seja o diálogo judicial, não se lhe pode pedir mais do que aquilo que é capaz de dar.

4. Conclusões

Do estudo realizado podem extrair-se as seguintes conclusões:

1. O TJUE considerou que a proibição do uso do véu islâmico no emprego pelo empregador não constitui uma discriminação direta, desde logo, porque essa proibição se aplica a todas as religiões e a todas as convicções filosóficas e políticas.
2. Se assim não for, infere-se da decisão do Tribunal que essa discriminação seria contrária ao direito da União Europeia.
3. Ora, este ponto de partida é criticável, desde logo, porque se estão a comparar religiões que não implicam qualquer manifestação exterior com outras em que isso é intrínseco à própria religião.
4. O TJUE aceita, todavia, que pode haver discriminação indireta, ou seja, que, apesar do critério aparentemente neutro – porque

[30] Ver, no mesmo sentido, acórdãos de 4/12/2008, *Dogru c.França*, queixa nº 27058/05 e *Kervanci c. França*, queixa nº 31645/04.

[31] Ac. De 26/11/2015, *Ebrahimian c. França*, queixa º 64846/11.

[32] Ac. de 1/7/2014, *S.A.S. c. França*, queixa nº 43835/11.

[33] Ac. de 11/07/2017, *Belcacemi e Oussar contra a Béligica*, queixa nº 37798/13.

abrange todas as religiões e convicções – afeta mais umas religiões que outras.

5. Assim sendo, o Tribunal aceita que a liberdade de empresa pode justificar a restrição da liberdade religiosa, sem ter procedido a testes muito rigorosos do controlo do princípio da proporcionalidade.

6. De qualquer modo, o Tribunal admite que é difícil justificar restrições a empregados que não estão em contacto com o público.

7. O facto de o TJUE ter indicado que o empregador deve ponderar se não pode mudar o empregado de função parece indicar que o empregador deve tentar a adaptação razoável do empregado, o que na diretiva só está previsto para a discriminação em função da deficiência.

8. No caso *Bougnaoui,* o Tribunal rejeitou que os desejos dos clientes se pudessem incluir no requisito essencial e determinante para o exercício da atividade profissional em causa, o que é positivo.

9. O TJUE deveria ter decidido com base num maior rigor quanto à justificação da discriminação indireta, como fez anteriormente com outras categorias suspeitas.

10. A religião como fundamento de discriminação não deve ser tratada de modo diferente dos outros fundamentos, sob pena de inconsistência que pode conduzir a uma menor proteção da liberdade religiosa em geral.

11. O TJUE poderia ter dado mais peso ao direito individual a manifestar a religião, o qual é garantido pelo artigo 10º da Carta.

12. A decisão coloca obstáculos ao exercício de direitos por parte das minorias e, em especial, por parte das mulheres islâmicas, podendo ser questionada a falta de referência à discriminação bem como aos valores da União consagrados no artigo 2º TUE, nomeadamente a dignidade humana, os direitos das pessoas pertencentes a uma minoria, o pluralismo e a tolerância.

13. Se, em termos de fundamentação, se pode aceitar que as decisões do TJUE são mais pobres do que as do TEDH sobre questões paralelas, a verdade é que convergem no que diz respeito ao resultado. O TEDH já aceitou, diversas vezes, a restrição do uso do véu islâmico no local de trabalho.

Parte III

O migrante, o refugiado e o trabalhador no Direito Internacional

VII
A igualdade e a não discriminação como fundamento dos direitos dos migrantes e dos refugiados no Direito Internacional*

1. Introdução

1.1. Objeto do presente estudo

O tema que nos propomos tratar é a igualdade e a não discriminação[1] como fundamento dos direitos dos migrantes e dos refugiados no direito internacional.

Tendo em conta que se assiste, atualmente, a uma das maiores crises, no domínio dos fluxos migratórios e de refugiados, a qual tem conduzido a um maior – ou, pelo menos, mais mediático – atropelo dos direitos fundamentais daqueles que se deslocam de um Estado para outro, quer o façam por razões políticas, religiosas, sociais, económicas ou outras, e

* O presente estudo encontra-se publicado em Eduardo Vera-Cruz Pinto e outros (coordenação) *Refugiados, Imigrantes e Igualdade dos Povos – Estudos em homenagem a António Guterres*, São Paulo, Editora Quartier Latin, 2017, p. 185-204.

[1] Já em anteriores estudos tivemos oportunidade de nos debruçar sobre a igualdade e a não discriminação. V. Ana Maria Guerra Martins, "O Tratado de Lisboa reforça o princípio da igualdade e da não discriminação?", *in Estudos em homenagem ao Prof. Doutor Martim de Albuquerque*, Volume I, Coimbra, Coimbra Editora, 2009, p. 55 e segs.; Ana Maria Guerra Martins, *A igualdade e a não discriminação dos nacionais dos Estados terceiros legalmente residentes na União Europeia – da origem na integração económica ao fundamento na dignidade do ser humano*, Coimbra, 2010, p. 39 e segs.; Ana Maria Guerra Martins, "Does the Treaty of Lisbon really implement equal and non-discriminatory treatment of Third-Country Nationals (TCN)? The case of legally resident TCN within a Member State of the Union", in Ingolf Pernice/José Maria Beneyto (org.), *Europe's Constitutional Challenges in the Light of the Recent Case-Law – Lisbon and Beyond*, vol. 8 of ECLN Series, Baden-Baden, Nomos, 2011, p. 327 e segs.

tendo presente que a igualdade e a não discriminação, a par da dignidade do ser humano e da liberdade, constituem a base em que se ancoram todos os direitos fundamentais, parece-nos que, numa obra sobre imigração, refugiados e direitos dos povos, não pode deixar de se investigar, por um lado, qual o verdadeiro significado da igualdade e da não discriminação e, por outro lado, se e em que medida elas podem constituir a base em que se ancoram os direitos fundamentais dos migrantes e dos refugiados[2]. Importa ainda esclarecer que, ao contrário do que temos sustentado em anteriores trabalhos[3], a nossa pesquisa se vai restringir ao direito internacional. Com efeito, apesar de considerarmos que, atualmente, qualquer estudo relativo à proteção e à tutela dos direitos fundamentais só faz sentido numa perspetiva multinível, a qual abarca os direitos constitucionais nacionais, o direito internacional regional e universal e o direito da União Europeia, o espaço de que dispomos nesta obra não permitiria essa amplitude de tratamento.

1.2. Indicação de sequência

Tendo em atenção o objetivo que nos move, começaremos, num primeiro momento, por enunciar sucintamente os marcos mais relevantes da evolução dos conceitos de igualdade e não discriminação, passando, num segundo momento, a estudar a distinção, do ponto de vista jurídico, entre igualdade e não discriminação em todas as suas vertentes. Num terceiro momento, trataremos da igualdade e da não discriminação como fundamento dos direitos fundamentais em geral e dos direitos dos migrantes e dos refugiados, em especial, no âmbito do direito internacional.

2. A herança cultural comum europeia em matéria de igualdade e de não discriminação – breve nota

A tarefa de averiguar em que consistem a igualdade e a não discriminação não se afigura fácil, na medida em que se trata de conceitos plurívo-

[2] A igualdade dos povos levanta problemas específicos, que não vão ser tratados no âmbito deste estudo.

[3] Ana Maria Guerra Martins/Miguel Prata Roque, "A tutela multinível dos direitos fundamentais", *Revista do Esmape*, vol. 19, nº 40, 2014, p. 35 e segs.

cos, com uma multiplicidade de conteúdos[4], que se expressam de formas muito diversas[5] e que encerram alguma ambiguidade[6]. Aliás, o modo como estes conceitos têm sido interpretados, ao longo dos tempos, varia, em função do espírito da época e das normas e valores que prevalecem numa determinada Ordem Jurídica, num dado momento[7]. A igualdade e a não discriminação não podem, portanto, ser consideradas em abstrato, devendo antes ser compreendidas no seu contexto histórico e político[8].

Pilar fundamental da tradição judaico-cristã, a igualdade faz parte, tal como a liberdade e a dignidade humana, da herança cultural comum europeia, tendo penetrado no discurso jurídico com o advento do Iluminismo.

Remontando as suas origens à Antiguidade clássica, têm estado, desde então, no âmago das preocupações da filosofia, da moral e da teologia. Autores de referência do pensamento europeu, como THOMAS MORUS (1478-1535), THOMAS HOBBES (1588-1679), JEAN-JACQUES ROUSSEAU (1712-1778) e IMMANUEL KANT (1724-1804), conferiram à igualdade um lugar cimeiro nas suas respetivas obras.

Os conceitos de igualdade e de não discriminação sofreram uma longa e profunda evolução, embora tenham mantido sempre uma ligação muito estreita com a Justiça, como afirma JOHN RAWLS[9]. É, pois, por essa evolução que vamos iniciar o presente trabalho.

2.1. Da Antiguidade ao liberalismo

A herança cultural comum europeia remonta à Antiguidade clássica (grega e romana). SÓCRATES (470-399 A.C), PLATÃO (c. 429–347 A.C.), CÍCERO (106-43 A.C.) e ARISTÓTELES (384–322 A.C) são algumas das

[4] Neste sentido, FERNANDO ALVES CORREIA, *O plano urbanístico e o princípio da igualdade*, Coimbra, 1989, p. 393.

[5] Neste sentido, EVELYN ELLIS, *EU Anti-Discrimination Law*, Oxford, 2005, p. 4; CHRISTA TOBLER, *Indirect Discrimination, A Case Study into the Development of the Legal Concept of Indirect Discrimination under EC Law*, Antuérpia/Oxford, 2005, p. 41.

[6] Ver XAVIER BIOY, «L'ambiguïté du concept de non-discrimination», *in* FREDERIC SUDRE/ HÈLÉNE SURREL, *Le droit à la non-discrimination au sens de la Convention européenne des droits de l'homme*, Bruxelas, 2008, p. 51.

[7] Ver J. H. GERARDS, *Judicial Review in Equal Treatment Cases*, Leiden, 2005, p. 5.

[8] Neste sentido, SANDRA FREDMAN, *Discrimination Law*, Oxford, 2002, p. 26.

[9] JOHN RAWLS, *A Theory of Justice* (original edition), Cambridge, Massachusetts, 1971, p. 54 e segs.

incontornáveis referências culturais europeias, a par de SANTO AGOSTINHO (354-430) ou de S. TOMÁS DE AQUINO (1225-1274).

No domínio da igualdade, as origens mais remotas do conceito podem encontrar-se em SÓLON (c. 640-560 A.C.), PÉRICLES (c. 460–429 A.C.) e PLATÃO[10-11], devendo-se, no entanto, a ARISTÓTELES a construção do conceito que mais influenciou a atualidade.

Para este Autor, "*se a injustiça é iniquidade, então a justiça é igualdade, coisa que é aceite por todos sem ser necessária demonstração. Por outro lado, a igualdade implica, pelo menos, dois termos*"[12]. Ou seja, o conceito de igualdade relaciona-se com a justiça e o juízo de igualdade requer a comparação de duas situações, com o intuito de avaliar as suas semelhanças e diferenças e daí retirar as devidas consequências.

Segundo ARISTÓTELES, "*porque se as pessoas não forem iguais não terão partes iguais e é daqui que resultam muitos conflitos e queixas, como quando pessoas iguais têm e partilham partes desiguais ou pessoas desiguais têm e partilham partes iguais*"[13]. Além disso, para o filósofo, a justiça implica proporção. Por outras palavras, a justiça impõe que situações iguais sejam tratadas de modo igual e situações diferentes sejam de modo diferente, na proporção da sua diferença[14].

Esta fórmula foi, contudo, alvo de muitas críticas que se podem sintetizar do seguinte modo: em primeiro lugar, o juízo do tratamento "idêntico" é abstrato, não equacionando as particularidades de cada indivíduo – a cor, a religião, as origens étnicas, o sexo, a língua, etc. Em segundo lugar, este juízo descura o tratamento da diferença, uma vez que só se impõe o tratamento igual dos iguais, não se dando indicações para a forma como devem ser tratados, nem se impondo um tratamento adequado dos diferentes. Em terceiro lugar, trata-se de uma conceção de igualdade individualista, que não tem em conta a relevância do grupo e da participação do indiví-

[10] Ver PLATÃO, *A República* (trad. ELÍSIO GALA), Lisboa, 2005, 359c; 453a; 558c; 561b-c e 561e. As referências são, contudo, escassas e circunstanciais.

[11] Neste sentido, MARTIM DE ALBUQUERQUE, *Da Igualdade, Introdução à Jurisprudência*, Coimbra, 1993, p. 11 e segs.

[12] ARISTÓTELES, *Ética a Nicómano*, (trad. de ANTÓNIO DE CASTRO CAEIRO), 3ª ed., Lisboa, 2009, cap. V 1131a10-20.

[13] ARISTÓTELES, *Ética a Nicómano...*, cap. V 1131a20-25.

[14] Note-se que a ideia de igualdade em Aristóteles só se aplica aos homens livres, admitindo-se a escravatura como uma instituição natural.

duo em grupos culturais, religiosos, étnicos reiteradamente desfavorecidos ao longo da História[15].

Há mesmo quem sustente o esgotamento da igualdade na ideia de não discriminação, e como tal a conceção aristotélica de igualdade não passaria de uma fórmula vazia de sentido[16].

Apesar das inúmeras críticas, o conceito aristotélico de igualdade, profundamente ligado à ideia de justiça, vai influenciar a moral, a política e o Direito até aos nossos dias.

Os estóicos (como SÉNECA (4-65)) vão desenvolver a ideia de igualdade entre todos os homens, alicerçada na existência de uma igualdade natural entre todos os homens e na centralidade da ideia de indivíduo em detrimento da ideia de cidadão[17].

A primeira grande rutura com a fórmula da igualdade prevalecente em toda a Antiguidade clássica vai ocorrer com o pensamento judaico-cristão, na medida em que, baseando-se na premissa de que todos os seres humanos são criados à imagem e semelhança de Deus, todos devem ser iguais. Ou seja, todos têm igual dignidade perante Deus sem distinção entre romanos e gregos e o resto do mundo nem entre escravos e homens livres[18].

Enquanto conceito jurídico, a igualdade é, no entanto, um produto do Iluminismo, o qual se baseou na ideia de que todos os homens nascem livres e iguais em direitos, pelo que a ideia de igualdade vai entroncar na ideia de liberdade. Além disso, a igualdade vai constituir uma das mais importantes marcas do Estado de Direito Liberal. Nas palavras de SANDRA FREDMAN, "*a igualdade como ideal brilha claramente na galáxia das aspirações liberais*"[19].

Ora, a igualdade no sentido liberal decorre claramente das Revoluções Inglesa (1640), Americana (1776) e Francesa (1789).

[15] Neste sentido, SANDRA FREDMAN, "Combating Racism with Human Rights: The Right to Equality", *in* SANDRA FREDMAN (ed), *Discrimination and Human Rights – The Case of Racism*, Oxford, 2001, p. 16 e 17.

[16] Neste sentido, PETER WESTEN, «The Empty Idea of Equality», *HLR*, vol. 95, 1982, p. 537 e segs.

[17] Cfr. PAULO OTERO, *Instituições políticas e constitucionais*, vol. I, Coimbra, 2007, p. 88.

[18] Para maiores desenvolvimentos, PAULO OTERO, *Instituições...*, p. 97 e 98.

[19] SANDRA FREDMAN, *Discrimination Law...*, p. 1.

Mas o conceito de igualdade liberal vai-se construindo anteriormente à Revolução Inglesa.

De entre os seus percursores deve mencionar-se, em primeiro lugar, Thomas Morus, o qual baseia a sociedade da ilha da Utopia no princípio da igualdade. Inspirando-se em Platão, preconiza a abolição da propriedade privada, defendendo uma distribuição igualitária dos bens – "os bens devem ser distribuídos por todos em pé de igualdade"[20]. Mais do que a igualdade perante as leis, Thomas Morus sustenta a igualdade na distribuição da riqueza, pois só assim se evitará a guerra e se atingirá a felicidade pública. Em segundo lugar, devem referir-se os *Levellers* – grupo relativamente radical – que, no âmbito da revolução inglesa, defenderam a igualdade política de todos os homens, a eliminação dos privilégios de classe e o direito universal de voto[21].

Mais tarde, o britânico Thomas Hobbes sustenta que "*a natureza fez os homens tão iguais, quanto às faculdades do corpo e do espírito*"[22], ou seja, os homens são todos iguais por natureza. "*A diferença entre um e outro homem não é suficientemente considerável para que qualquer pessoa possa com base nela reclamar qualquer benefício a que outro não possa igualmente aspirar*"[23]. Ou seja, todos os homens iguais têm direitos e "*da igualdade da justiça faz parte também a igual cobrança de impostos*"[24-25].

[20] Thomas Morus, *A Utopia*, Lisboa, 2006, liv. I, p. 479.

[21] Paulo Otero, *Instituições...*, p. 176.

[22] Thomas Hobbes, *Leviatã* (trad. de João Paulo Monteiro e Maria Beatriz Nizza da Silva), 2ª ed., Lisboa, s.d., p. 109.

[23] *Idem, ibidem.*

[24] Thomas Hobbes, *Leviatã...*, p. 271.

[25] Thomas Hobbes assenta a construção da sociedade e do Estado na vontade do Homem. Para ele a natureza humana é essencialmente imperfeita, negativa. O Homem é um ser mau por natureza, sendo as paixões o verdadeiro motor da natureza humana. A principal paixão que move os homens é a defesa da vida. Além disso, o homem é por natureza ambicioso. Só um poder exterior ao Homem pode evitar estas tendências malévolas.
O *«estado de natureza»* é a situação em que os homens se encontrariam se não houvesse poder político. O *«estado de natureza»* ocorre sempre que falta um poder capaz de manter a ordem, a paz e a segurança entre os homens. O *«estado de natureza»* é um estado de liberdade absoluta, de direitos individuais ilimitados, em que cada um tem direito a tudo, incluindo a vida dos outros. É a guerra de todos contra todos.
Mas a vida em sociedade impõe ao Homem, por imperativo da razão, o acatamento de regras tendentes à salvaguarda da paz e da segurança. Essas regras são, em primeiro lugar, as leis

O alemão SAMUEL PUFENDORF (1632-1694), partindo do princípio de que o homem tem de viver em sociedade, desenvolve, ao nível dos deveres do homem para com os outros homens, duas das ideias mais marcantes da sua filosofia e que mais vão influenciar o pensamento europeu: a ideia de igualdade e a ideia de dignidade[26].

Para PUFENDORF, os homens são iguais por natureza, uma vez que participam de uma natureza comum, pelo que cada um tem o dever de tratar os outros como iguais. A igualdade e a dignidade devem ser objeto de um reconhecimento mútuo[27].

O princípio da igualdade aparece, na obra deste filósofo, relacionado com a justiça. Quem tem a autoridade suprema deve prescrever as leis adequadas, assim como punir os que não as cumprem, sendo "*injusto (...) tratar de maneira desigual aqueles que merecem igual tratamento*"[28].

Do ponto de vista da constituição material britânica, o *Bill of Rights* (1689), ao proibir o rei de, unilateralmente, suspender as leis ou dispensar a sua obediência, consagra a génese do princípio da igualdade perante a lei.

A Revolução Americana vai permitir "*a materialização constitucional dos valores liberais no domínio dos direitos da pessoa humana*"[29] que encontram a sua "*primeira expressão jurídico-positiva na Declaração de Direitos da Virgínia*"[30], de 12 de Junho de 1776. De acordo com a sua secção 1ª, "*todos os homens são por natureza igualmente livres e têm certos direitos inatos*". Por sua vez, a Declaração de Independência dos EUA, de 4 de Julho de 1776, vai reafirmar o princípio de que todos os homens são iguais.

naturais limitativas do Direito, mas como as leis naturais ditadas pela razão não chegam para garantir a paz e a segurança entre os homens são necessárias determinações precisas, ou seja «*mandatos do soberano*».
Assim, cada cidadão vai renunciar ao direito de se determinar por si mesmo e vai cedê-lo ao soberano, sob condição de que todos os outros cidadãos cedam também esse direito e o coloquem nas mãos do soberano. Com fundamento nesse contrato coletivo («*contrato de sujeição*»), os cidadãos renunciam aos seus direitos e liberdades e conferem o poder de soberania a um terceiro – o soberano. Ver THOMAS HOBBES, *Leviatã...*, p. 109 e segs.

[26] SAMUEL PUFENDORF, *De los deberes del hombre y del cidadano según la ley natural, en dos libros*, Madrid, 2002, p. 58 e segs. (livro I, cap. VII).

[27] SAMUEL PUFENDORF, *De los deberes del hombre...*, p. 59.

[28] SAMUEL PUFENDORF, *De los deberes del hombre...*, p. 139.

[29] PAULO OTERO, *Instituições...*, p. 237.

[30] PAULO OTERO, *Instituições...*, p. 237.

Em França, a Declaração dos Direitos do Homem e do Cidadão, de 26 de Agosto de 1789, vai reproduzir os ideais da Revolução Francesa, abrindo com a declaração de que "*os homens nascem e são livres e iguais em direitos*" (artigo 1º).

Embora as bases filosóficas da Revolução Francesa se ancorem mais diretamente na obra de JEAN-JACQUES ROUSSEAU, a referência ao inglês JOHN LOCKE (1632-1704) afigura-se, neste contexto, incontornável. Admitindo uma fase primitiva da vida humana que é o *«estado de natureza»*, em que não há poder político e em que os homens vivem entregues a si próprios, sem qualquer organização política em que se afirme um poder capaz de governar a comunidade, J. LOCKE, embora, à partida, não qualifique o *«estado de natureza»* como negativo nem como positivo, acabará por o considerar negativo. A inexistência de leis e de tribunais não permitirá aos homens uma defesa dos seus direitos, nem lhes garante a liberdade e a propriedade. Daí que os homens que vivem em estado de natureza cheguem racionalmente à conclusão de que é necessário passar ao "estado de sociedade"[31].

Mas a grande inovação de J. LOCKE, para o que agora nos interessa, é a afirmação de que todos os homens nascem livres e iguais e, portanto, todo o governo deve ser limitado no seu poder[32].

Tal como JOHN LOCKE, JEAN-JACQUES ROUSSEAU parte do princípio que, no *«estado de natureza»*, há indivíduos isolados que são livres e iguais. Isto é, todo o homem nasce livre e no estado de natureza, a desigualdade é quase nula. A passagem do *«estado de natureza»* para o *«estado civil»* faz-se através do contrato social[33-34].

O maior contributo de ROUSSEAU assenta na diferente conceção, sentido e função da propriedade privada. Sendo o elemento fundador da sociedade civil, é ela a origem de toda a desigualdade entre os homens e a causadora de um estado permanente de guerra. Por isso a sociedade tem

[31] JOHN LOCKE, *Traité du gouvernement civil* (trad. francesa), Paris, 1992, cap. II a V.

[32] *Idem, ibidem*, cap. VIII e IX.

[33] JEAN-JACQUES ROUSSEAU, *Du contrat social*, Paris, 1973, p. 72 e segs. (livro I, cap. IV).

[34] O contrato social é um acordo unânime dos homens, pelo qual procuram encontrar uma forma de associação que defenda e proteja com força comum a pessoa e os bens de cada membro e, de tal modo, que cada um unido a todos só obedeça a si mesmo e permaneça livre como antes. Este acordo exige uma alienação total de cada membro à comunidade. Tal alienação é a única forma de cada um garantir os seus direitos.

de se organizar de acordo com leis, abdicando cada um da sua liberdade natural a favor de uma força comum, garante dos direitos de todos e de cada um. Esta força comum, que é a soberania, permanece nas mãos de todos e de cada um dos cidadãos[35].

Immanuel Kant, o expoente máximo do Idealismo alemão, funda a constituição "*em primeiro lugar, segundo os princípios da* liberdade *dos membros de uma sociedade (enquanto homens); em segundo lugar, em conformidade com os princípios da* dependência *de todos em relação a uma única legislação comum (enquanto súbditos); e em terceiro lugar, segundo a lei da* igualdade *dos mesmos (enquanto cidadãos)*"[36]. A constituição republicana tem em vista alcançar a paz perpétua[37].

A liberdade de cada membro da sociedade, como homem, a igualdade deste com todos os outros, como súbdito, e a independência de cada membro de uma comunidade, como cidadão, são as leis que permitem uma instituição estável, segundo os puros princípios racionais do direito humano externo em geral[38].

A igualdade, em Kant, significa que "*segundo o direito (que enquanto expressão da vontade geral só pode ser um único (...)) são enquanto súbditos todos iguais; porque nenhum pode constranger a quem quer que seja, exceto mediante lei pública (...), mas através desta também todos os outros se lhe contrapõem em igual medida (...))*"[39]. Deste excerto resulta claro que a noção de igualdade adotada por Kant é meramente formal, apontando no sentido da igualdade perante a lei. Como afirma Paulo Otero, não há em Kant qualquer dimensão material da igualdade[40].

Como é óbvio, muito mais se poderia dizer sobre a herança cultural comum europeia desde a Antiguidade até ao liberalismo, mas esta não é a sede própria para esse efeito. O que acaba de se expor já permite extrair duas conclusões: em primeiro lugar, a igualdade, em ligação com a justiça, tem sido uma preocupação constante do pensamento europeu ao longo

[35] Jean-Jacques Rousseau, *Du contrat...*, p. 83 e segs. (livro II, cap. I).

[36] Immanuel Kant, *A Paz Perpétua e Outros Opúsculos*, Lisboa, 2008, p. 137 e 138 e segs.

[37] Immanuel Kant, *A Paz Perpétua...*, p. 139.

[38] Immanuel Kant, "Sobre a expressão corrente: isto pode ser correto na teoria, mas nada vale na prática (1793)", *in A Paz Perpétua...*, p. 79.

[39] Immanuel Kant, "Sobre a expressão corrente: isto pode ser correcto na teoria, mas nada vale na prática (1793)", *in A Paz Perpétua...*, p. 81.

[40] Paulo Otero, *Instituições...*, p. 206.

dos tempos e, em segundo lugar, a ausência de um consenso geral quanto ao conteúdo da igualdade vem de tempos remotos.

2.2. Do liberalismo à atualidade

Como já se disse, a noção de igualdade não é, todavia, estanque. Pelo contrário, tem vindo a alterar-se ao longo da História[41].

Assim, a igualdade, reclamada nos finais do séc. XVIII e durante todo o séc. XIX, pelo Estado de Direito liberal, limita-se a impor que a lei seja a mesma para todos, independentemente do seu conteúdo e das condições específicas sociais e económicas dos indivíduos. A igualdade perante a lei atinge-se, pois, através da generalidade e da universalidade da lei, tornando-se num princípio da prevalência da mesma. Ora, o entendimento da igualdade como mera aplicação uniforme da lei é meramente formal e suscetível de conduzir a situações profundamente discriminatórias[42].

Note-se que as limitações inerentes à igualdade perante a lei têm na sua base uma conceção abstencionista ou não intervencionista do Estado, a qual subjaz à garantia de todo e qualquer direito fundamental no liberalismo.

Ora, a insuficiência da noção liberal de igualdade é, por demais, evidente, além de ser desmentida pela observação da realidade da vida. As desigualdades sociais, económicas e culturais a que conduziu o liberalismo, levaram sectores muito díspares (desde a Igreja Católica aos movimentos socialistas) à reivindicação de uma maior intervenção do Estado, designadamente, na economia, de modo a promover a melhoria das condições de vida, em especial, dos mais pobres.

E assim, no início do séc. XX, surgem as primeiras manifestações do Estado social – um Estado mais intervencionista nos domínios económico,

[41] Como afirma JORGE REIS NOVAIS, "o princípio da igualdade é, porventura, dos princípios estruturantes do Estado de Direito, o de presença mais constante e mais antiga nos textos constitucionais, mas também é, mesmo em consequência dessa *longevidade* constitucional, o que tem experimentado uma evolução mais pronunciada e multifacetada". *In Os Princípios Constitucionais Estruturantes da República Portuguesa*, Coimbra, 2004, p. 101.

[42] Ver MARIA DA GLÓRIA F. P. D. GARCIA, "Princípio da igualdade: fórmula vazia ou fórmula "carregada" de sentido?", *in Estudos sobre o Princípio da Igualdade*, Coimbra, 2005, p. 36 e segs; *Idem*, "Princípio da Igualdade: da Uniformidade à Diferenciação ou a interminável história de Abel e Caim, dois irmãos marcados pela diferença", *Estudos...*, p. 10 e segs.

social e cultural – que obriga à reformulação do conceito de igualdade, o qual evolui, passando a levar em conta a situação dos indivíduos em face da lei ou na lei. Ou seja, a igualdade centra-se na própria lei e no seu conteúdo, bem como nas condições específicas dos indivíduos em face dela. As situações diferentes devem ser tratadas diferentemente, pois só assim se pode atingir a igualdade social. Esta dimensão da igualdade já não se dirige apenas à Administração e aos Tribunais na fase da aplicação da lei, mas dirige-se também ao Legislador na fase da sua criação. Deixa de se aceitar a indiferenciação jurídica entre as pessoas, para se passar a exigir a existência de diferenças fundamentadas entre elas[43]. Franqueado este passo, assume relevo a distinção entre igualdade e não discriminação.

Deve realçar-se, todavia, que nem todas as diferenças de tratamento são admissíveis[44]. Estas diferenças de tratamento podem ocorrer por determinação da própria lei, pela forma como a lei é aplicada pela Administração ou nas relações entre privados.

O controlo da aplicação do princípio da igualdade cabe aos tribunais, os quais devem testar as eventuais diferenças de tratamento com base em critérios tão previsíveis, objetivos e seguros quanto possível, pois só assim se garantirá a certeza jurídica[45]. Por conseguinte, uma medida discriminatória só pode ser justificada se prosseguir um fim legítimo e se respeitar o princípio da proporcionalidade[46] nas suas três vertentes de adequação, necessidade e proporcionalidade *stricto sensu*[47]. Mas daqui não decorre qualquer confusão entre o princípio da igualdade (e da não discriminação) e o princípio da proporcionalidade. Trata-se de dois princípios distintos[48].

[43] Neste sentido, Maria Lúcia Amaral, "O princípio da igualdade na Constituição Portuguesa", in *Estudos em Homenagem ao Prof. Doutor Armando Marques Guedes*, Coimbra, 2004, p. 39.

[44] Ver J. H. Gerards, *Judicial Review in Equal Treatment Cases*, Leiden, 2005, p. 1 e 2.

[45] Neste sentido, J. H. Gerards, *Judicial Review...*, p. 4.

[46] Sobre o princípio da proporcionalidade como modo de justificação objectiva da discriminação ver Sheldon Leader, "Proportionality and the Justification of Discrimination", *in* Janet Dine/Bob Watt (ed.), *Discrimination Law, Concepts, Limitations and Justifications*, Londres/Nova Iorque, 1996, p. 110 e segs.

[47] Para maiores desenvolvimentos sobre a forma como os tribunais devem aplicar estes critérios, ver J. H. Gerards, *Judicial Review...*, p. 28 a 102.

[48] Ver Mathias Herdegen, "The Relation between the Principles of Equality and Proportionality", *CMLR*, 1985, p. 686 e segs.

Após a Segunda Guerra Mundial, com a introdução, nos textos constitucionais (*maxime*, europeus), da cláusula de bem-estar social, o Estado passou a assumir as tarefas necessárias à realização da justiça social e da solidariedade. Ou seja, o Estado (no modelo de Estado-Providência) torna-se responsável pela criação das condições económicas, sociais, culturais e ambientais que permitam a todos os seres humanos uma existência condigna. Se assim é, a eliminação das desigualdades transforma-se num objetivo central do Estado, pois será o meio para atingir a justiça social. Daqui decorre que a realização do princípio da igualdade desempenha um papel primordial no Estado-Providência.

Mas que igualdade? A igualdade formal do liberalismo revela-se insuficiente, pois, como vimos, é geradora de uma maior injustiça social. A igualdade, na sua vertente de não discriminação *tout court*, a qual proíbe à lei diferenciar com base em critérios considerados suspeitos, admitindo-se, ainda assim, justificações objetivas, razoáveis e proporcionais, também não permitirá eliminar as desigualdades, uma vez que o ponto de partida de cada um é diferente (ou seja, o ambiente social, económico, cultural, educacional, familiar, etc., em que cada um vive é condicionante).

A igualdade relevante no Estado-Providência é a igualdade substancial, material ou de facto. Mas se se verifica um certo consenso no sentido de que, na distribuição do rendimento e dos bens, a justiça social impõe ao Estado o dever de ter em consideração que nem todos dispõem, à partida, das mesmas condições, ou seja, o ponto de partida de cada um é diferente, o mesmo já não se pode asseverar quanto ao papel que o Estado deve ser chamado a desempenhar. Enquanto para alguns, a intervenção do Estado se deve limitar a assegurar a igualdade de oportunidades, independentemente do resultado final, para outros, de entre os quais se destaca JOHN RAWLS, esta revela-se insuficiente para eliminar a desigualdade dos menos favorecidos[49], pelo que a igualdade de oportunidades tem de ser concatenada com o "princípio da diferença"[50]. O Estado deve intervir na redistribuição da riqueza[51], de modo a alcançar a igualdade de resultados, isto é, na promoção da igualdade real entre as pessoas.

[49] JOHN RAWLS, *A Theory*..., p. 87.

[50] JOHN RAWLS, *A Theory*..., p. 75.

[51] JOHN RAWLS, *A Theory*..., p. 100.

Em síntese, diremos que, atualmente, a herança cultural comum europeia acolhe o princípio da igualdade na sua vertente aristotélica e liberal, ligando-o à ideia de justiça, à luta contra os privilégios e à dignidade humana[52]. Aliás, porque "*o princípio da igualdade é inerente a qualquer noção desenvolvida de direito e justiça. Situações idênticas devem ser tratadas de modo idêntico. Se um sistema jurídico não aceitar esta premissa básica, então não se deve considerar como tal*"[53].

Mas para além desta vertente formal da igualdade, a herança cultural comum europeia evoluiu, abrindo-se a novas perspetivas. A conceção dominante da igualdade nos Estados sociais e democráticos de Direito cumpre três funções: uma função de liberdade (proíbe o arbítrio), uma função democrática (impede a marginalização das minorias) e uma função social (proporciona a igualdade não só à partida como à chegada, ou seja, a igualdade de oportunidades e a igualdade de resultados)[54].

Assim, a igualdade de cariz formal requer a igualdade perante a lei, enquanto a igualdade substancial, a igualdade de oportunidades e a igualdade de resultados exigem a igualdade através da lei[55].

3. As diferentes vertentes da igualdade e a não discriminação na atualidade

Tendo em conta a evolução acabada de traçar, importa esclarecer as diversas vertentes da igualdade e da não discriminação, as quais estão intrinsecamente ligadas, não se entendendo, porém, a doutrina quanto à natureza dessa ligação.

[52] Com efeito, no Estado Moderno o princípio da igualdade é um princípio estruturante do Estado de Direito, o qual acompanha a evolução do constitucionalismo, a que está intrinsecamente ligado. Neste sentido, ver, JORGE REIS NOVAIS, *Os Princípios Constitucionais...*, p. 101; MARIA DA GLÓRIA F. P. D. GARCIA, "Princípio da igualdade: fórmula vazia..., p. 32 e segs.; MARIA LÚCIA AMARAL, "O princípio da igualdade...", p. 35 e segs.

[53] F. G. JACOBS, "An Introduction to the General Principle of Equality in EC Law", *in* ALAN DASHWOOD/SÌOFRA'LEARY, *The Principle of Equal Treatment in EC Law*, Londres, 1997, p. 8.

[54] FERNANDO REY MARTINEZ, "La Discriminación positiva de mujeres (Comentario a propósito de la sentencia del Tribunal de Justicia de la Comunidad de 17 de Octubre de 1995, asunto Kalanke)", *REDC*, 1996, p. 319.

[55] Neste sentido, TAKIS TRIDIMAS, *The General Principles of EU Law*, 2ª ed., Oxford, 2006, p. 61.

Assim, há quem considere que se existe discriminação é porque não existe igualdade. Parafraseando Michel Mine, "*Uma discriminação é uma rutura da igualdade por motivo proibido. O conceito de discriminação depende, portanto, do de igualdade*"[56]. A proibição da discriminação baseia-se, pois, no facto de que todas as pessoas são iguais[57].

Há, no entanto, quem entenda que "*à medida que se passa da igualdade formal para a igualdade concreta, da igualdade pela generalidade para a igualdade pela diferença e da igualdade em Direito para a igualdade de facto, a discriminação como conceito jurídico deixa de se poder definir como a violação de um princípio de igualdade, cujo âmbito é cada vez mais fluido. Nem toda a diferença de tratamento é constitutiva de discriminação.*"[58]

Mas também há quem sustente que não se devem distinguir os dois conceitos, considerando-os sinónimos ou equiparando-os[59]. Para esta doutrina, a proibição da discriminação é a outra face da moeda do igual tratamento. A discriminação é a expressão negativa da violação de um dever positivo de tratamento igual[60]. Nicole Belloubet-Frier afirma mesmo que "*a igualdade é concebida como um princípio de não discriminação*"[61].

[56] Michel Miné, «Les concepts de discrimination directe et indirecte», *ERA*, 3/2003, p. 32.

[57] Cfr. Erica Howard, *The EU Race Directive – Developing the protection against racial discrimination within the EU*, Londres, 2010, p. 109.

[58] Danièle Lochak, «Réflexions sur la notion de discrimination», *DS*, 1987, p. 779.

[59] Neste sentido, Dagmar Schiek/Lisa Waddington/Mark Bell, «Introductory Chapter – A Comparative Perspective on Non-discrimination Law», *in* Dagmar Schiek/Lisa Waddington/Mark Bell, *Cases, Materials, and Text on National, Supranational and International Non-discrimination Law*, Oxford, 2007, p. 26; J. H. Jans/R. de Lange,/S. Prechal/R.J.G. M. Widdershoven, *Europeanisation of Public Law*, Groningen, 2007, p. 130; Edouard Dubout, *L'article 13 du traité CE – La clause communautaire de lutte contre les discriminations*, Bruxelas, 2006, p. 20; Denis Martin, *Égalité et non-discrimination dans la jurisprudence communautaire – Étude critique à la lumière d'une approche comparatiste*, Bruxelas, 2006, p. 515 e 516; Mark Bell, «Walking in the Same Direction? The Contribution of the European Social Charter and the European Union to Combating Discrimination», *in* Grainne De Búrca/Bruno De Witte (ed.), *Social Rights in Europe*, Oxford, 2005, p. 267; Paul Cassia, «Contrats publics et principe communautaire d'égalité de traitement», *RTDE*, 2002, p. 415 e segs.; Sophie Robin-Olivier, *Le principe d'égalité en Droit Communautaire – Étude à partir des libertés économiques*, Marselha, 1999, p. 18 e segs.; Koen Lenaerts, «L'égalité de traitement en droit communautaire: un principe unique aux apparences multiples», *CDE*, 1991, p. 21.

[60] Cfr. Michael Meyer, *Das Diskriminierungsverbot des Gemeinschaftsrechts als Grundsatznorm und Gleichheitsrecht*, Frankfurt, 2002, p. 35.

[61] Nicole Belloubet-Frier, «Le principe d'égalité», *AJDA*, 1998, p. 154.

Christopher McCruden sustenta que a igualdade e a não discriminação – indistintamente – apresentam quatro sentidos diversos[62], que não só não se excluem como podem até estar em tensão uns com os outros[63].

Para este Autor, o sentido de igualdade como impedimento ao "estado de prejuízo ou desvantagem" deve ter em conta: *i)* a justiça individual; *ii)* a justiça de grupo; *iii)* o reconhecimento da diversidade; *iv)* a igualdade como participação[64]. Segundo Mccrudden, a dimensão total da igualdade só se conseguirá atingir se se levar em consideração todos estes conteúdos[65].

Como ponto de partida, admitamos que a igualdade aponta num sentido positivo que pode ir ao ponto de impor uma obrigação de assegurar a igualdade de facto entre os indivíduos e pode até legitimar uma obrigação positiva de ação, enquanto a não discriminação se contenta em exigir um comportamento negativo de abstenção, apontando num sentido negativo de proibição de tratamento diferenciado de situações idênticas, com base em determinados critérios considerados suspeitos (as chamadas *distinções, classificações ou categorias suspeitas*) pela Ordem Jurídica em causa[66].

Já a afirmação generalizada de que a igualdade e a não discriminação são duas faces da mesma moeda, ou seja, são a afirmação positiva e nega-

[62] O Autor refere-se ao Direito da União Europeia.

[63] Os quatro sentidos da igualdade e da não discriminação são, para McCruden, os seguintes:

a) a igualdade como "racionalidade" ("*rationality*") – corresponde à ideia aristotélica de igualdade e aplica-se sem atender às circunstâncias nem às limitações com base nas quais se chegou à diferença;

b) a igualdade como "protectora de direitos" – os iguais devem ser tratados de modo idêntico, excepto quando um tratamento diferente possa ser justificado;

c) a igualdade como impedimento ao "estado de "prejuízo"/desvantagem" que decorre da discriminação com fundamento em certas categorias – tem-se em vista evitar a discriminação sofrida por aqueles que têm essas características;

d) a igualdade como promoção pro-activa da igualdade de oportunidades entre grupos particulares.

Crhistopher Mccrudden, "The New Concept of Equality", *ERA*, 3/2003, p. 16 e segs.

[64] Crhistopher Mccrudden, "The New Concept...", p. 21 e segs.

[65] Crhistopher Mccrudden, "The New Concept...", p. 27.

[66] Ver Takis Tridimas, *The General Principles...*, p. 64. Embora o Autor considere que para o TJ a distinção é irrelevante.

tiva do mesmo princípio[67] é, na nossa opinião, mais duvidosa. Com efeito, determinadas vertentes da igualdade até podem colidir com a não discriminação, sem que sejam proibidas. É o caso da igualdade substancial, da igualdade de oportunidades e da igualdade de resultados.

Discriminar vem do latim *discriminare* que significa "diferenciar, distinguir, separar, destrinçar, discernir, segregar"[68].

O conceito de discriminação raramente se define em termos gerais. Por facilidade de exposição, partamos da definição apresentada por XAVIER BIOY (importada de VALÉRIE DOUMENG). "*A (discriminação) pode definir-se como uma desigualdade de atribuição e de exercício de direitos, mais precisamente, uma distinção entre pessoas, colocadas em condições ou situações semelhantes, fundada sobre um critério proibido ou neutro, mas tendo um efeito discriminatório sobre um grupo de pessoas, sem que haja qualquer motivo legítimo ou justificação objetiva e razoável. Para haver discriminação devem estar cumulativamente reunidos dois elementos. O primeiro consiste numa distinção entre indivíduos, fundada num critério inaceitável. Esta distinção pode traduzir-se quer numa exclusão, quer numa preferência, discriminação positiva ou à rebours. Pode fundar-se num critério proibido – discriminação direta – ou num critério neutro – discriminação indireta*".[69]

A discriminação pressupõe, portanto, um tratamento diferenciado de situações idênticas sem justificação objetiva, razoável e proporcional.

Dito isto, passemos à distinção das várias vertentes da igualdade e da não discriminação.

3.1. A igualdade formal e a igualdade substancial

A ideia aristotélica de tratamento igual de situações iguais e de tratamento diferente de situações diferentes identifica-se com a igualdade formal, assim chamada por não atender aos resultados a que a lei conduz.

[67] Neste sentido, FRÉDÉRIC SUDRE, «Rapport Introductif», *in* FREDERIC SUDRE/HÈLÉNE SURREL, *Le droit à la non-discrimination...*, p. 18; XAVIER BIOY, «L'ambiguïté du concept...», p. 64; ODDNÝ MJÖLL ARNARDÓTTIR, *Equality and Non-Discrimination under the European Convention on Human Rights*, Haia, 2003, p. 113; ANNE F. BAYEFSKY, "The Principle of Equality or Non-Discrimination in International Law", *HRLJ*, 1990, p. 1, n. 1; WARWICK MCKEAN, *Equality and Discrimination under International Law*, Oxford, 1983, p. 287; MARC BOSSUYT, *L'interdiction de la discrimination dans le droit international des droits de l'homme*, Bruxelas, 1976, p. 37.

[68] *Dicionário de Língua Portuguesa*, 8ª ed., Porto Editora, 1999.

[69] XAVIER BIOY, «L'ambiguïté du concept...», p. 51 e 52.

A igualdade formal, de inspiração liberal, apenas impõe às autoridades públicas que apliquem a lei de forma a tratar igualmente os cidadãos que estão em idêntica posição. A igualdade formal resolve, essencialmente, o problema da reivindicação de um ordenamento jurídico composto de leis indiferentes à condição das pessoas e, portanto, formuladas em termos subjetivamente universais. A igualdade formal contenta-se e requer apenas a igualdade perante a lei, pressupondo, portanto, um modelo de justiça individual[70].

A ideia da igualdade formal corresponde, no pensamento de RONALD DWORKIN, ao *direito ao tratamento igual*, o qual é concebido, pelo Autor, como o direito a uma igual distribuição de oportunidades, recursos ou obrigações. Todo o cidadão tem, por exemplo, um igual direito de voto em democracia[71].

A igualdade formal é, todavia, uma noção muito limitada e tem sido muito criticada[72]. Em primeiro lugar, a lei não consegue, pura e simplesmente, levar em conta todas as diferenças que existem entre as pessoas, nem se exige que as pessoas sejam tratadas adequadamente para acomodar as suas diferenças. Por maioria de razão, não se admitem medidas positivas que valorizem a diferença para atingir a genuína igualdade[73]. Em segundo lugar, nem todas as diferenças são discriminatórias. O legislador pode classificar as pessoas por grupos pelas mais diversas razões, algumas das quais são legítimas. Em terceiro lugar, a igualdade é um conceito relativo, uma vez que se contenta que iguais sejam tratados de modo igual e diferentes sejam tratados de modo diferente, não levando em linha de conta o modo como as pessoas são tratadas nem o facto de, à partida, se situarem, quer individualmente quer na sociedade, em planos diferentes[74]. Isto é, tratar igualmente duas pessoas não significa tratá-las bem.

[70] Neste sentido, MARK BELL/LISA WADDINGTON, "Reflecting on Inequalities in European Equality Law", *ELR*, 2003, p. 351 e segs.

[71] Cfr. RONALD DWORKIN, *Taking Rights Seriously*, Londres, 1977, p. 227.

[72] ELISA HOLMES, "Anti-Discrimination Rights Without Equality", *MLR*, 2005, p. 182 e segs.; MARK BELL, "Equality and the European Union Constitution", *ILJ*, 2004, p. 246 e 247; SANDRA FREDMAN, "Combating Racism with Human Rights...", p. 16.

[73] Neste sentido, SANDRA FREDMAN, *Discrimination Law...*, p. 10.

[74] Neste sentido, EVELYN ELLIS, *EU Anti-Discrimination Law...*, p. 4; SANDRA FREDMAN, *Discrimination Law...*, p. 8; HELEN FENWICK, "From Formal to Substantive Equality: the Place of Affirmative Action in the European Union Sex Equality Law", *EPL*, 1998, p. 508.

A igualdade formal não contempla qualquer garantia de melhoria no tratamento. É um princípio essencialmente estático[75]. Em quarto lugar, a igualdade formal pressupõe sempre um termo de comparação, ou seja, tem de se demonstrar que uma determinada pessoa numa situação similar é pior tratada do que outra de raça, sexo, religião, etc. diferentes. Ora, em certos casos, é muito difícil – ou mesmo impossível – encontrar um termo de comparação adequado (veja-se o caso das mulheres grávidas)[76].

De notar que, no contexto da igualdade de sexos, a escolha do termo de comparação toma normalmente o homem como regra, devendo a mulher assumir a mesma posição que o homem, o que, em certos casos, não faz qualquer sentido e até é desvantajoso para a mulher[77].

Ao contrário da igualdade formal, a igualdade substancial, mais do que com a forma, preocupa-se com o conteúdo da norma e com o impacto que ela vai ter nas pessoas[78]. O que conta não é já um tratamento igual de todos no plano jurídico, mas sim no plano fáctico, por isso, certos autores, como, por exemplo, Robert Alexy, preferem usar as expressões igualdade jurídica (ou *de jure*) para designar a igualdade formal e igualdade de facto para denominar a igualdade substancial[79].

A igualdade substancial preocupa-se, assim, com a criação das condições sociais necessárias para assegurar que as pessoas sejam tratadas de modo igual. Enquanto para alguns, a igualdade de oportunidades é suficiente para atingir esse objetivo, para outros só a igualdade de resultados o pode alcançar plenamente.

A igualdade substancial pressupõe um modelo de justiça de grupo[80]. Daí que se tenham em conta as diferenças e em que medida certas barrei-

[75] Neste sentido, Gavin Barrett, "Re-examining the Concept and Principle of Equality in EC Law", *YEL*, 2003, p. 122 e 123; Sandra Fredman, "Combating Racism with Human Rights...", p. 18.

[76] Neste sentido, Erica Howard, "The European Year of Equal Opportunities for All – 2007: Is the EU Moving Away from a Formal Idea of Equality?", *ELJ*, 2008, p. 170; Sandra Fredman, *Discrimination Law...*, p. 9.

[77] Neste sentido, Catherine Barnard, "Gender Equality in the EU: A Balance Sheet", *in* Philip Alston, *The EU and Human Rights*, Oxford, 1999, p. 245 e 246.

[78] Neste sentido, Takis Tridimas, *The General Principles...* , p. 61.

[79] Robert Alexy, *Theorie der Grundrechte*, 1ª ed., Frankfurt, 1986, p. 377 e segs.

[80] Neste sentido, Mark Bell/Lisa Waddington, "Reflecting on Inequalities...", p. 353 e segs.

ras individuais e sociais inibem a participação de um determinado indivíduo ou grupo em certa atividade. Avalia-se, portanto, o impacto que certas normas têm nos membros de determinados grupos[81].

Em contraste com a igualdade formal, a igualdade substancial permite acomodar a ação positiva[82], não como uma exceção mas como um componente do princípio da igualdade[83].

A ideia da igualdade substancial expressa-se, na obra de Ronald Dworkin, no *direito ao tratamento como igual*, o qual significa o direito – não a receber a mesma distribuição de obrigações e benefícios – mas a ser tratado com o mesmo respeito e consideração como qualquer outra pessoa[84]. O direito ao tratamento como igual é encarado, pelo Autor, como um direito fundamental, enquanto o direito a igual tratamento é "derivado". Nem sempre o direito a tratamento como igual implica o direito a igual tratamento[85].

Na prática, numa dada Ordem Jurídica, encontram-se, normalmente, exemplos de aplicação tanto da igualdade formal como substancial. No âmbito deste estudo não é possível prosseguir com a apresentação desses casos concretos.

3.2. A discriminação negativa e a vertente positiva da igualdade

A discriminação negativa tem como contraponto a igualdade formal, pelo que as críticas dirigidas a esta aplicam-se também àquela.

A discriminação negativa aponta no sentido da abstenção de comportamentos que impliquem um tratamento diferenciado de idênticas situações e categorias de pessoas, com base em critérios considerados suspeitos num Estado de direito, nos quais se incluem o sexo, a raça, a religião, a deficiência e a orientação sexual.

[81] Ver Klaartje Wentholt, "Formal and Substantive Equal Treatment: the Limitations and the Potential of the Legal Concept of Equality", *in* Titia Loenen/Peter Rodrigues, *Non-Discrimination Law: Comparative Perspectives*, Haia, 1999, p. 58.

[82] Neste sentido, Helen Fenwick, "From Formal to Substantive Equality..." , p. 598.

[83] Neste sentido, Klaartje Wentholt, "Formal and Substantive Equal...", p. 60.

[84] Cfr. Ronald Dworkin, *Taking Rights...*, p. 227.

[85] *Idem, ibidem.*

A proibição da discriminação pode constar de cláusulas específicas, as quais podem conter um número, mais ou menos alargado, de *categorias suspeitas,* cuja enumeração pode ser exemplificativa ou taxativa.

Antes de avançar, importa esclarecer o que se entende por *categoria suspeita.*

A distinção entre classificações ou *categorias razoáveis* e classificações ou *categorias suspeitas* surgiu nos EUA, na sequência da aplicação, pelo Supremo Tribunal, da cláusula da igual proteção (*equal protection clause*) prevista na XIV emenda à Constituição e daí irradiou para o resto do Mundo.

Em 1949, Joseph Tussman e Jacobus tenBroek, tendo em conta o aumento da utilização da referida cláusula por parte do Supremo Tribunal, num artigo publicado, na *Califórnia Law Review,* analisaram a *equal protection clause,* numa perspetiva crítica da jurisprudência do STEUA e de futuro desenvolvimento das suas potencialidades[86].

Segundo estes Autores, não obstante a legislação classificar as pessoas a partir de certos critérios, na ótica da igualdade, há classificações que são razoáveis enquanto outras são suspeitas de serem proibidas.

Assim, a doutrina da *classificação razoável* procura resolver a aparente contradição entre o princípio da igualdade e o poder do legislador de classificar os indivíduos, de acordo com a sua situação[87]. Não se verifica, porém, qualquer contradição entre a igualdade e a classificação ou categorização dos indivíduos, em função das suas diferenças. Antes pelo contrário, a igualdade pressupõe essa categorização.

A *classificação suspeita* é aquela que usa critérios diferenciadores do tratamento, como é o caso do sexo, da raça, da crença ou outro que a dignidade humana impede que seja tido como classificação razoável. Sendo, por natureza, suspeitos, estes critérios gozam de uma presunção de inconstitucionalidade[88], a qual, em certos casos, é mais difícil de ilidir do que noutros.

Numa conceção tradicional de discriminação, para se saber se uma determinada norma se aplica de modo diferenciado sem justificação,

[86] Joseph Tussman/Jacobus tenBroek, "The Equal Protection of Laws", *CLR*, 1949, p. 342.

[87] Joseph Tussman/Jacobus tenBroek, "The Equal...", p. 344.

[88] Joseph Tussman/Jacobus tenBroek, "The Equal...", p. 356.

isto é, se discrimina as pessoas, devido a certas características que elas possuem, averigua-se como é que a norma se aplica em relação às outras pessoas, isto é, àquelas que não se integrem na dita *categoria suspeita*. A verificação da discriminação relativamente a certa(s) categoria(s) de pessoas passa, portanto, por definir com rigor os termos da comparação, os quais assumem um relevo muito particular[89]. Ora, uma análise imprópria da comparabilidade conduz a avaliações inadequadas da discriminação.

Recorde-se que há casos em que é impossível a comparação com situações idênticas por elas não existirem. A título de exemplo, refira-se que, no caso da discriminação da mulher com fundamento na gravidez, não é adequada qualquer comparação com a incapacidade do homem para o trabalho, por exemplo, por razões médicas[90].

Aliás, durante anos o debate na Europa acerca da igualdade de tratamento entre ambos os sexos centrou-se na questão de saber se a mulher deveria aspirar a ser igual ao homem, devendo ter os mesmos direitos (tratamento simétrico), ou se, pelo contrário, a mulher deveria lutar para ver as suas diferenças reconhecidas pelo Direito (tratamento assimétrico)[91] e talvez ainda não se tenha chegado a uma inequívoca conclusão a este respeito.

Além da tutela negativa em que se traduziu a proibição da discriminação, a partir da II Guerra, o jurista vê-se confrontado com a tutela positiva da igualdade[92], a qual, em última análise, tem como objetivo atingir a igualdade substancial.

A tutela positiva da igualdade parte do princípio que, sendo as condições de partida dos diferentes grupos diversas nunca se conseguirá atingir a igualdade sem um certo intervencionismo público. Não se verifica, toda-

[89] "A igualdade é um conceito comparativo, ou, o mesmo é dizer, toda a afirmação de igualdade pressupõe uma comparação". V. Maria Da Glória F. P. D. Garcia, "Princípio da igualdade: fórmula vazia...", p. 46. No mesmo sentido, Fernando Alves Correia, *O plano urbanístico...*, p. 397.

[90] Ver Acórdãos do Tribunal de Justiça da União Europeia, *Dekker* (ac. de 08/11/90, proc. C-177/88, Col. 1990, p. I-3941) e *Webb* (ac. de 14/07/94, proc. C-32/93, Col. 1994, p. I--3567.

[91] Neste sentido, Catherine Barnard, "Gender Equality in the EU...", p. 215.

[92] Alessandro Pizzorusso, *Il patrimonio costituzionale europeu*, Bolonha, 2002, p. 71.

via, um consenso quanto à medida desse intervencionismo. Para alguns, a tutela positiva da igualdade só pode visar a criação da igualdade de oportunidades entre os diferentes grupos sociais. Ou seja, para quem assim entenda, a igualdade positiva procura atingir a igualdade substancial ou material através da criação de condições de partida idênticas para os diferentes grupos, não devendo o intervencionismo público ultrapassar esta fronteira. Para outros, a igualdade de partida não é suficiente, pois ainda deixa subsistir flagrantes injustiças sociais, pelo que o poder público deve preocupar-se com o resultado a que se vai chegar com as medidas que adotou e, no caso de não se ter conseguido atingir a justiça, deve tomar medidas dirigidas ao resultado. Isto é, a tutela positiva da igualdade exige a igualdade de resultados, o que implica uma maior intervenção pública.

Assim, a igualdade positiva implica que o acesso das pessoas aos bens e aos direitos não dependa de critérios arbitrários como ser branco ou negro, homem ou mulher, deficiente ou não. A ideia da igualdade positiva implica, portanto, para os poderes públicos a obrigação, não só de eliminarem as discriminações, como também de criarem as condições necessárias para que todos possam usufruir das vantagens sociais, desde que assim o queiram. Isto significa que pode ser necessário tomar medidas especiais para o grupo que se encontra em desvantagem[93].

Em suma, a ideia de igualdade de oportunidades deve ser vista como uma noção de compromisso, que se encontra a meio caminho entre a igualdade formal e a igualdade substancial, enquanto a ideia da igualdade de resultados visa claramente a igualdade substancial[94]. A diferença entre uma e outra é, antes de mais, de grau, mas não deixa de ser também qualitativa, uma vez que implica uma diferente conceção da atuação do poder público.

93 Neste sentido, SANDRA FREDMAN, "Combating Racism with Human Rights...", p. 20.

94 Neste sentido, GAVIN BARRETT, "Re-examining the Concept...", p. 128; SANDRA FREDMAN, "Combating Racism with Human Rights...", p. 20; CATHERINE BARNARD, "Gender Equality in the EU...", p. 226.

Aliás, a igualdade de resultados[95] tem sido objeto de muita controvérsia, dado que parece contradizer a própria ideia de igualdade[96], conduzindo ao que ROBERT ALEXY designa por paradoxo da igualdade[97]. Todo o tratamento desigual *de jure* para a criação da igualdade de facto é uma restrição à realização da igualdade jurídica[98]. Com efeito, do ponto de vista da igualdade formal, o tratamento preferencial das pessoas afro-americanas ou das mulheres discrimina aparentemente as de raça branca ou os homens. Já assim não é na ótica da igualdade substancial[99]. Um meio de promover um direito fundamental – por exemplo, o direito à não discriminação em função do sexo – não se vê como possa ser encarado como uma derrogação a esse mesmo direito. Aliás, qualquer interpretação restritiva das medidas de ação positiva tem como consequência a restrição do direito em si[100].

Note-se que a fronteira entre a igualdade de oportunidades e a igualdade de resultados nem sempre é fácil de delimitar[101], tendo em conta que um dos meios de que as autoridades dispõem para as assegurar é, precisamente, a realização de medidas de ação positiva em relação ao grupo desfavorecido. Ou seja, os poderes públicos têm ao seu dispor diversos meios para atingir a igualdade positiva, sendo que um desses meios é, indubitavelmente, a adoção de medidas de ação positiva, com o objetivo de incentivar um determinado grupo a praticar determinado ato, sem que

[95] A igualdade de resultados pode ser usada em três sentidos diferentes. O primeiro avalia o impacto no indivíduo do tratamento aparentemente igual. O segundo foca-se no grupo e partindo do princípio que num ambiente não discriminatório qualquer organismo, seja ele empresa, estabelecimento de ensino ou órgão de decisão deve incluir um número alargado de membros dos vários grupos raciais, religiosos e dos dois sexos. Daí que a ausência de um grupo numa determinada actividade é um indício de discriminação. O terceiro sentido da igualdade de resultados procura a igualdade de representação de homens e mulheres. Neste sentido, SANDRA FREDMAN, "Combating Racism with Human Rights...", p. 19.

[96] Neste sentido, GAVIN BARRETT, "Re-examining the Concept...", p. 126.

[97] ROBERT ALEXY, *Theorie der Grundrechte...*, p. 379.

[98] ROBERT ALEXY, *Theorie der Grundrechte...*, p. 383 e 384.

[99] Neste sentido, MARIANNE GIJZEN, *Selected Issues...*, p. 220.

[100] Neste sentido, SOPHIA KOUKOULIS-SPILIOTOPOULOS, "The Amended Equal Treatment Directive (2002/73): An Expression of Constitutional Principles/Fundamentals Rights", *MJ*, 2005, p. 339.

[101] ERICA HOWARD, "The European Year...", p. 173.

se crie diretamente uma discriminação contra o grupo que delas não beneficia[102].

As ações positivas podem admitir o tratamento diferente de situações aparentemente idênticas, se elas tiverem como resultado compensar desigualdades antigas e persistentes, afastar obstáculos discriminatórios atuais[103] e ainda promover a diversidade ou a representação proporcional em áreas em que todos os grupos devem estar representados[104]. Neste caso, a ação positiva é, antes de mais, uma forma de discriminação justificada por razões objetivas e razoáveis[105]. Através dela, o legislador procura compensar a desvantagem, o *handicap* inicial de que são vítimas certas categorias de pessoas[106].

O objetivo das medidas de ação positiva tanto pode ser restabelecer a igualdade de oportunidades que o respeito restrito do princípio da igualdade de tratamento não só não asseguraria como tornaria ilusório, como obter uma igualdade de resultados[107]. As pessoas sobre as quais incidem as medidas de ação positiva encontram-se, à partida, numa situação diferente, pelo que, para chegarem a uma situação igual, necessitam de um tratamento diferente e mais favorável[108]. No fundo, trata-se de promover, para além da igualdade formal dos direitos, uma real igualdade social. Por outras palavras, tenta-se corrigir as desigualdades sociais através do Direito[109].

A ação positiva é supostamente temporária, deixando de ter sentido quando o grupo que se encontra em desvantagem deixa de o estar. Para

[102] A título de exemplo, podem referir-se anúncios de emprego que incentivam expressamente as mulheres a concorrer.

[103] Neste sentido, Sandra Fredman, *Discrimination Law...*, p. 150 e segs.

[104] Neste sentido, Olivier De Schutter, "Three Models of Equality and European Anti-Discrimination Law", *NILQ*, 2006, p. 33 e segs.

[105] Evelyn Ellis, *EU Anti-Discrimination Law...*, p. 3 e 4 .

[106] A título de exemplo, refira-se o sistema de quotas (rígido ou flexível) a favor das mulheres em matéria de emprego.

[107] Neste sentido, Marianne Gijzen, *Selected Issues in Equal Treatment Law: a Multi-Layered Comparison of European, English and Dutch Law*, Antuérpia, 2006, p. 211.

[108] Gwénaële Calvès, *L'affirmative action dans la jurisprudence de la Cour Suprême des Etats-Unis. Le problème de la discrimination positive*, Paris, 1998, p. 10.

[109] Neste sentido, Jacques Chevallier, «Réflexions sur la notion de discrimination positive», *in Mélanges en hommage au Doyen Gérard* Cohen-Jonathan, *Libertés, Justice, Tolérance*, Bruxelas, 2004, p. 419.

alguns, a ação positiva deve ser uma resposta excecional e conjuntural a um problema (desigualdade social) das sociedades contemporâneas. Se assim não for, arrisca-se a contribuir para a perpetuação das desigualdades[110].

A ação positiva apresenta uma dimensão eminentemente coletiva. O indivíduo apaga-se em benefício do grupo ao qual está irremediavelmente ligado[111]. Além disso, a ação positiva deve ser encarada como uma forma de implementar um novo valor sócio-político de igualdade que está para além da originária dimensão económica[112].

A ação positiva procura atingir a igualdade substancial, afastando-se tanto mais da igualdade formal quanto promove a igualdade de resultados (veja-se o caso, por exemplo, do emprego).

Antes de concluir este ponto, note-se que a problemática da *affirmative action* (ação positiva) teve a sua origem, nos EUA. Embora se tenha colocado com mais acuidade a propósito dos cidadãos afro-americanos[113],

[110] Neste sentido, JACQUES CHEVALLIER, «Réflexions sur la notion de discrimination...», p. 428.

[111] Neste sentido, XAVIER BIOY, «L'ambiguïté du concept ...», p. 79.

[112] Neste sentido, ERIKA SZYSZCZAK, "On Equal Treatment, Positive Action and the Significance of a Person's Sex, Comments on Ann Numhauser-Henning's Article", *in* ANN NUMHAUSER-HENNING, *Legal Perspectives on Equal Treatment and Non-Discrimination*, Haia, 2001, p. 256.

[113] Sobre a jurisprudência do Supremo Tribunal dos EUA relativa à *affirmative action*, cfr. RICHARD H. FALLON, JR., *The Dynamic Constitution – An Introduction to American Constitutional Law*, Cambridge, 2004, p. 123 e segs.; GERALD STOURZH, "... égaux en droits": The Place of Non-Discrimination in the History of Human Rights", *HRLJ*, 2004, p. 8 e segs.; JOHN HASNAS, "Equal Opportunity, Affirmative Action, and the Anti-Discrimination Principle: The Philosophical Basis for Legal Prohibition of Discrimination", *Fordham L. Rev.*, 2002-2003, p. 481 e segs.; JEROME A. BARRON/C. THOMAS DIENES, *Constitutional Law in a Nutshell*, 4ª ed., St. Paul, Minn., 1999, p. 268 e segs.; DENIS MARTIN, *Égalité et non-discrimination...*, p. 342 e segs. e 391 e segs.; DAVID A. J. RICHARDS, *Conscience and the Constitution – History, Theory, and Law of the Reconstruction Amendments*, Princeton, s.d., p. 174 e segs.; MARÍA ÁNGELES MARTÍN VIDA, "Evolución del principio de igualdad en Estados Unidos. Nacimiento y desarrollo de las medidas de acción afirmativa en derecho estadounidense", *REDC*, 2003, p. 167 e segs.; GWÉNAËLE CALVÈS, *L'affirmative action...*, *maxime* p. 97 e segs.; WILLIAM B. LOCKHART *e.a.*, *Constitutional Law, Cases – Comments – Questions*, 7ª ed., St. Paul Minn., 1992, p. 1279 e segs.

o Supremo Tribunal também teve oportunidade de a reconhecer em relação às mulheres[114-115].

Assim, o Supremo Tribunal viu-se confrontado com uma série de casos em que foi chamado a decidir se determinadas ações ou medidas a favor dos cidadãos afro-americanos eram, ou não, contrárias à XIV emenda da Constituição, a qual consagra a cláusula de igual proteção das leis (*Equal Protection Clause*)[116-117]. Esta cláusula tem sido, predominantemente, interpretada no sentido de que acolhe o princípio da não discriminação, o que não se pode sequer inferir da sua letra[118].

O primeiro aresto do Supremo Tribunal, neste domínio, foi proferido no caso *University of Califórnia Regents v. Bakke*[119]. Estava em causa o acesso à universidade de um indivíduo de raça branca, o qual foi prete-

[114] Foi em 1873 que, pela primeira vez, o STEUA se pronunciou sobre uma questão de discriminação sexual. No caso *Bradwell v. Illinois* (83 U.S. 130 (1873)) decidiu que a restrição da profissão de advogado às mulheres não era contrária à Constituição. A inversão desta jurisprudência demorou quase um século. Com efeito, o reconhecimento por parte do STEUA de que a discriminação sexual viola a *equal protection clause* e, como tal, uma lei que nela se baseia é inconstitucional data de 1971 (cfr. caso *Reed v. Reed* (404 U.S. 71 (1971)).

[115] No caso *Johnston c/Transportation Agency* (480 U.S. 616 (1987)), o Supremo confirmou uma série de medidas de acção positiva a favor do emprego das mulheres na função pública, de entre as quais se incluía a promoção preferencial de uma mulher numa função tradicionalmente reservada aos homens. Para mais desenvolvimentos sobre a evolução da jurisprudência Supremo Tribunal dos EUA, no que diz respeito à *affirmative action* a favor das mulheres, cfr. Jerome A. Barron/C. Thomas Dienes, *Constitutional Law...*, p. 297 e segs.; David A. J. Richards, *Conscience and the Constitution...*, p. 178 e segs.; Michel Rosenfeld, "Le principe d'égalité appliqué aux femmes dans la jurisprudence de la Cour Suprême Américaine", *Les cahiers du Conseil Constitutionnel*, 1998, p. 67 e segs.

[116] Sobre a XIV emenda da Constituição dos Estados Unidos da América, cfr. Richard H. Fallon, Jr., *The Dynamic Constitution...*, p. 106 e segs.; Jerome A. Barron/C. Thomas Dienes, *Constitutional Law...*, p. 244 e segs.; Michael J. Perry, *The Constitution in the Courts – Law or Politics?*, Nova Iorque, 1994, p. 116 e segs.; William B. Lockhart *e.a.*, *Constitutional Law...*, p. 1202 e segs.; Owen M. Fiss, "Groups and the Equal Protection Clause", *Phil. & Pub. Af.*, 1976, p. 107 e segs.

[117] A XIV emenda foi introduzida na sequência da abolição da escravatura, sendo tributária da ideia de que o poder político deve ser razoavelmente justificado em termos de igual respeito dos direitos humanos e da prossecução do interesse público. Para maiores desenvolvimentos sobre a génese desta emenda, cfr. David A. J. Richards, *Conscience and the Constitution ...*, p. 149 e segs.

[118] Neste sentido, Owen M. Fiss, "Groups...", p. 118.

[119] 438 U.S. 265 (1978).

rido, com fundamento no programa especial de admissão à Universidade – menos exigente para as minorias raciais. *Bakke* recorreu dessa decisão, com base na violação da XIV emenda. Os tribunais do Estado da Califórnia consideraram que ele tinha razão e ordenaram a sua integração na Universidade, o que foi confirmado pelo Supremo Tribunal dos EUA e considerado uma derrota para as minorias raciais. No entanto, o Supremo Tribunal não se limitou a negar a *affirmative action* no caso concreto, tendo acrescentado que o objetivo de ultrapassar a sub-representação crónica e substancial das minorias na profissão de médico era legítimo para justificar o direito da Universidade usar o critério da raça como fator a ter em conta nas candidaturas dos estudantes. Em consequência, não invalidou o programa especial de admissão da Universidade. O Tribunal reconheceu, nesta parte do acórdão, o princípio da *affirmative action* a favor das minorias raciais, o qual virá a ser desenvolvido na sua posterior jurisprudência.

Assim, no caso *Steelworkers v. Weber*[120], estando em causa um programa voluntário de *affirmative action* levado a efeito por empresas privadas, o Tribunal admitiu que elas podiam instaurar as preferências com base na raça se tivessem como objetivo eliminar "um desequilíbrio racial manifesto" resultante "de velhas estruturas e de hierarquização racial", desde que as medidas em causa fossem temporárias e os direitos e interesses dos assalariados brancos não fossem "excessivamente afetados", isto é, que não fossem despedidos nem excluídos da competição.

Este entendimento da *affirmative action* foi reiterado, posteriormente, em vários acórdãos[121].

Mas, se é verdade que a jurisprudência do Supremo Tribunal se mostrou inicialmente (década de 80) bastante favorável à *affirmative action*, acabou por evoluir num sentido mais restritivo (década de 90)[122]. De notar que esta evolução não é linear, antes teve alguns sobressaltos e oscilações, por vezes, dificilmente explicáveis. Após um acórdão restritivo, surge,

[120] 443 U.S. 193 (1979).

[121] Ver, por exemplo, o caso *Johnston v. Transportation Agency Santa Clara County* (480 U.S.616 (1987)), em que o Tribunal transpôs a jurisprudência *Weber* para a política de *affirmative action* que uma empresa pública adoptou em relação a certas categorias de pessoas sub-representadas – as mulheres, as minorias e os deficientes.

[122] Ver, por exemplo, os casos *Adarand Constructors v. Pena* – 515 U.S. 200 (1995) e *Richmond v. J. A. Croson* – 488 U.S. 469 (1989).

muito próximo no tempo, um outro que reconhece a constitucionalidade de certas medidas de *affirmative action*[123].

Mais recentemente, o Supremo Tribunal dos EUA pronunciou-se sobre os programas de *affirmative action* em matéria de acesso às escolas e às universidades, tendo clarificado em que condições esses programas são suscetíveis de passar o teste da constitucionalidade. Note-se que esta jurisprudência é limitada ao acesso à educação, tendo o Tribunal sido perentório na afirmação da sua intransponilidade para o domínio do acesso ao emprego.

Assim, no caso *Grutter v. Bollinger*[124], confrontado com a constitucionalidade do programa de *affirmative actions* da Faculdade de Direito da Universidade de Michigan, o qual tinha como objetivo atingir a diversidade (racial e étnica) do corpo de estudantes (*student body diversity*), o Supremo Tribunal apreciou a questão de saber se a diversidade poderia constituir um interesse imperioso que justificasse uma utilização estritamente delimitada da raça na seleção dos candidatos a admitir nas universidades públicas. Reafirmando a sua anterior jurisprudência *Adarand*[125] e *Croson*[126], que, sublinhe-se, era bastante restritiva, o Supremo considerou que o interesse imperioso (*compelling interest*) de atingir a diversidade justifica o recurso ao critério da raça, desde que a admissão ou a recusa dos candidatos não seja automática. A raça deverá ser um entre vários critérios e o programa deve ser temporário. O Tribunal concluiu que todos estes limites se encontravam observados, pelo que o programa era conforme à Constituição.

Note-se que os limites impostos pelo Supremo Tribunal não são fáceis de respeitar, como se pode inferir do caso *Gratz v. Bollinger*[127], em que o mesmo Tribunal considerou contrário à Constituição um programa de *affirmative action*, cujo objetivo era também a diversidade do corpo de estudantes, mas os meios utilizados eram muito diferentes, uma vez que se

[123] Ver, por exemplo, caso *Metro Broadcasting v. FCC* – 497 U.S. 547 (1990).

[124] 539 U.S. 306 (2003).

[125] Segundo este acórdão, as classificações fundadas na raça devem estar submetidas ao teste de constitucionalidade mais restrito.

[126] Uma vez satisfeito o teste do escrutínio restrito (*strict scrutiny test*), os meios utilizados para atingir o interesse imperioso (*compelling interest*) devem ser estritamente adaptados (*narrowly tailored*).

[127] 539 U.S. 244 (2003).

conferiam automaticamente 20 pontos sobre 100 aos candidatos de minorias étnicas que possuíssem as qualificações mínimas necessárias. O acesso à universidade das minorias étnicas acabava, portanto, por ser automático, o que levou o Tribunal a decidir que aquele programa não satisfazia o teste da proporcionalidade estrita.

3.3. A discriminação direta e a discriminação indireta

A discriminação direta ocorre quando uma pessoa é tratada de forma menos favorável do que outra que se encontra nas mesmas condições e circunstâncias, apenas porque possui características particulares, como sejam, a raça, o sexo, a religião, a orientação sexual ou outras. Ora, as considerações sobre a raça, o sexo, a deficiência, etc. não podem ser tidas em conta no processo legislativo, devendo antes ser ignoradas. Como estas características não podem ser critério relevante para tratar as pessoas diferentemente, o tratamento menos favorável, em função disso, constitui uma discriminação direta, que não pode ser objetivamente justificada (ao contrário do que sucede com a discriminação indireta), a menos que esteja expressamente prevista na legislação alguma derrogação[128-129].

A ideia de discriminação indireta foi, pela primeira vez, aflorada nos EUA, ainda no séc. XIX. Em 1886, no caso *Yick Wo v. Hopkins*[130], o Supremo

[128] Neste sentido, MARIANNE GIJZEN, *Selected Issues...*, p. 53 e segs.; LISA WADDINGTON/AART HENDRIKS, "The Expanding Concept of Employment Discrimination in Europe – From Direct Effect and Indirect Discrimination to Reasonable Accommodation Discrimination", *The Int'l J. Comp. Lab. Law and Industrial Relations*, 2002, p. 407.

[129] Sobre a discriminação direta, ver CRISEIDE NOVI, "La parità di trattamento tra uomo e donna in materia di occupazione e condizioni di lavoro nel diritto comunitario: il felice connubio tra codificazione e innovazione", *Dir. Pubb. Comp. Eur.*, 2004, 1251 e segs.; MICHEL MINÉ, "Les concepts de discrimination..., p. 34 e 35; ANNA CHRISTENSEN, "Structural Aspects of Anti-Discriminatory Legislation and Processes of Normative Change", *in* ANN NUMHAUSER-HENNING, *Legal Perspectives ...*, p. 39 e segs.; EVELYN ELLIS, "Gender Discrimination Law in the European Community", *in* JANET DINE/BOB WATT (ed.), *Discrimination Law, Concepts, Limitations and Justifications*, Londres/Nova Iorque, 1996, p. 16 e segs.; EVELYN ELLIS, "The Definition of Discrimination in European Community Sex Equality Law", *ELR*, 1994, p. 565 e segs.

[130] 118 U.S. 356 (1886).

Tribunal dos EUA aceitou que uma classificação aparentemente neutra, mas que tinha como objetivo evidente estabelecer que uma discriminação com base na raça deve ser submetida a *strict scrutiny review*, conduzirá muito provavelmente à invalidade da lei em causa. Este acórdão colocava o acento tónico na intenção discriminatória, o que não se afigurou satisfatório.

Daí que a jurisprudência do Supremo Tribunal dos EUA tenha sofrido uma evolução (tal como, aliás, aconteceu no Direito da UE). O nó górdio do problema deslocou-se para o impacto desproporcionado (*disparate impact*) da medida em causa em relação a uma certa raça ou a um determinado sexo. Com este entendimento, o conceito de discriminação indireta foi usado, pela primeira vez, nos EUA, em 1971, a propósito da discriminação racial, no caso *Griggs v. Duke Power*[131]. Neste caso, o Supremo Tribunal considerou que as exigências de um empregador relativas a elevadas qualificações académicas ou testes de literacia no acesso a um emprego tinham um impacto desproporcionado nas pessoas de raça negra, dado que o sistema de ensino americano favorecia as pessoas de raça branca (não se exigia a intenção de discriminar, mas apenas o impacto desproporcionado)[132].

A intenção discriminatória foi, porém, retomada na jurisprudência posterior do Supremo Tribunal dos EUA, no caso *Washington v. Davis*[133], em 1976, em que se exige, para além do impacto racial desproporcionado, a intenção discriminatória racial. Um ano depois, no caso *Village of Arlington Heights v. Metropolitan Housing Inc.*[134], o Tribunal vem matizar a exigência de prova da intenção discriminatória, ao afirmar que não é necessário que o recorrente prove que a medida em causa se baseie exclusivamente nessa intenção.

131 401 U.S. 424 (1971).

132 Cfr. Denis Martin, *Égalité et non-discrimination...*, p. 337 e segs. e 385 e segs.; Alan David Freeman, "Legitimizing Racial Discrimination Through Antidiscrimination Law: A Critical Review of Supreme Court Doctrine", *Minn. L. Rev.*, 1978, p. 1093 e segs.

133 426 U.S. 229 (1976).

134 429 U.S. 256 (1977).

Note-se, contudo, que a jurisprudência do Supremo Tribunal EUA não é linear neste domínio[135-136].

A discriminação indireta tem vindo a ser entendida de duas formas diversas que, aliás, não se excluem.

Assim, em primeiro lugar, haverá discriminação indireta quando uma medida tiver um impacto desproporcionado num determinado grupo. Ou seja, uma medida aparentemente neutra atinge *de facto* um número muito maior de indivíduos de um determinado grupo, sendo que essa medida só poderá ser mantida se tiver uma justificação objetiva e razoável[137]. Através de critérios aparentemente neutros para diferenciar acaba-se por prejudicar o grupo que se visa proteger com as normas anti-discriminação em comparação com outro grupo, sem que haja justificação objetiva para essa desvantagem.[138]. A estatística é um importante meio de prova deste tipo de discriminação.

Em segundo lugar, haverá discriminação indireta se se adotarem medidas, por natureza, ou intrinsecamente, suscetíveis de desfavorecer os que pertencem à categoria protegida contra a discriminação. Neste caso, não se afigura necessário usar a estatística como meio de prova da discriminação[139].

A decisão quanto à existência ou não de justificação objetiva compete aos tribunais nacionais[140], uma vez que se trata de uma questão de facto.

[135] No caso *Personal Administrator of Massachusetts v. Feeney* (442 U.S. 256 (1979)), o Tribunal voltou a reforçar as exigências de prova da intenção discriminatória.

[136] Para maiores desenvolvimentos sobre a jurisprudência do Supremo Tribunal dos EUA, no que diz respeito à discriminação indirecta, ver RICHARD H. FALLON, JR., *The Dynamic Constitution...*, p. 122 e segs.; JEROME A. BARRON/C. THOMAS DIENES, *Constitutional Law...*, p. 253 e segs.; DENIS MARTIN, *Égalité et non-discrimination...*, p. 337 e segs.; MARÍA ÁNGELES MARTÍN VIDA, "Evolución del principio de igualdad...", p. 162 e segs.; JOHN HASNAS, "Equal Opportunity...", *maxime*, p. 474 e segs.; WILLIAM B. LOCKHART *e.a.*, *Constitutional Law...*, p. 1240 e segs.; PAUL BREST, "In Defense of the Antidiscrimination Principle", *HLR*, vol. 90, 1976, p. 22 e segs.

[137] Neste sentido, OLIVIER DE SCHUTTER, «Prouver la discrimination», *ERA*, 3/2003, p. 46.

[138] Neste sentido, MARIANNE GIJZEN, *Selected Issues...*, p. 57; LISA WADDINGTON/AART HENDRIKS, "The Expanding Concept...", p. 407.

[139] Neste sentido, OLIVIER DE SCHUTTER, «Prouver...», p. 46.

[140] Neste sentido, TITIA LOENEN, "Indirect Discrimination: Oscillating between Containment and Revolution", *in* TITIA LOENEN/PETER RODRIGUES, *Non-Discrimination Law: Comparative Perspectives*, Haia, 1999, p. 208.

Tal não impede o Tribunal de Justiça de, frequentemente, dar ao tribunal nacional diretrizes precisas quanto ao modo como deve ponderar o princípio da não discriminação e os outros interesses em causa[141].

A possibilidade de justificação objetiva é, pois, um dos fatores que distingue a discriminação direta da discriminação indireta[142].

A proibição da discriminação indireta representa o reconhecimento dos limites do modelo liberal da igualdade[143].

A noção de discriminação indireta aproxima-se mais da de igualdade substancial ou igualdade de facto do que da de igualdade formal, uma vez que se preocupa com as diferenças materiais que se verificam entre as pessoas e com os resultados a que conduz uma determinada forma de tratamento[144-145].

4. A igualdade e a não discriminação como base dos direitos fundamentais dos migrantes e dos refugiados no direito internacional

Antes de mais, importa notar que os refugiados e os migrantes se encontram abrangidos, como qualquer outra pessoa, pelo direito internacional dos direitos humanos. Porém, nem sempre a proteção e a tutela internacional dos direitos humanos em geral se revela como sendo a mais ade-

[141] Neste sentido, Marianne Gijzen, *Selected Issues...*, p. 87; Steve Anderman, "Constitutional Law...", p. 107.

[142] Para uma tentativa de construção dogmática do conceito de discriminação indirecta a partir da jurisprudência do Tribunal de Justiça, ver Christa Tobler, *Indirect Discrimination...*, p. 99 e segs.; Pierre Garrone, "La discrimination indirecte en droit communautaire: vers une théorie générale", *RTDE*, 1994, p. 426 e segs.

[143] Neste sentido, Marianne Gijzen, *Selected Issues...*, p. 60.

[144] Neste sentido, Erica Howard, "The European Year...", p. 171; Marianne Gijzen, *Selected Issues...*, p. 62; Christa Tobler, *Indirect Discrimination...*, p. 85 e 86; Dagmar Schiek, "A New Framework on Equal Treatment of Persons in EC Law? Directives 2000/43/EC, 2000/78/EC and 2002/???/EC changing Directive 76/207/EEC in context", *ELJ*, 2002, p. 305; Karin Lundström, "Indirect Sex Discrimination ...", p. 147.

[145] Sobre a discriminação indireta ver, para além da bibliografia citada nas notas precedentes, Criseide Novi, "La parità di trattamento...", p. 1246 e segs.; Sacha Prechal, "Equality of Treatment, Non-Discrimination and Social Policy: Achievements in Three Themes", *CMLR*, 2004, p. 534 a 537; Michel Miné, "Les concepts de discrimination...", p. 37 e segs.; Sandra Fredman, *Discrimination Law...*, p. 106 e segs.; Anna Christensen, "Structural Aspects of Anti-Discriminatory...", p. 42 e segs.; Mark Bell, "Walking in the Same Direction?..., p. 264 e segs.; Evelyn Ellis, "The Definition of Discrimination...", p. 572 e segs.

quada à situação muito particular destas pessoas. Daí que, sobretudo, após a Segunda Guerra Mundial – devido aos fluxos migratórios e de refugiados que ela provocou – se tenha assistido ao desenvolvimento de um direito internacional dos direitos humanos dos refugiados e dos migrantes. Vejamos então em que medida este direito internacional tem na sua base a igualdade e a não discriminação.

4.1. A igualdade e a não discriminação no direito internacional dos direitos humanos em geral

A igualdade e a não discriminação são afirmadas no direito internacional quer ao nível universal quer ao nível regional. Porém, não o são de forma unívoca e uniforme[146]. Além disso, também não se encontram definições claras de igualdade e de não discriminação assim como são raras as referências à igualdade perante a lei.

De entre os textos internacionais que mencionam a igualdade perante a lei, devem destacar-se o artigo 7º da DUDH, que determina que "*todos são iguais perante a lei*", o artigo 24º da Convenção Americana sobre Direitos Humanos, o qual estabelece que "*todas as pessoas são iguais perante a lei. Por conseguinte, têm direito, sem discriminação a igual proteção da lei*" e o artigo 26º do PIDCP, o qual dispõe que "*todos são iguais perante a lei e têm direito, sem discriminação a igual proteção da lei*". O protocolo nº 12 à CEDH, no preâmbulo, afirma que todas as pessoas são iguais perante a lei e têm direito a uma igual proteção pela lei.

O direito internacional ocupa-se, primordialmente, da proibição da discriminação (ver, por exemplo, artigo 2º PIDCP), existindo mesmo tratados internacionais, que definem o conceito de discriminação relevante para efeitos de aplicação da convenção, como é o caso da Convenção das Nações Unidas para a eliminação de todas as formas de discriminação racial, da Convenção das Nações Unidas para a eliminação de todas as formas de discriminação contra as mulheres, da Convenção nº 111 da OIT relativa à discriminação no trabalho e no emprego e da Convenção da UNESCO contra a discriminação na educação[147].

[146] Neste sentido, Anne F. Bayefsky, "The Principle of Equality...", p. 2.

[147] Sobre a definição de discriminação nestas convenções, cfr. Martin MacEwen, *Tackling Racism in Europe, An Examination of Anti-Discrimination Law in Practice*, Oxford, 1995, p. 47 e segs.

A referida Convenção para a eliminação de todas as formas de discriminação racial entende por discriminação (racial) toda a distinção, exclusão, restrição ou preferência fundada na raça, cor, ascendência, origem nacional ou étnica que tenha por objetivo ou como efeito destruir ou comprometer o reconhecimento, o gozo ou o exercício, em condições de igualdade, dos direitos do homem e das liberdades fundamentais nos domínios político, económico, social e cultural ou em qualquer outro domínio da vida pública.

Este conceito de discriminação não difere muito do consagrado nas outras convenções mencionadas. O principal problema que se colocou a propósito da definição de discriminação foi o de saber se esta abrangia apenas a discriminação direta ou se se deveria considerar incluída também a discriminação indireta, uma vez que, esta última não se baseia propriamente na raça ou noutro critério suspeito, mas antes resulta de um impacto desproporcionado de uma determinada medida num grupo que tem em comum, por exemplo, uma certa raça[148]. Não parece que o argumento literal seja suficiente para afastar a proibição da discriminação indireta.

No direito internacional, a destrinça entre igualdade e não discriminação também não é muito clara, dado que o próprio termo igualdade faz parte da definição de discriminação.

No Conselho da Europa, o artigo 14º da CEDH estabelece que «*o gozo dos direitos e liberdades reconhecidos na presente Convenção deve ser assegurado sem quaisquer distinções, tais como as fundadas no sexo, cor, língua, religião, opiniões públicas ou outras, a origem nacional ou social, a pertença a uma minoria nacional, a riqueza, o nascimento ou qualquer outra situação*». Do ponto de vista literal, o preceito não consagra a existência independente do princípio da não discriminação, uma vez que se ele aplica unicamente aos direitos e liberdades garantidos pela Convenção[149]. Ao contrário do que sucede com os preceitos da DUDH e do PIDCP – que se aplicam autonomamente –, a

[148] Neste sentido, MARTIN MACEWEN, *Tackling Racism in Europe...*, p. 51.

[149] A invocação do artigo 14º CEDH, no Tribunal de Estrasburgo, é relativamente frequente e o seu âmbito de aplicação tem vindo a ser alargado (ver caso *Affaire linguistique belge*, de 23/07/1968, A 8, par. 9). Na prática, o artigo 14º CEDH veio a adquirir, progressivamente, autonomia. Para maiores desenvolvimentos, ver ANA MARIA GUERRA MARTINS, *Direito Internacional dos Direitos Humanos*, Coimbra, 2006, p. 202, bem como a bibliografia aí citada.

letra do artigo 14º da CEDH só garante o direito a não ser discriminado no contexto da violação dos direitos ou liberdades reconhecidos na própria Convenção.

Refira-se ainda que no direito internacional não é muito comum a imposição da igualdade positiva aos Estados partes nas convenções. Assim, se analisarmos o artigo 14º da CEDH, o protocolo nº 12, os Pactos das Nações Unidas dificilmente conseguiremos descortinar um dever nesse sentido, quer de modo expresso quer implícito. Somente nas Convenções das Nações Unidas específicas em matéria de eliminação de todas as formas de discriminação, seja racial, seja contra as mulheres, encontramos disposições – os artigos 1º, nº 4, e 2º, nº 2 e o artigo 4º, respetivamente – que se inserem nessa vertente da igualdade, prevendo a tomada de medidas de ação positiva por parte dos Estados[150].

A igualdade de oportunidades encontra-se consagrada no direito internacional dos direitos humanos, em vários instrumentos internacionais, dos quais cumpre destacar a Declaração de Filadélfia, de 10 de Maio de 1944, anexa à Constituição da OIT, sobre os fins da Organização e os princípios que devem inspirar a ação dos Estados-Membros (pontos II, a), e III, j))[151], a convenção nº 111 da OIT (artigo 5º, nº 2) e a convenção sobre todas as formas de eliminação das discriminações contra as mulheres (artigo 4º).

4.2. O direito internacional relativo à igualdade e à não discriminação dos migrantes e dos refugiados

No que diz respeito aos migrantes e aos refugiados, várias são as convenções internacionais tanto ao nível universal como regional que se debruçam especificamente sobre os seus direitos, incluindo o princípio da igualdade nas suas várias vertentes bem como cláusulas de não discriminação, sendo de destacar as seguintes:

[150] Sobre a vertente positiva da igualdade no Direito Internacional, ver Marc De Vos, "Beyond Formal Equality – Positive Action under Directives 2000/43/EC and 2000/78/EC, *in European Commission – Directorate-General for Employment, Social Affairs and Equal Opportunities*, Luxemburgo, Office for Publications of the European Communities, 2007, p. 50 e segs., disponível no sítio http://europa.eu.

[151] Esta declaração está disponível no sítio http://www.ilo.org/ilolex/english/constq

a) Convenções das Nações Unidas:
   - A Convenção relativa ao Estatuto dos Refugiados, adotada em 28 de julho de 1951, a qual entrou em vigor em 22 de abril de 1954;
   - A Convenção internacional sobre a proteção dos direitos de todos os trabalhadores migrantes e dos membros das suas famílias, adotada em 18 de dezembro de 1990, a qual entrou em vigor em 1 de julho de 2003.

b) Convenções da Organização Internacional do Trabalho:
   - A Convenção nº 97, relativa aos trabalhadores migrantes, adotada em 1 de julho de 1949, que entrou em vigor em 22 de janeiro de 1952;
   - A Convenção nº 143 relativa às migrações em condições abusivas e à promoção de igualdade de oportunidades e de tratamento dos trabalhadores migrantes, adotada em 24 de junho de 1975, a qual entrou em vigor em 9 de dezembro de 1979.

c) Convenções do Conselho da Europa:
   - A Convenção Europeia relativa ao estatuto jurídico do trabalhador migrante adotada, em 24 de novembro de 1977, e entrada em vigor em 1 de maio de 1993.

Começando pela Convenção Relativa ao Estatuto dos Refugiados, importa referir que o artigo 3º da referida convenção é bem claro ao afirmar que "*os Estados Contratantes aplicarão as disposições desta Convenção aos refugiados sem discriminação quanto à raça, religião ou país de origem*", equiparando-os, no que diz respeito ao exercício dos direitos, em concreto, aos nacionais ou aos estrangeiros, consoante os direitos que estejam em causa. Assim, relativamente à liberdade religiosa e à liberdade de educação dos filhos, o artigo 4º da Convenção estabelece que "*os Estados Contratantes concederão aos refugiados nos seus territórios um tratamento pelo menos tão favorável como o concedido aos nacionais no que diz respeito à liberdade de praticar a sua religião e no que se refere à liberdade de instrução religiosa dos seus filhos*". O mesmo sucede no que diz respeito à propriedade intelectual e industrial (cf. artigo 14º), ao acesso aos tribunais (artigo 16º), ao direito à educação pública primária (artigo 22º, nº 1). Já em relação a outros direitos, como sejam, por exemplo, o direito de propriedade mobiliária e imobiliária (artigo 13º), o direito ao trabalho (artigos 17º a 19º), o direito a prestações sociais (artigo 23º) e o direito à habitação (artigo 21º), a Convenção proíbe um tratamento menos favorável do que o concedido aos estrangeiros.

A Convenção internacional sobre a proteção dos direitos de todos os trabalhadores migrantes e dos membros das suas famílias começa por afirmar no artigo 1º, nº 1, que "*salvo disposição em contrário constante do seu próprio texto, a presente Convenção aplica-se a todos os trabalhadores migrantes e aos membros das suas famílias sem qualquer distinção, fundada nomeadamente no sexo, raça, cor, língua, religião ou convicção, opinião política ou outra, origem nacional, étnica ou social, nacionalidade, idade, posição económica, património, estado civil, nascimento ou outra situação*" para no artigo 7º especificar que "*os Estados Partes comprometem-se, em conformidade com os instrumentos internacionais relativos aos direitos humanos, a respeitar e a garantir os direitos previstos na presente Convenção a todos os trabalhadores migrantes e membros da sua família que se encontrem no seu território e sujeitos à sua jurisdição, sem distinção alguma, independentemente de qualquer consideração de raça, cor, sexo, língua, religião ou convicção, opinião política ou outra, origem nacional, étnica ou social, nacionalidade, idade, posição económica, património, estado civil, nascimento ou de qualquer outra situação*". Em seguida, a Convenção enumera os direitos dos trabalhadores migrantes e das suas famílias, os quais, *grosso modo*, são importados de outros instrumentos internacionais, designadamente de instrumentos das Nações Unidas, como é o caso, entre outros, da Declaração Universal dos Direitos Humanos, do Pacto Internacional sobre os Direitos Económicos, Sociais e Culturais, do Pacto Internacional sobre os Direitos Civis e Políticos, da Convenção Internacional sobre a Eliminação de Todas as Formas de Discriminação Racial, da Convenção sobre a Eliminação de Todas as Formas de Discriminação contra as Mulheres e da Convenção sobre os Direitos da Criança ou da Organização Internacional do Trabalho, em particular a Convenção relativa aos Trabalhadores Migrantes (nº 97), a Convenção relativa às Migrações em Condições Abusivas e à Promoção da Igualdade de Oportunidades e de Tratamento dos Trabalhadores Migrantes (nº 143), a Recomendação relativa à Migração para o Emprego (nº 86), a Recomendação relativa aos Trabalhadores Migrantes (nº 151), a Convenção sobre Trabalho Forçado ou Obrigatório (nº 29) e a Convenção sobre a Abolição do Trabalho Forçado (nº 105).

Deve notar-se que a afirmação do princípio da não discriminação na Convenção Relativa ao Estatuto do Refugiado é manifestamente insuficiente como fundamento dos direitos dos refugiados, desde logo, porque, tendo em conta as suas atuais motivações, o conceito de refugiado constante da convenção – ainda que com as alterações inseridas pelo Protocolo de Nova Iorque de Dezembro de 1967 – não consegue abrange a maior parte das pessoas que fogem de guerras, sejam elas civis ou não, de condições económicas miseráveis, pois não foi para isso que ele foi criado. Por outro lado, a convenção admite reservas (artigo 42º), pelo que as normas que ela consagra não vigoram de modo idêntico em todos os Estados contratantes. Além disso, a convenção admite denúncia (artigo 44º), o que implica que, em qualquer momento, os refugiados podem ver os seus direitos restringidos pela legislação nacional, sem que o Estado esteja a incumprir o direito internacional (desde que, naturalmente, siga os trâmites do artigo 44º da convenção).

Já a Convenção internacional sobre a proteção dos direitos de todos os trabalhadores migrantes e dos membros das suas famílias, como o próprio nome indica, não se aplica a qualquer migrante mas sim aos trabalhadores e às suas famílias, ou seja, também não se aplica à maior parte das pessoas que se deslocam no âmbito dos fluxos migratórios atuais. Esta Convenção parece excluir as reservas (artigo 88º), mas admite a denúncia (artigo 89º), ainda que sujeita a critérios mais rigorosos dos que os da Convenção relativa ao Estatuto dos Refugiados.

Em relação às convenções da OIT acima referidas, deve mencionar-se que a Convenção nº 97, relativa aos trabalhadores migrantes, se limita a consagrar, no artigo 6º, o princípio da não discriminação, enquanto a Convenção nº 143 relativa às migrações em condições abusivas e à promoção de igualdade de oportunidades e de tratamento dos trabalhadores migrantes estabelece no artigo 10º que "*os Membros para os quais a presente Convenção esteja em vigor comprometem-se a formular e a aplicar uma política nacional que se proponha promover e garantir, por métodos adaptados às circunstâncias e aos costumes nacionais, a igualdade de oportunidades e de tratamento em matéria de emprego e de profissão, de segurança social, de direitos sindicais e culturais e de liberdades individuais e coletivas para aqueles que se encontram legalmente nos seus territórios na qualidade de emigrantes ou de familiares destes*".

Estas duas convenções aplicam-se igualmente apenas aos trabalhadores, com exceção dos que estão excluídos do seu âmbito de aplicação (cf. artigos 11º, nº 2, de ambas as Convenções) e não a qualquer migrante, sendo certo que a segunda – a Convenção nº 143 da OIT – já não se limita a afirmar um princípio da não discriminação meramente formal, como sucede nos outros casos mencionados, mas inclui claramente a igualdade substancial. Dito isto, importa notar que esta convenção admite que todo o Estado Membro que ratifique a Convenção possa excluir da sua aplicação a parte I ou a parte II da Convenção por meio de uma declaração anexa à sua ratificação, o que, obviamente, enfraquece a efetivação da mesma.

O princípio que rege a Convenção do Conselho da Europa relativa ao estatuto jurídico dos trabalhadores migrantes é o da igualdade de direitos destes trabalhadores em relação aos trabalhadores nacionais. Assim, eles gozam, na mesma situação, de direitos idênticos aos trabalhadores nacionais.

Em conclusão, quer o direito internacional dos direitos humanos em geral quer o direito internacional dos refugiados e migrantes se fundamentam na igualdade e a não discriminação, delas derivando – por equiparação com os direitos dos nacionais ou dos estrangeiros – alguns direitos fundamentais dos migrantes e dos refugiados. Isto não significa que a igualdade e a não discriminação sejam a única base em que assentam os direitos dos migrantes e dos refugiados, na medida em que existem indubitavelmente outros fundamentos, como é o caso da dignidade da pessoa humana[152], com tanta ou mais importância, mas a verdade é que quando se trata de fundamentar os direitos dos migrantes e dos refugiados não se pode prescindir da igualdade e a não discriminação.

[152] Para maiores desenvolvimentos, v. ANA MARIA GUERRA MARTINS, *A igualdade e a não discriminação...*, p. 499 e segs.

VIII
A Organização Internacional do Trabalho e a União Europeia*

1. Introdução

1.1. Razões da escolha do tema

Num livro comemorativo do centenário da Organização Internacional do Trabalho (OIT), a escolha de um tema que convoca a União Europeia (UE) necessita de uma explicação.

A OIT e a UE têm mais em comum mais do que aquilo que, numa primeira análise, se vislumbra, na medida em que ambas trouxeram ao direito internacional soluções inovadoras e muito criativas para os problemas com que a comunidade internacional se defrontava ao tempo em que foram criadas.

A OIT surge, em 1919, no final da Primeira Guerra Mundial, tendo a sua Constituição sido integrada no Tratado de Versalhes. Desde logo, a designação do seu tratado institutivo como Constituição[1] revela um avanço em relação ao que existia até então no contexto do direito internacional, dominado, antes de mais, pela ideia de soberania absoluta dos Estados.

* O presente estudo está em vias de publicação no Brasil numa obra coordenada por Nelson Mannrich (USP)/Jouberto de Quadros Pessoa Cavalcante (Mackenzie) e Marco Antônio César Villatore (PUC/PR), cujo título é *Direito Internacional do Trabalho e a Organização Internacional do Trabalho: OIT 100 anos.*

[1] Já em anterior trabalho tivemos oportunidade de nos debruçar sobre a aplicação do conceito de constituição em direito internacional, designadamente em relação aos tratados institutivos de organizações internacionais. Ver Guerra Martins, Ana Maria, *A natureza jurídica da revisão do Tratado da União Europeia*, Lisboa, Lex, 2000, p. 290 e segs.

Os seus órgãos assentam numa estrutura tripartida, única no Mundo, que inclui Estados, trabalhadores e empregadores. Ou seja, a OIT ultrapassa *avant la lettre* a visão clássica do direito internacional como um direito criado pelos Estados e para os Estados.

Daí que ao longo dos tempos tenha atraído a atenção de juristas das mais diversas áreas, com especial destaque para os cultores do direito do trabalho. No entanto, também os jus internacionalistas a encaram como uma percursora das organizações internacionais, tal como as conhecemos hoje, e até como fonte de inspiração de sujeitos de direito internacional mais evoluídos que já ultrapassaram a natureza de meras organizações internacionais, como é o caso da União Europeia. Além disso, as normas provenientes das convenções e das recomendações da OIT são negociadas a um nível tripartido e ainda que tenham de ser ratificadas pelos Estados para neles vigorarem, destinam-se, essencialmente, aos trabalhadores e aos empregadores.

Acrescente-se ainda que a OIT constitui um terreno muito fértil para os investigadores da teoria geral dos direitos fundamentais bem como do direito internacional dos direitos humanos, uma vez que, ao introduzir os direitos económicos e sociais, *maxime* os direitos dos trabalhadores, no âmbito do direito internacional, fê-lo muito antes de terem sido reconhecidos internacionalmente os direitos civis e políticos. Daí que as convenções da OIT ponham em causa certa doutrina que tende a considerar os direitos económicos e sociais como de segunda geração e, consequentemente, de segunda categoria.

Em suma, a OIT abriu novas perspetivas ao direito internacional[2].

Por seu turno, a UE[3], ao nível regional, ombreia com a OIT em termos de inovação no plano internacional. Ainda que este não seja o local próprio para aprofundar esta questão[4], sempre diremos que a União Europeia é o sujeito de direito internacional, com exceção do Estado,

[2] Sobre a evolução da OIT e as suas caraterísticas atuais ver Diez de Velasco, Manuel, *Las Organizaciones Internacionales*, 12ª ed., 2002, p. 355 e segs.

[3] A UE sucedeu à Comunidade Europeia (artigo 1º do TUE).

[4] Já o fizemos em anteriores trabalhos, dos quais se destaca Guerra Martins, Ana Maria, *Manual de Direito da União Europeia*, 2ª edição, Coimbra, Almedina, 2017, p. 224 e segs bem como toda a bibliografia aí citada.

que possui o mais amplo leque de objetivos[5], o quadro institucional mais independente dos Estados-Membros[6], em que um dos seus órgãos (o Parlamento Europeu) é eleito por sufrágio direto e universal pelos cidadãos da União[7], o sistema de fontes[8] mais original, em que muitas delas se aplicam diretamente aos indivíduos, sem necessidade de transposição por parte dos Estados-Membros, como é o caso dos regulamentos[9] e outras podem ser invocadas pelos particulares mesmo antes de serem transpostas para os ordenamentos jurídicos internos, como, por exemplo, as diretivas[10], e o sistema de fiscalização judicial obrigatório mais completo e eficaz[11]. Além disso, a União Europeia, embora tenha surgido inicialmente com preocupações, essencialmente, económicas – a construção do mercado comum – desde cedo percebeu que não podia descurar a proteção dos direitos fundamentais[12] das pessoas e, por isso, esta foi assumindo, ao longo dos tempos, o caráter de objetivo primordial da União.

Em suma, a OIT e a União Europeia comungam de uma certa originalidade, especialmente se atendermos ao tempo em que foram criadas. Além da originalidade, a OIT e a UE têm alguns objetivos em comum e partilham certos valores e princípios.

Do exposto resulta pois que o estudo da relação entre a OIT e a UE faz todo o sentido.

[5] Sobre os objetivos da União ver GUERRA MARTINS, Ana Maria, *Manual de Direito da União Europeia*, p. 218 e segs bem como toda a bibliografia aí citada.

[6] Sobre o quadro institucional da UE ver GUERRA MARTINS, Ana Maria, *Manual de Direito da União Europeia*, p. 391 e segs bem como toda a bibliografia aí citada.

[7] Sobre o Parlamento Europeu ver GUERRA MARTINS, Ana Maria, *Manual de Direito da União Europeia*, p. 399 e segs bem como toda a bibliografia aí citada.

[8] Sobre o sistema de fontes de direito da UE ver GUERRA MARTINS, Ana Maria, *Manual de Direito da União Europeia*, p. 481 e segs bem como toda a bibliografia aí citada.

[9] Sobre as particularidades dos regulamentos ver GUERRA MARTINS, Ana Maria, *Manual de Direito da União Europeia*, p. 498 e segs bem como toda a bibliografia aí citada.

[10] Sobre as diretivas e o seu efeito direto ver GUERRA MARTINS, Ana Maria, *Manual de Direito da União Europeia*, p. 499 e segs bem como toda a bibliografia aí citada.

[11] Sobre o sistema judicial da UE, GUERRA MARTINS, Ana Maria, *Manual de Direito da União Europeia*, p. 423 e segs bem como toda a bibliografia aí citada.

[12] Sobre a proteção dos direitos fundamentais na UE ver GUERRA MARTINS, Ana Maria, *Manual de Direito da União Europeia*, p. 259 e segs bem como toda a bibliografia aí citada.

1.2. O objeto do presente estudo

O presente estudo tem por objeto a relação que, desde os primórdios da integração europeia, se estabeleceu entre a OIT e a UE. Relação essa que, baseando-se numa comunhão de objetivos, valores e princípios, se tem vindo a estreitar, ao longo dos tempos.

Na verdade, a OIT é a agência especializada das Nações Unidas (ONU) para as questões de emprego e laborais, operando a um nível universal. A sua principal missão é promover a justiça social através da melhoria das condições de trabalho. Por seu turno, antes as Comunidades Europeias, e atualmente a UE, sempre dispuseram de uma dimensão social, a qual abrange, desde logo, o progresso económico e social, a justiça social e os direitos sociais dos trabalhadores.

Assim, muitas matérias que são objeto de convenções ou recomendações da OIT coincidem com a esfera de atuação da UE, no domínio das políticas social e de emprego, abrangendo a primeira a melhoria, principalmente, do ambiente de trabalho, a fim de proteger a saúde e a segurança dos trabalhadores, as condições de trabalho, a segurança social e proteção social dos trabalhadores, a proteção dos trabalhadores em caso de rescisão do contrato de trabalho, a informação e consulta dos trabalhadores, a representação e defesa coletiva dos interesses dos trabalhadores e das entidades patronais, incluindo a cogestão, as condições de emprego dos nacionais de países terceiros que residam legalmente no território da União, a integração das pessoas excluídas do mercado de trabalho, a igualdade entre homens e mulheres quanto às oportunidades no mercado de trabalho e ao tratamento no trabalho, a luta contra a exclusão social e a modernização dos sistemas de proteção social[13].

Além disso, há casos em que, não fazendo parte da política social nem da política de emprego, determinadas atribuições da União se encontram em estreita conexão com o âmbito temático da OIT, como, por exemplo, a igualdade e da não discriminação, o mercado interno, a segurança social, a liberdade de circulação de trabalhadores, a liberdade de estabelecimento e a livre prestação de serviços e os direitos fundamentais.

Note-se, contudo, que há igualmente matérias que estão excluídas do âmbito de aplicação do direito social da União Europeia – as remunera-

[13] Ver artigo 153º, nº 1, do TFUE.

ções, o direito sindical, o direito à greve e o direito ao *lock out*[14] que estão abrangidas no domínio material da OIT.

Do exposto resulta que as normas provenientes da OIT podem justapor-se às normas de direito da UE, o que, naturalmente, não levanta qualquer problema e até reforça a proteção dos direitos, se houver convergência de pontos de vista, mas já pode tornar-se problemático se se verificarem divergências que conduzam a conflitos entre os direitos consagrados, designadamente, nas convenções da OIT e os direitos reconhecidos pelo direito da União Europeia. Ora, é precisamente este tópico que pretendemos tratar neste estudo.

1.3. Indicação de sequência

Antes de nos debruçarmos sobre a questão acabada de enunciar, vamos proceder a uma breve análise dos objetivos comuns da União Europeia e da OIT, no que diz respeito ao trabalho e ao emprego. Chegados a este ponto, será o momento de estudar o estatuto da UE na OIT. Não sendo a União Europeia membro da OIT, verifica-se que o objeto de algumas convenções e recomendações da OIT faz parte do cerne das atribuições partilhadas – e até exclusivas – da UE. Assim sendo, coloca-se a questão de saber se a União deve/pode participar nessas convenções ou se o terá de fazer através dos Estados-Membros e quais as razões que justificam esta prática.

Como veremos, não obstante a personalidade e capacidade jurídicas internacionais da UE, a Constituição da OIT só admite como membros os Estados e só os membros podem negociar e ratificar as suas convenções. Assim sendo, independentemente da matéria que estiver em causa, a participação da União nunca é direta, ocorrendo, antes, por intermédio dos seus Estados-Membros. Porém, através de mecanismos de coordenação dos Estados, a UE acaba por influenciar o direito produzido pela OIT, o que contribui para uma ampla convergência. Porém, também se verificam alguns casos de convenções da OIT que claramente conflituam com o direito da União Europeia, o que será estudado no último ponto deste estudo.

No final, apresentaremos algumas conclusões.

[14] Ver artigo 153º, nº 5, do TFUE.

2. Breve referência aos objetivos da UE e da OIT

2.1. Os objetivos da UE

Como já referimos, verifica-se uma certa coincidência de objetivos entre a OIT e a UE.

Começando pelos objetivos da UE, logo na versão originária do Tratado da Comunidade Económica Europeia (CEE), os objetivos enunciados no preâmbulo incluíam a paz e a união cada vez mais estreita entre os povos europeus, o estabelecimento de bases comuns do desenvolvimento económico, o progresso económico e social e a melhoria constante das condições de vida e de emprego dos povos da Europa.

As sucessivas revisões dos Tratados aditaram novos objetivos à Comunidade Europeia (CE) e enumeraram os objetivos da UE, sendo de realçar o crescimento sustentável e não inflacionista que respeite o ambiente, um elevado nível de emprego e de proteção social, o aumento do nível da qualidade de vida, a coesão económica e social e a solidariedade entre os Estados-Membros.

Também os objetivos da UE – segundo o Tratado de Maastricht – abrangiam a promoção de um progresso económico e social, equilibrado e sustentável, nomeadamente mediante a criação de um espaço sem fronteiras internas, o reforço da coesão económica e social e o estabelecimento de uma união económica e monetária, que incluirá a prazo uma moeda única, a afirmação da União na cena internacional, o reforço da defesa dos direitos e dos interesses dos nacionais dos Estados-Membros, através da instituição de uma cidadania da União, o desenvolvimento de uma estreita cooperação no domínio da justiça e dos assuntos internos e a manutenção da integralidade do acervo comunitário.

Após o Tratado de Amesterdão a igualdade entre homens e mulheres foi alcandorada a objetivo da CE (cfr. artigo 2º do TCE) e o Tratado de Lisboa introduziu modificações muito significativas, as quais refletiram a passagem de uma estrutura tripartida para uma estrutura unitária da União.

Assim, a partir do Tratado de Lisboa passou a existir uma lista única de objetivos da UE, a qual consta do artigo 3º TUE. Além disso, ao contrário dos seus antecessores, o Tratado de Lisboa estabelece, nos artigos 2º a 6º do TFUE, regras mais claras relativas às categorias e aos domínios de competências da União.

Para o que ora nos interessa, os objetivos relevantes são a promoção da paz, dos valores da União e do bem-estar dos seus povos, previstos no artigo 3º, nº 1, do TUE, o estabelecimento do mercado interno que inclui as questões sociais, ambientais e culturais bem como o empenho no desenvolvimento sustentável, assente num crescimento económico equilibrado e na estabilidade de preços, numa economia social de mercado altamente competitiva que tenha por meta o pleno emprego e o progresso social e a melhoria da qualidade do ambiente e que a União fomenta o progresso científico e tecnológico, previstos no artigo 3º, nº 3, par. 1º, do TUE, e ainda o combate à exclusão social e às discriminações, a promoção da justiça e da proteção sociais, da igualdade entre homens e mulheres e da solidariedade entre gerações e da proteção dos direitos das crianças (artigo 3º, nº 3, parágrafo 2º, do TUE).

Se compararmos estes objetivos com as missões da OIT facilmente encontramos aspetos coincidentes. Senão vejamos.

2.2. Os objetivos da OIT

De acordo com o artigo 1º da sua Constituição, a OIT tem como missão promover os objetivos constantes do preâmbulo bem como os constantes da Declaração relativa aos objetivos e fins da OIT, adotada em Filadélfia em 10 de maio de 1944.

Ora, nos termos desta Declaração e do preâmbulo, a justiça social é condição *sine qua non* para atingir a paz mundial e duradoura. A melhoria das condições de trabalho é uma necessidade e abrange, entre outras, matérias como a regulamentação do horário de trabalho, a fixação de uma duração máxima do dia e da semana de trabalho, o recrutamento da mão-de-obra, a luta contra o desemprego, a garantia de um salário que assegure condições de existência convenientes, a proteção dos trabalhadores contra as doenças graves ou profissionais e os acidentes do trabalho, a proteção das crianças, dos adolescentes e das mulheres, as pensões de velhice e de invalidez, a defesa dos interesses dos trabalhadores empregados no estrangeiro, a afirmação do princípio "para igual trabalho, salário igual", a afirmação do princípio de liberdade sindical, a organização do ensino profissional e técnico.

Como se vê, a maior parte dos objetivos da OIT coincidem com os da UE.

3. O estatuto da União Europeia no seio da OIT

O estatuto da UE na OIT depende, desde logo, do TUE e do TFUE[15], prevendo este último a possibilidade de a União e os seus Estados-Membros, no âmbito das suas respetivas competências, cooperarem com as organizações internacionais (artigo 211º TFUE). Por seu turno, o artigo 220º, nºs 1 e 2, TFUE prevê a "cooperação útil" com certas organizações internacionais e o estabelecimento de "ligações oportunas" com outras. O nº 3 do mesmo preceito define quem é competente ao nível da União para promover as referidas "cooperação útil" e "ligações oportunas" – o Alto Representante da União para os Negócios Estrangeiros e a Política de Segurança e a Comissão.

A ideia da cooperação da União com organizações internacionais aplica-se em vários domínios, sendo que alguns deles relevam nas relações com a OIT. É o caso, por exemplo, da formação profissional (artigo 166º, nº 3, TFUE), da saúde pública (artigo 168º, nº 3, TFUE) e da política social (artigo 156º TFUE).

O artigo 220º do TFUE explicita quais as organizações internacionais com as quais a União deve desenvolver a cooperação útil, aí incluindo os órgãos das Nações Unidas e das suas agências especializadas. O que distingue a cooperação útil da ligação oportuna é, no fundo, o grau de intensidade da relação. Os Tratados preconizam, portanto, uma relação intensa com a OIT.

O tipo de relação que se estabelece entre a União e uma qualquer organização internacional não tem diretamente a ver com o estatuto da União nessa organização. Ou seja, a União pode não ser membro de uma organização e estabelecer cooperação útil, enquanto sendo membro pode estabelecer apenas ligações oportunas.

Além da cooperação útil e das ligações oportunas, a União pode participar como membro de uma determinada organização internacional. Porém, a participação da UE em determinada organização internacional depende, em primeiro lugar, da repartição de atribuições entre os Esta-

[15] V. Wessel, Ramses A./Blockmans, Steven, "The Legal Status and Influence of Decisions of International Organizations and other Bodies in the European Union", in Piet Eeckhout/ Manuel Lopez-Escudero (ed.), *The European Union's External Action in Times of Crisis,* Oxford, Hart, 2016, p. 228 e segs; Wessel, Ramses A., "The Legal Framework for the Participation of the European Union in International Institutions", *European Integration,* 2011, p. 626 e segs.

dos-Membros e a União e, em segundo lugar, do facto de a organização internacional em causa permitir, ou não, a entidades, como a UE, dela fazerem parte[16]. Na verdade, só um número muito reduzido de organizações internacionais permite a participação da União em pleno[17].

No caso em apreço, só os Estados podem ser membros da OIT (artigo 1º, nºs 2 e 3, da Constituição da OIT). Logo, a UE não pode ser – e não é – membro da OIT, porque esta não o permite, uma vez que só está aberta aos Estados.

Porém, a União Europeia, ou melhor, a Comissão tem um estatuto de observador não votante.

Nos termos do artigo 34º, nº 1, TUE, a/o Alta/o Representante da União para os Negócios Estrangeiros e a Política de Segurança assegura a organização da coordenação dos Estados-Membros da União nas organizações internacionais e em conferências internacionais, incluindo aquelas em que não tomem parte todos os Estados-Membros, no sentido da defesa das posições da União.

Os Estados-Membros representados em organizações internacionais ou conferências internacionais em que nem todos os Estados-Membros o estejam, manterão estes últimos, bem como a/o Alta/o Representante, informados sobre todas as questões que se revistam de interesse comum.

Esta função de coordenação é particularmente relevante na OIT.

Independentemente dos constrangimentos normativos, a União promove o desenvolvimento económico e social sustentável e o trabalho digno fora das fronteiras da UE, em consonância com os valores da UE, com o Pilar Europeu dos Direitos Sociais e com os Objetivos de Desenvolvimento Sustentável.

Para tanto, colabora com a OIT no sentido de promover o trabalho digno para todos, fomentar a dimensão social da globalização e implementar a dimensão externa das políticas europeias. Além disso, fomenta uma globalização justa, nomeadamente, contribuindo para a adoção de normas internacionais do trabalho e a supervisão da sua aplicação, incluindo dis-

[16] V. WESSEL, Ramses A., "The Legal Framework for the Participation of the European Union...", p. 625.

[17] Sobre as várias modalidades de participação da UE nas organizações internacionais ver GUERRA MARTINS, Ana Maria, *Os Desafios Contemporâneos à Ação Externa da União Europeia – Lições de Direito Internacional Público II*, Coimbra, Almedina, 2018, p. 271 e segs bem como a bibliografia aí citada.

posições em matéria laboral, nos acordos comerciais da UE, e assegurando o respetivo acompanhamento.

A Comissão Europeia vela para que as questões sociais e de emprego sejam tidas em conta na política externa da UE.

4. As atribuições da União Europeia no domínio de atuação da OIT

Recorde-se que, não sendo membro da OIT, a UE estabelece uma relação estratégica de longa data com a OIT[18], a qual se concentra na promoção dos princípios e direitos fundamentais no trabalho, nomeadamente no domínio do comércio, e noutras áreas de política social. Acresce que a UE leva a cabo projetos conjuntos com a OIT e contribui para o seu trabalho, em conjunto com os países da UE, nomeadamente através de declarações da UE.

Aliás, a relação da UE com a OIT é propiciada pelo conjunto de atribuições de que a primeira dispõe, nos domínios de atuação da segunda.

Para melhor compreensão do que acaba de se afirmar, vejamos como se repartem as atribuições entre a União e os seus Estados-Membros nos domínios social, de trabalho e de emprego. Antes, porém, cumpre indicar quais os princípios que regem essa repartição de atribuições.

4.1. Os princípios

O princípio fundamental, neste domínio, é o da atribuição (ou especialidade), o qual se encontra, expressamente, consagrado no artigo 5º do TUE[19]. O nº 2 do mesmo preceito esclarece que "*em virtude do princípio da atribuição, a União atua unicamente dentro dos limites das competências que os Estados-Membros lhe tenham atribuído nos Tratados para alcançar os objetivos fixados por estes últimos*"[20].

[18] Sobre a evolução histórica da relação entre a UE e a OIT ver AART, Marieke van, *Relations EU – ILO – Cooperation or Conflict?*, Tilburg University, 2011, p. 44 e segs.

[19] O preceito estabelece o seguinte: "*A delimitação das competências da União rege-se pelo princípio da atribuição.*"

[20] Sobre o princípio da atribuição na União Europeia, cfr. GUERRA MARTINS, Ana Maria, *Manual de Direito da União Europeia*, p. 316 e segs; LENAERTS, Koen/NUFFEL, Piet Van, *European Union Law*, 3ª ed., Londres, Sweet & Maxwell, 2011, p. 112 e segs; WYATT & DASHWOOD'S, *European Union Law*, 6ª ed., Oxford, 2011, p. 97 e segs; HARTLEY, T C, *The Foundations of European Union Law*, 7ª ed., Oxford, 2010, p.110 e segs.

Em matéria de exercício de atribuições regem os princípios da subsidiariedade, da preempção, da cooperação leal e da proporcionalidade.

O primeiro atua quando se trata de atribuições não exclusivas da União, admitindo-se a intervenção da União"*apenas se e na medida em que os objetivos da ação encarada não possam ser suficientemente alcançados pelos Estados-membros, tanto ao nível central como ao nível regional ou local, podendo contudo, devido às dimensões ou efeitos da ação considerada, ser mais bem alcançados ao nível da União*" (artigo 5º, nº 3, par. 1º do TUE)[21].

O segundo aplica-se às atribuições partilhadas e está implícito no artigo 2º, nº 2, do TFUE, o qual determina que "*os Estados-Membros exercem a sua competência na medida em que a União não tenha exercido a sua*".

O terceiro está definido no artigo 4º, nº 3, do TUE, o qual estabelece que a União e os Estados-Membros se respeitam e assistem mutuamente no cumprimento das missões decorrentes dos Tratados, comprometendo-se os Estados-Membros a adotar todas as medidas gerais ou específicas adequadas para garantir a execução das obrigações decorrentes dos Tratados ou dos atos das instituições da União bem como a facilitar à União o cumprimento dos objetivos constantes dos Tratados e abster-se de adotar quaisquer medidas que ponham em causa esses objetivos[22].

Por último, o princípio da proporcionalidade encontra-se atualmente previsto no par. 1º do nº 4 do artigo 5º do TUE, o qual impõe que "*o conteúdo e a forma da ação da União não devem exceder o necessário para alcançar os objetivos do Tratado*"[23].

4.2. As categorias de atribuições da União

Além disso, ao contrário do que sucedia anteriormente[24], os artigos 2º a 6º do TFUE, introduzidos pelo Tratado de Lisboa, enumeram as categorias

[21] Sobre o princípio da subsidiariedade ver Guerra Martins, Ana Maria, *Manual de Direito da União Europeia*, p. 318 e segs bem como toda a bibliografia aí citada.

[22] Sobre o princípio da cooperação leal ver Guerra Martins, Ana Maria, *Manual de Direito da União Europeia*, p. 309 e segs bem como toda a bibliografia aí citada.

[23] Sobre o princípio da proporcionalidade ver Guerra Martins, Ana Maria, *Manual de Direito da União Europeia*, p. 322 e segs bem como toda a bibliografia aí citada.

[24] Os Tratados institutivos das Comunidades Europeias bem como o Tratado da União Europeia não continham qualquer cláusula de repartição de atribuições entre os Estados-Membros e as Comunidades e a União. Os Tratados baseavam-se no método da enumeração dos objetivos e enunciavam os instrumentos necessários para os atingir bem como consagravam

de atribuições, especificam quais as consequências para a União e para os Estados-Membros da inserção de uma determinada matéria em cada uma dessas categorias e indicam qual o domínio material de cada uma delas[25]. Além disso, ao longo do TFUE desenvolvem-se as bases jurídicas das diversas matérias que integram cada uma das categorias de atribuições.

As categorias de atribuições enunciadas no artigo 2º do TFUE que relevam, em sede de relações entre a UE e a OIT, são, essencialmente, as seguintes:

- As atribuições exclusivas (nº 1);
- As atribuições partilhadas (nº 2);
- As atribuições de coordenação das políticas económicas e de emprego dos Estados-membros (nº 3);
- As atribuições para desenvolver ações destinadas a apoiar, a coordenar e a completar a ação dos Estados-Membros (nº 5).

as diversas bases jurídicas de implementação desses objetivos e desses instrumentos. Este método revelou-se, desde muito cedo, propício a conflitos, quer positivos quer negativos, de atribuições entre a União Europeia/as Comunidades Europeias e os seus Estados-Membros.

[25] Sobre as atribuições da União, ver, entre outros, Rossi, Lucia Serena «Does the Treaty of Lisbon Provide a Clearer Separation of Competences between EU and Member States?», *in* Andrea Biondi/Piet Eeckhout/Stefanie Ripley, *EU Law after Lisbon,* Oxford, Oxford Univ. Press, 2012, p. 85 e segs; Tridimas, Takis, «Competence after Lisbon: The elusive search for bright lines», *in* Diamond Ashiagbor/Nicola Countouris/Ioannis Lianos, *The European Union after the Treaty of Lisbon,* Cambridge, Cambridge Univ. Press, 2012, p. 47 e segs; Craig, Paul, *The Lisbon Treaty – Law, Politics and Treaty Reform,* Oxford, Oxford Univ. Press, 2010, p. 155 e segs; Rangel de Mesquita, Maria José, *A União Europeia após o Tratado de Lisboa,* Coimbra, Almedina, 2010, p. 57 e segs; Edjaharan, Vérane, "Les compétences dans le Traité de Lisbonne: la constitutionnalisation de l'Union intérrogée", *in* E. Brosset/C. Chevallier-Govers/V. Edjaharian/C. Schneider (dir.), *Le Traité de Lisbonne – Reconfiguration ou déconstitutionnalisation de l'Union européenne?,* Bruxelas, Bruylant, 2009, p. 227 e segs; Bosse-Platière, Isabelle, "Traité de Lisbonne et clarification des compétences", *RMCUE,* 2008, p. 443 e segs; Pasquale, Patrizia de, "Il riparto di competenze tra Unione europea e Stati membri", *Dir. Pubb. Comp. Eur.,* 2008, p. 60 e segs; Craig, Paul, "The Treaty of Lisbon: Process, architecture and substance", *ELR,* 2008, p. 144 e segs e ainda o nosso *Manual de Direito da União Europeia,* p. 347 e segs.

Na verdade, ainda que a maior parte dos domínios abrangidos pelas ações da OIT façam parte das atribuições partilhadas da União, há algumas matérias, das quais se destacam a igualdade e da não discriminação, objeto da Convenção nº 100 da OIT, alguns aspetos do mercado interno, como, por exemplo, a isenção de vistos regulada pela Convenção nº 185 da OIT, a coordenação da segurança social, a liberdade de circulação de trabalhadores, a liberdade de estabelecimento, a livre prestação de serviços e a contratação pública (especialmente as cláusulas sociais, previstas na Convenção nº 94), os direitos fundamentais previstos na Carta de Direitos Fundamentais da União Europeia, que se inserem nas atribuições exclusivas da União[26]. Ora, nesses casos, só a União pode legislar e adotar atos juridicamente vinculativos, sendo que os Estados-Membros só podem fazê-lo mediante habilitação da União ou para implementar os atos da União (artigo 2º, nº 1, do TFUE)[27]. Não sendo a União membro da OIT está identificado o primeiro obstáculo ao relacionamento entre ambas.

A maior parte das matérias abrangidas pela OIT e pelo seu direito derivado integram-se, todavia, nas atribuições partilhadas entre a União e os seus Estados-Membros, o que implica que a União e os Estados-Membros podem legislar e adotar atos juridicamente vinculativos. Como já vimos, os Estados-Membros só exercem a sua competência na medida em que a União não tenha exercido a sua e só voltam a exercê-la na medida em que a União tenha deixado de exercer a sua (artigo 2º, nº 2, do TFUE). Ou seja, uma atribuição partilhada, por força do princípio da preempção pode tornar-se, pelo menos, temporariamente, exclusiva.

[26] Nos termos do artigo 3º, nº 1, do TFUE fazem parte das atribuições exclusivas a união aduaneira, o estabelecimento das regras de concorrência necessárias ao funcionamento do mercado interno, a política monetária para os Estados-membros cuja moeda é o euro, a conservação dos recursos biológicos do mar, no âmbito da política comum de pescas e a política comercial comum.

[27] Sobre as atribuições internas exclusivas da União, cfr. Schütze, Robert, *European Constitutional Law*, 2ª ed., Cambridge, Cambridge Univ. Press, 2015, p. 164 e segs; Craig, Paul/De Búrca, Gráinne, *European Union Law, Text, Cases and Materials,* 6ª ed., Oxford, Oxford University Press, 2015 p. 78 e segs; Craig, Paul, *The Lisbon Treaty*, cit, p. 159 e segs; Rideau, Joël, *Droit institutionnel de l'Union européenne,* 6ª ed., Paris, LGDJ, 2010, p. 633 e segs; Hartley, T. C.,*The Foundations,* cit., p. 116 e segs.

O artigo 4º, nº 2, do TFUE enumera a lista das matérias que se incorporam nas atribuições partilhadas[28], a qual é meramente exemplificativa. Assim, o mercado interno, a política social no que se refere aos aspetos definidos no TFUE e a coesão económica, social e territorial fazem parte das atribuições partilhadas que consubstanciam áreas temáticas igualmente relevantes no âmbito da relação entre a OIT e a UE. Ora, não sendo a União membro da OIT mas podendo atuar com os seus Estados-Membros nos domínios partilhados é importante determinar, por exemplo, quem deve vincular-se às convenções da OIT.

Mas as dificuldades levantadas pela repartição de atribuições entre a UE e os seus Estados-Membros que se repercutem na relação da UE com a OIT não se esgotam nas atribuições partilhadas. Pelo contrário, as atribuições previstas no artigo 2º, nº 3, do TFUE relativas à coordenação das políticas económicas e de emprego dos Estados-Membros também se revelam decisivas.

Acresce que o artigo 5º, nº 3, do TFUE ao estabelecer que a União pode tomar iniciativas para garantir a coordenação das políticas sociais dos Estados-membros, terá obviamente implicações nos domínios de atuação da OIT. Como se vê, no domínio da política social, cuja relevância para o presente estudo está fora de dúvida, afigura-se, por vezes, difícil traçar uma linha de demarcação clara entre as diferentes categorias de atribuições da União, na medida em que há aspetos dessa política que se incluem nas atribuições partilhadas, outros incluem-se na ações de coordenação do artigo 5º e para complicar ainda mais este quadro, há matérias que se inserem nas ações de apoio, coordenação e complemento, ainda que não façam parte da lista constante do artigo 6º do TFUE[29]. Se compaginarmos

[28] Sobre as atribuições partilhadas entre a União e os seus Estados-Membros, cfr. Schütze, Robert, *European Constitutional Law*, cit., p. 166 e segs; Craig, Paul/De Búrca, Gráinne, *EU Law*, cit., p. 83 e segs; Craig, Paul, *The Lisbon Treaty*, cit., p. 167 e segs; Rideau, Joël, *Droit institutionnel*, cit., p. 636 e segs; Hartley, T. C., *The Foundation*, cit., p. 117 e segs.

[29] O artigo 6º do TFUE enumera as matérias sobre as quais podem incidir ações da União destinadas a apoiar, a coordenar e a completar a ação dos Estados-membros, a saber:
- A proteção e melhoria da saúde humana;
- Indústria;
- Cultura;
- Turismo;
- Educação, formação profissional, juventude e desporto;

as disposições gerais relativas às categorias de atribuições da União com as disposições específicas relativas à política social, constantes dos artigos 151º a 161º do TFUE, a obscuridade desta solução torna-se ainda mais evidente.

O artigo 2º, nº 5, par. 1º, parte final, do TFUE estabelece expressamente que as medidas de apoio, coordenação e complemento das ações dos Estados-Membros não substituem a competência dos Estados-Membros e o par. 2º do mesmo preceito exclui a harmonização das disposições legislativas e regulamentares desta categoria de atribuições da União. Porém, o âmbito de atuação da União, ao abrigo desta categoria de atribuições, varia consoante a matéria que está em causa, podendo, inclusivamente, vir a ser adotados atos jurídicos vinculativos pela União Europeia. Ou seja, está excluída a harmonização, mas já não a adoção de atos jurídicos vinculativos por parte da União, desde que fundados nas disposições específicas do TFUE, o que vai necessariamente ter repercussões nas competências que, no futuro, os Estados-Membros poderão vir a exercer[30].

No fundo, para definir a existência ou não de atribuição da União num determinado domínio o que mais importa é o que estabelecem as disposições específicas do TFUE.

Em conclusão, dispondo a UE de atribuições nos domínios de atuação da OIT, o relacionamento com esta organização internacional é imperativo. Vejamos então as bases jurídicas das atribuições externas da União.

4.3. As atribuições externas da União nos domínios de atuação da OIT

4.3.1. Questão prévia: a subjetividade internacional da União Europeia

Em primeiro lugar, deve sublinhar-se que a UE tem personalidade jurídica internacional, ou seja, é suscetível de ser titular de direitos e de estar adstrita a deveres diretamente provenientes da norma jurídica internacional.

- Proteção civil;
- Cooperação administrativa.

[30] Sobre as ações da União destinadas a apoiar, a coordenar ou a completar a ação dos Estados--Membros, cfr. Schütze, Robert, *European Constitutional Law*, cit., p. 168; Craig, Paul/De Búrca, Gráinne, *EU Law*, cit., p. 85 e segs; Craig, Paul, *The Lisbon Treaty*, cit., p. 173 e segs; Rideau, Joël, *Droit institutionnel*, cit., p. 640 e segs.

Se até ao Tratado de Lisboa, essa personalidade não estava claramente afirmada nos Tratados, embora tenha sido deles inferida pela jurisprudência do Tribunal de Justiça da União Europeia (TJUE), hoje em dia, esta questão está esclarecida no artigo 47º do TUE. A União Europeia detém personalidade jurídica internacional, o que significa que é suscetível e goza dos direitos e prerrogativas que lhe são inerentes[31].

Além da personalidade jurídica internacional, a União também é detentora de uma ampla capacidade internacional, ainda que, ao contrário do que sucede com os Estados, não detenha a capacidade internacional plena. A UE tem, pois, o direito de celebrar convenções internacionais, o direito de legação ativo e passivo e o direito de participação em organizações internacionais. O exercício desses direitos depende, designadamente, da repartição de atribuições externas entre a União e os seus Estados-Membros assim como da aceitação por parte dos terceiros com quem pretende relacionar-se.

Em suma, não basta que a União seja um sujeito de direito internacional, é necessário que detenha a competência externa necessária para atuar em determinado domínio e que o terceiro aceite negociar e estabelecer relações com a União.

Importa, portanto, averiguar se a União é titular de atribuições externas nos domínios de atuação da OIT.

4.3.2. O princípio do paralelismo de atribuições internas e externas

Até ao Tratado de Lisboa, o princípio que dominou a matéria da capacidade internacional das Comunidades Europeias foi de criação jurisprudencial – o princípio do paralelismo de atribuições internas e externas[32].

[31] Para um estudo desenvolvido da subjetividade internacional da União Europeia, cfr. GUERRA MARTINS, Ana Maria, *Os Desafios Contemporâneos à Ação Externa da União Europeia – Lições de Direito Internacional Público II*, Coimbra, Almedina, 2018, p. 47 e segs; RANGEL DE MESQUITA, Maria José, *A atuação externa da União Europeia depois do Tratado de Lisboa*, Coimbra, 2011, *maxime* p. 35 a 140 e da mesma Autora, "Anotação ao artigo 47º do TUE", *in* MANUEL LOPES PORTO/GONÇALO ANASTÁCIO (coord.), *Tratado de Lisboa – Anotado e comentado*, Coimbra, Almedina, 2012, p. 172 a 174.

[32] Para um estudo desenvolvido da jurisprudência do TJ no domínio deste princípio ver GUERRA MARTINS, Ana Maria, *Os Desafios Contemporâneos à Ação Externa da União Europeia – Lições de Direito Internacional Público II*, cit., p. 141 e segs bem como toda a bibliografia aí citada.

Segundo jurisprudência firme e constante do TJ, nas matérias em que existia competência exclusiva ao nível interno, como é o caso, por exemplo, da política comercial comum, essa exclusividade transmitia-se à conclusão de acordos internacionais com terceiros Estados. Aliás, quer as competências internas fossem exclusivas, quer não, as atribuições externas existiam, podendo ser expressas ou implícitas. Neste último caso, não resultariam de disposições expressas dos Tratados, mas sim implicitamente de outras disposições dos Tratados ou dos atos adotados pelos órgãos comunitários. Na ausência de legislação interna, a Comunidade podia celebrar acordos internacionais se forem necessários para atingir algum dos objetivos previstos no Tratado.

4.3.3. O direito de celebração de convenções internacionais após o Tratado de Lisboa

A jurisprudência do TJ acabou por ser, de algum modo, transposta para os Tratados. Assim, nos termos do artigo 3º, nº 2, do TFUE a União dispõe igualmente de competência exclusiva para celebrar acordos internacionais quando tal celebração esteja prevista num ato legislativo; quando seja necessária para dar à União a possibilidade de exercer a sua competência interna e quando seja suscetível de afetar regras comuns ou de alterar o alcance das mesmas.

De acordo com o artigo 216º, nº 1, TFUE, a União pode celebrar acordos com um ou mais países terceiros ou organizações internacionais quando os tratados o prevejam, quando a celebração do acordo for necessária para alcançar, no âmbito das políticas, um dos objetivos estabelecidos pelos Tratados, quando a celebração do acordo estiver prevista num ato juridicamente vinculativo da União e quando for suscetível de afetar regras comuns ou de alterar o seu alcance.

Apesar de uma parte da redação do artigo 216º, nº 1, TFUE não diferir muito da redação do artigo 3º, nº 2, TFUE, o âmbito de aplicação das duas disposições é distinto. Enquanto o artigo 216º, nº 1, TFUE não procede a qualquer categorização da atribuição, ou seja, não se debruça sobre o caráter exclusivo ou partilhado da mesma; o artigo 3º, nº 2, TFUE somente diz respeito às atribuições externas exclusivas. A competência externa da União não se esgota, portanto, nas situações previstas no artigo 3º, nº 2, TFUE.

Os Tratados preveem ainda a possibilidade de a União e os seus Estados-Membros cooperarem com as organizações internacionais competentes (artigo 211º TFUE) assim como a possibilidade de a União celebrar acordos com organizações internacionais que criem uma associação caracterizada por direitos e obrigações recíprocos, ações comuns e procedimentos especiais (artigo 217º TFUE).

O artigo 216º, nº 1, TFUE prevê que a União pode celebrar acordos com organizações internacionais e para isso não necessita de uma competência expressa, podendo resultar de uma competência interna. O processo para concluir esses acordos está previsto no artigo 218º TFUE.

Os Tratados preveem ainda a conclusão de tratados com organizações internacionais no domínio de políticas específicas, como, por exemplo, em matéria de política de ambiente (artigo 191º, nº 4, TFUE), em matéria de política comercial comum (artigo 207º, nº 3, TFUE), no âmbito da cooperação ao desenvolvimento (artigo 209º, nº 2, TFUE), no domínio da cooperação económica, financeira e técnica com países terceiros (artigo 212º, nº 3, TFUE) e em sede de ajuda humanitária (artigo 214º, nº 4, TFUE)[33].

4.3.4. As dificuldades inerentes às convenções da OIT

Aplicando as regras acabadas de enunciar às convenções da OIT importa notar que algumas – poucas[34] – caem no âmbito das atribuições externas exclusivas, quer expressas quer implícitas, da União Europeia, outras, pelo contrário, só parcialmente farão parte das atribuições externas da União para celebrar convenções internacionais[35].

Porém, o artigo 15º, nº 5, da Constituição da OIT é bem claro quando afirma que só os membros da OIT, ou seja, os Estados podem ratificar as convenções, o que significa que a União, mesmo que se trate de uma

[33] Sobre as atribuições externas da União após o Tratado de Lisboa ver GUERRA MARTINS, Ana Maria, *Os Desafios Contemporâneos à Ação Externa da União Europeia – Lições de Direito Internacional Público II*, cit., p. 173 e segs bem como toda a bibliografia aí citada.

[34] Sobre as convenções da OIT em que a União tem competência exclusiva ver BLOMMÉ, Linnéa, *The impact of European Community law on the work within the ILO*, Estocolmo, April 2008, p. 13 e segs.

[35] Sobre as convenções da OIT em que a União detém competência partilhada com os Estados-Membros ver BLOMMÉ, Linnéa, *The impact of European Community law on the work within the ILO*, p. 16 e segs.

convenção cuja matéria é totalmente da sua competência, não participará na sua negociação nem a poderá vir a ratificar. Mas, do ponto de vista do direito da União Europeia, não é admissível que sejam os Estados-Membros a negociar, a ratificar e até a executar uma tal convenção. Daí que a única forma de ultrapassar o obstáculo à participação da União, constante da Constituição da OIT, é a prévia autorização dos órgãos da União aos Estados-Membros para negociarem e ratificarem a referida convenção no interesse e em nome da União. Esta regra aplica-se igualmente quando se trata de uma convenção em sede de atribuições partilhadas na parte em que a competência cabe à União.

Aliás, o Tribunal de Justiça já teve oportunidade de se pronunciar sobre a competência da então CE no âmbito das convenções da OIT. Fê-lo no parecer 2/91[36], no qual estava em causa a conclusão da convenção nº 170 da OIT relativa à segurança da utilização de produtos químicos no trabalho. O Tribunal decidiu que esta matéria pertencia em conjunto aos Estados--Membros e à Comunidade, dado que o domínio em apreço resultava da política social. Ora, o ex-artigo 118ºA do TCEE apenas conferia à Comunidade poderes para aprovar diretivas que fixassem *standards* mínimos, pelo que o direito comunitário deixava aos Estados-Membros a liberdade de aplicarem normas mais exigentes.

5. Os eventuais conflitos entre as convenções da OIT e o direito da UE

São várias as convenções da OIT em relação às quais se têm detetado eventuais incompatibilidades com o direito da União[37], o que levou até à modificação de algumas convenções com o intuito de ultrapassar a situação.

Foi precisamente o caso do Protocolo à Convenção nº 89 relativa ao trabalho noturno das mulheres na indústria que procurou adequar os parâmetros da OIT ao princípio da igualdade homem-mulher vigente no direito da União. Apesar de existir esse protocolo, a convenção ainda

[36] Parecer de 19/3/92, *parecer nº 2/91*, Col. 1992, p. 1061 e segs.

[37] Sobre as convenções da OIT potencialmente incompatíveis com o direito da União ver *Analysis – in the light of the European Union acquis–of the ILO Conventions that have been classified by the International Labour Organisation as up to date*, European Commission, Directorate-General for Employment, Social Affairs and Inclusion Unit A.4 Manuscript completed in June 2013, p. 69 segs.

mantém algumas desigualdades que dificilmente podem ser aceites pela União Europeia.

A convenção nº 94 sobre cláusulas de trabalho nos contratos firmados por entidades públicas contem algumas disposições potencialmente incompatíveis com as normas da UE relativas aos trabalhadores deslocados e com as normas relativas à liberdade de prestação de serviços consagrada no direito da União Europeia.

A convenção nº 97 sobre os trabalhadores migrantes impõe uma série de condições à deslocação de trabalhadores entre Estados que não se harmonizam totalmente com as regras de livre circulação de trabalhadores prevista na União Europeia nem com o princípio da não discriminação em função da nacionalidade que se aplica aos trabalhadores.

A convenção nº 110 sobre as condições de emprego dos trabalhadores agrícolas exige, por exemplo, exames médicos aos trabalhadores, os quais são incompatíveis com o direito da UE.

Assim sendo, os Estados-Membros não devem ratificar estas convenções e se já o tiverem feito, antes de se tornarem membros da União, deverão socorrer-se do artigo 351º TFUE, o qual dispõe, no seu par. 1º, que as disposições dos Tratados não prejudicam os direitos e obrigações que decorrem de convenções concluídas antes de 1 de janeiro de 1958 ou, em relação aos Estados que aderem à União, anteriormente à data da respetiva adesão entre, por um lado, um ou vários Estados-Membros e, por outro, um ou mais Estados terceiros. Ou seja, estes acordos, em princípio, mantêm-se em vigor, em obediência ao princípio *pacta sunt servanda* (artigo 26º da Convenção de Viena sobre Direito dos Tratados (CVDT)) e ao princípio da relatividade dos tratados (artigo 34º, nº 4, alínea b), da CVDT).

Todavia, se tais convenções não forem compatíveis com os Tratados, como é o caso das convenções da OIT, acabadas de mencionar, o par. 2º do mesmo preceito impõe aos Estados-Membros a obrigação de recorrerem a todos os meios apropriados para eliminarem as eventuais incompatibilidades.

Caso seja necessário, os Estados-Membros auxiliar-se-ão mutuamente para atingir essa finalidade, adotando, se for caso disso, uma atitude comum (artigo 351º, par. 2º, do TFUE).

O par. 3º do mesmo preceito acrescenta ainda que, ao aplicar os acordos pré-comunitários ou pré-União, os Estados-Membros terão em conta o facto de as vantagens concedidas nos Tratados por cada um dos Estados-Membros fazerem parte integrante do estabelecimento da União, estando inseparavelmente ligadas à criação de instituições comuns, à atribuição de competências em seu favor e à concessão das mesmas vantagens por todos os outros Estados-Membros.

As convenções nº 185 relativa à emissão de documentos de identificação para trabalhadores marítimos, nº 186 sobre trabalho marítimo, nº 188 sobre trabalho na pesca e nº 189 sobre trabalho doméstico também são suscetíveis de conter normas incompatíveis com o direito de livre circulação de trabalhadores e de livre prestação de serviços reconhecido pela UE.

Tanto a UE como a OIT têm procurado ultrapassar os eventuais conflitos. Do lado da OIT, certas convenções, como, por exemplo, a convenção nº 189 da OIT, contêm cláusulas de salvaguarda no sentido de afastarem a aplicação de certas regras aos Estados que façam de organizações de integração económica regional. A União Europeia, por seu lado, incentiva os Estados-Membros (e até os não membros) a ratificarem o maior número possível de convenções da OIT.

6. Conclusões

Do presente estudo é possível extrair as seguintes conclusões.

Em primeiro lugar, deve sublinhar-se que a OIT e a UE inovaram no âmbito do direito internacional. A estrutura tripartida dos órgãos da OIT é disso exemplo. Do lado da União as novidades foram ainda maiores, tendo levado ao seu afastamento progressivo de todas as organizações internacionais.

Além disto, a OIT e a UE partilham princípios, valores e objetivos, o que significa que estão predestinadas a estabelecerem relações, o que, aliás, sempre se verificou, e tem sido bastante implementado ultimamente.

Porém, o estatuto formal da UE na OIT é muito delicado, na medida em que não sendo um Estado, não pode ser membro de pleno direito da organização e, consequentemente, não pode negociar, ratificar e ser responsável pelo não cumprimento das convenções da OIT.

Sucede, porém, que a União detém amplas atribuições nos domínios de atuação da OIT, ou seja, os domínios social, de emprego e de trabalho, algumas delas até exclusivas, o que implica que tenha de existir uma enorme coordenação dos Estados-Membros por parte da União, a qual é assegurada pela Comissão. Nem sempre se afigura fácil.

Do ponto de vista da União, não haveria nenhum entrave à adesão à OIT, na medida em que tem personalidade jurídica internacional e atribuições nos domínios de atuação da OIT, mas o mesmo não se verifica do lado da OIT. Esta organização só admite Estados como membros. Daí que a relação entre a OIT e a UE, por vezes, se torne de uma enorme complexidade. Se a OIT e a União regulam a mesma matéria de modo diferente surgem conflitos que têm de ser resolvidos. Do lado da União, o direito internacional dos Estados-Membros nas matérias que estes transferiram total, ou parcialmente, para a União deve conformar-se com o direito da União, o que significa que as convenções da OIT devem ser afastadas.

Note-se, porém, que são raros os casos em que isso acontece, pelo que a relações da OIT com a UE são bastante harmónicas, sendo a UE um catalisador de desenvolvimento da OIT.

Parte IV

A Convenção Europeia dos Direitos do Homem

IX
Opinion 2/13 of the European Court of Justice in the Context of Multilevel Protection of Fundamental Rights and Multilevel Constitutionalism Revisited*

Abstract

In Opinion 2/13 on the draft agreement on the European Union's accession to the European Convention on Human Rights (ECHR), the Court of Justice of the European Union (CJEU) held that the draft agreement was not compatible with European Union law (EU law), that is to say, with Article 6(2) of the Treaty on European Union (TEU) or with Protocol No 8 relating to Article 6(2) TEU. This is without doubt one of the most significant rulings in the history of the European integration process, due to its legal and political consequences. In this study, however, we will not elaborate on the future of the EU accession to the ECHR after Opinion 2/13. We will focus instead on the question of whether the conclusions of the Court could have been different if it had taken into account the multilevel protection of fundamental rights and multilevel constitutionalism, which is a theory that tries to explain how the legitimacy of public authority is rooted in individuals, as citizens of Member States and citizens of the Union.

* Este artigo corresponde à versão publicada em Lina Papadopoulou/Ingolf Pernice/Joseph H. H. Weiler (eds.), *Legitimacy Issues of the European Union in the Face of Crisis – Dimitris Tsatsos memoriam*, Baden-Baden, Hart/Nomos, 2017, p. 233-270.

I. Introduction

A. The background of Opinion 2/13

On 18 December 2014, the CJEU delivered Opinion 2/13[1] on whether the draft agreement on the European Union's accession to the ECHR was compatible with EU law. It concluded that it was not compatible with Article 6(2) of the Treaty on European Union (TEU) nor with Protocol No 8 relating to Article 6(2) TEU.

For the second time in the history of its case law,[2] the Court has blocked the Union's accession to the ECHR, in spite of the explicit competence conferred on the Union by the TEU after Lisbon.[3] According to the Court, the draft agreement providing for accession was, *grosso modo*, contrary to the specific characteristics of EU law[4] and its legal autonomy.[5]

[1] ECLI:EU:C:2014:2454.

[2] See Opinion 2/94 of 28 March 1996, ECLI:EU:C:1996:140.

[3] Cf. Article 6 (2) TEU. On the EU's accession to the ECHR in the Treaty of Lisbon compare T Lock, 'Accession of the EU to the ECHR – Who Would be Responsible in Strasbourg?' in D Ashiagbor et al (eds), *The European Union after the Treaty of Lisbon* (Cambridge, Cambridge University Press, 2012) 109 et seq; G Gaja, 'Accession to the ECHR' in A Biondi et al (eds), *EU Law after Lisbon* (Oxford, Oxford University Press, 2012) 180 et seq; MJR de Mesquita, *A União Europeia após o Tratado de Lisboa* (Coimbra, Almedina, 2010) 83 et seq; E Bribosia, 'Le traité de Lisbonne: un pas supplémentaire dans le processus de constitutionnalisation des droits fondamentaux' in P Magnette and A Weyembergh (eds), *L'Union européenne: la fin d'une crise?* (L'Université de Bruxelles, Brussels 2008) 195 et seq; FB Rohmer, 'Valeurs et droits fondamentaux' in E Brosset et al (eds), *Le Traité de Lisbonne – Reconfiguration ou déconstitutionnalisation de l'Union européenne?* (Émile Bruylant, Brussels, 2009) 158 et seq.

[4] According to the Court, 'these characteristics include those relating to the constitutional structure of the EU, which is seen in the principle of conferral of powers referred to in Articles 4(1) TEU and 5(1) and (2) TEU, and in the institutional framework established in Articles 13 TEU to 19 TEU' and 'EU law is characterised by the fact that it stems from an independent source of law, the Treaties, by its primacy over the laws of the Member States.' See, to that effect, the judgments in C-6/64 Costa EU:C:1964:66, 594 and C-11/70 Internationale Handelsgesellschaft EU:C:1970:114 para 3; Opinions 1/91 EU:C:1991:490 para 21 and 1/09 EU:C:2011:123 para 65; and the judgment in C-399/11 Melloni EU:C:2013:107 para 59, and the direct effect of a whole series of provisions which are applicable to their nationals and to the Member States themselves (the judgment in C-26/62 van Gend & Loos, EU:C:1963:1, 12 and Opinion 1/09 EU:C:2011:123 para 65).' See paras 165-166 of Opinion 2/13.

[5] On the autonomy of EU law see, among others, I Pernice, 'The Autonomy of the EU Legal Order – Fifty Years After *Van Gend*' in A Tizzano et al (eds), *50ème Anniversaire de l'arrêt Van*

To be perfectly honest, this was not completely surprising, taking into account that a number of previous rulings[6] had been in a similar direction. Even so, most people would have expected that the Court would not apply its case law on human rights matters and would weigh up the advantages of EU accession to the ECHR, which have been noted by scholars[7] and some European institutions, such as the Commission,[8] for decades. Among these advantages should be included a greater adherence to the multilevel protection of fundamental rights, which would surely increase the legitimacy of the EU, since it would effectively have to abide by the same international catalogue of fundamental human rights – the ECHR – and come under the same international jurisdiction – the ECtHR – as its Member States. Furthermore, possible gaps in either the EU or national fundamental rights systems could be filled in by the ECHR. Finally, individuals would be able to hold the EU itself and not only the Member States responsible in Strasbourg, which would contribute to a better pro-

Gend en Loos 1963-2003 (Luxemburg, Office des publications de l'Union européenne, 2013) 55 et seq; P Gragl, *The Accession of the European Union to the European Convention on Human Rights* (Oxford, Hart Publishing, 2013) *maxime* 19-49; P Craig, 'EU Accession to the ECHR: Competence, Procedure and Substance' (2013) 36 (1) *Fordham International Law Journal* 1142 et seq; JP Terhechte, 'Autonomie und Kohärenz – Die Eigenständigkeit der Unionsgrundrechte im Zuge des EMRK-Beitritts der Europäischen Union', in J Iliopoulos-Strangas et al (eds), *Der Beitritt der Europäischen Union zur EMRK* (Baden-Baden, Nomos, 2013) 34 et seq; T Lock, 'Walking on a Tightrope: The Draft ECHR Accession Agreement and the Autonomy of the EU Legal Order' (2011) 48 (4) *CML Rev* 1028 et seq; T Schilling, 'The Autonomy of the Community Legal Order: An Analysis of Possible Foundations' (1996) 37 (2) *Harvard International Law Journal* 380 et seq; JHH Weiler, 'The Autonomy of the Community Legal Order – Through the Looking Glass' (1996) 37 (2) *Harvard International Law Journal* 411 et seq; FE Dowrick, 'A Model of the European Communities Legal System' (1983) *Yearbook of European Law* 169 et seq.

[6] See Opinion 1/91 of 14 December 1991, ECLI:EU:C:1991:490; and Opinion 1/09 of 8 March 2011, ECLI:EU:C:2011:123.

[7] See, among others, G Cohen-Jonathan, 'Le problème de l'adhésion des Communautés européennes à la Convention européeenne des droits de l'homme', in *Mélanges offerts à Pierre--Henri Teitgen* (Paris, Pedone, 1984) 82 et seq; JP Jacqué, 'The Convention and the European Communities' in RSt Macdonald et al (eds), *The European System for the Protection of Human Rights* (Dordrecht, Nijhof, 1993) 889 et seq.

[8] See the Memorandum on the Accession of the European Communities to the Convention for the Protection of Human Rights and Fundamental Freedoms COM (79) 200 final, 2 May 1979, in *Bulletin of the European Communities*, Supplement 2/79.

tection of their fundamental rights and to an increase in the legal certainty of the system.[9]

In this context, the legal and political significance of Opinion 2/13 is unquestionable. It is '*without a shadow of doubt one of the most important rulings of the Court of Justice*'[10] and few rulings of the CJEU have aroused so much immediate criticism as Opinion 2/13.

B. Scholars' Reactions

Apart from the blogosphere,[11] one of the most prestigious EU law reviews – the Common Market Law Review – published an editorial comment claiming '[t]he Opinion of the Court, (...), appears to reflect a somewhat formalistic and sometimes uncooperative attitude in defence of its own powers vis-à-vis the European Human Rights Court (ECtHR)'.[12] Steve Peers characterises the Court's Opinion as 'a clear and present danger to human rights protection'[13] and Sionaidh Douglas-Scott agrees with him, adding that 'Opinion 2/13 does not take rights seriously'.[14] Piet Eeckhout

[9] On the reasons for accession, see, among others, M Claes and Š Imamovic, 'National Courts in the New European Fundamental Rights Architecture' in V Kosta et al (eds), *The EU Accession to the ECHR* (Oxford, Hart Publishing, 2014) 164; E Steiner and I R'tescu, 'The Long Way to Strasbourg – The Impact of CJEU's Opinion on EU's Accession to the ECHR' (2015) *European Yearbook on Human Rights* 53-55.

[10] A Łazowski and RA Wessel, 'When Caveats Turn into Locks: Opinion 2/13 on Accession of the European Union to the ECHR' (2015) 16 (1) *German Law Journal* 179-212, at 210. Also available at www.utwente.nl/bms/pa/research/wessel/wessel108.pdf.

[11] The blogosphere reacted immediately. See S Peers, 'The CJEU and the EU's Accession to the ECHR: a Clear and Present Danger to Human Rights Protection', www.eulawanalysis.blogspot.pt/2014/12/the-cjeu-and-eus-accession-to-echr.html; M Wendel, 'Mehr Offenheit wagen! Eine Kritische Annäherung an das Gutachten des EuGH zum EMRK-Beitritt', *VerfBlog*, 2014/12/21, www.verfassungblog.de/mehr-offenheit-wagen-eine-kritische-annäherung-das-gutachten-des-eugh-zum-emrk-beitritt/; LFM Besselink, 'Acceding to the ECHR Notwithstanding the Court of Justice Opinion 2/13', *VerfBlog*, 2014/12/23, www.verfassungsblog.de/acceding-echr-notwithstanding-court-justice-opinion-213/.

[12] 'Editorial Comments: The EU's Accession to the ECHR – A "NO" from the ECJ!' (2015) 52 (1), *CML Rev* 1.

[13] S Peers, 'The EU's Accession to the ECHR: the Dream Becomes a Nightmare' (2015) 16 (1) *German Law Journal* 219 et seq.

[14] S Douglas-Scott, 'Opinion 2/13 on EU Accession to the ECHR: a Christmas Bombshell from the European Court of Justice', p. 5, *UK Constitutional Law Blog*, 2014/12/24 www.

claims that 'the CJEU's objections to the Accession Agreement do not persuade, and are not in accordance with the limited conditions imposed by Art 6(2) TEU and by Protocol 8'.[15] For the same author, 'Opinion 2/13 is based on a concept of autonomy which borders on autarky'.[16] Paul Gragl – who is an expert on the subject of the EU's accession to the ECHR – wrote that 'Opinion 2/13 leaves a bitter taste and a fair share of pessimism among all those who are interested in human rights and their effective protection and enforcement'.[17] Even Finisk Korenica – who recently wrote a PhD thesis on EU Accession to the ECHR, in which he often agrees with the Court – believes that 'the opinion confirms (...) the very allergic tendency of the Luxembourg Court to recognize external control from an international court. Such aversion, as shown in this Opinion, goes far beyond the likely situations that may emerge in practice'.[18]

In fact, few scholars have entirely supported Opinion 2/13.[19]

ukconstitutionallaw.org, available also at www.verfassungsblog.de/author/sionaidh-douglas--scott.

[15] P Eeckhout, 'Opinion 2/13 on EU Accession to the ECHR and Judicial Dialogue – Autonomy or Autarky?', *Jean Monnet Working Paper* 01/15, 39, available at www.jeanmonnetprogram.org/papers/15/documents/JMWP01Eeckhout.pdf.

[16] Ibid.

[17] P Gragl, 'The Reasonableness of Jealousy: Opinion 2/13 and EU Accession to the ECHR', 2015 *European Yearbook on Human Rights* 47.

[18] F Korenica, *The EU Accession to the ECHR – Between Luxembourg's Search for Autonomy and Strasbourg's Credibility on Human Rights Protection* (Heidelberg, Springer, 2015) 408.

[19] See D Halberstam, '"It's the Autonomy, Stupid!" A Modest Defense of Opinion 2/13 on EU Accession to the ECHR, and the Way Forward', *University of Michigan Law School, Public Law and Legal Theory Research Paper Series*, No 432, February 2015, available at papers.ssrn.com/sol3/papers.cfm?abstract_id=2567591; D Halberstam, 'A Constitutional Defense of CJEU Opinion 2/13 on EU Accession to the ECHR (and the Way Forward)', *VerfBlog*, 2015/3/12, www.verfassungsblog.de/a-constitutional-defense-of-cjeu-opinion-213-on-eu-accession-to--the-echr-and-the-way-forward/#.VgbS528g9dg; C Krenn, 'Autonomy and Effectiveness as a Common Concern: A Path to ECHR Accession After Opinion 2/13' (2015) 16 (1) *German Law Journal* 147 et seq.

C. Purpose of the Present Study

It is not our intention here to join our voice to this chorus of protests.[20] The main purpose of this study is neither to criticise the Court's views in general nor to seek solutions[21] in order to solve the legal and political problems that Opinion 2/13 has created either for the EU or for the ECHR. On the contrary, bearing in mind two statements made by the Court – the Union is not a State[22] but it has a '*constitutional structure*'[23] – we think that it makes perfect sense to assess whether the final decision of the Court is consistent with these two starting points. In other words, we intend to assess whether an adequate constitutional theory, which includes the multilevel protection of fundamental rights in Europe, as one factor of legitimacy, among others, could have led the Court to other conclusions.

Before continuing, we would like to stress that, independently of the political consequences of Opinion 2/13, which are somewhat catastrophic for the EU's accession to the ECHR – since, according to Article 218 (11) TFEU, the agreement may not enter into force unless it is amended or the Treaties are revised, which will be a somewhat difficult task –, the decision of the Court must be respected. That is to say, we cannot accept the idea

[20] See also J Nergelius, *The Accession of the EU to the European Convention on Human Rights – A Critical View of the Opinion of the Court of Justice*, SIEPS, 2015:3, 27 et seq, available at www.sieps.se;_E Dubout, 'Une question de confiance: nature juridique de l'Union européenne et adhésion à la Convention européenne des droits de l'homme' (2015) 51 *Cahiers de droit européen* 73 et seq.

[21] Some articles have already been published with this aim in mind. See I Pernice, 'L'adhésion de l'Union européenne à la Convention européenne des droits de l'homme est suspendue – Remarques à propos d'un avis surprenant de la Cour de Justice de l'Union européenne du 18 décembre 2014' (2015) 51 *Cahiers de droit européen* 47 et seq; JP Jacqué, 'Pride and/or Prejudice? Les lectures possibles de l'avis 2/13 de la Cour de Justice' (2015) 51 *Cahiers de droit européen* 19 et seq; T Lock, 'The Future of the EU Accession to the ECHR after Opinion 2/13: Is it Still Possible and is it Still Desirable?', *University of Edinburgh School of Law Research Paper* No 2015/18 (*Europa Working Paper* No 2015/02), available at ssrn.com.abstract=2616175.

[22] See para 156 of the Opinion – 'the EU is, under international law, precluded by its very nature from being considered a State.'.

[23] See para 165 of the Opinion – '(...) these characteristics include those relating to the constitutional structure of the EU.'.

that Opinion 2/13 does not prevent the accession.[24] In our view, it does. In a political entity such as the EU, which has to submit itself to the rule of law, the decisions of the courts must be respected regardless of whether we find their content pleasing or not.

In the following sections we will begin by providing a brief description of the multilevel protection of fundamental rights in Europe in the context of multilevel constitutionalism. Then we will go on to give a brief summary of the seven issues in the draft agreement that the Court's Opinion considers contrary to the Treaties. Finally, we will set out the reasons why we believe that the Court would have reached different conclusions if it had taken multilevel constitutionalism into account.

II. Multilevel Protection of Fundamental Rights in the Context of Multilevel Constitutionalism

A. Multilevel Protection of Fundamental Rights and EU Accession to the ECHR

Before analysing Opinion 2/13, we briefly need to clarify what is meant by the multilevel protection of fundamental rights and multilevel constitutionalism in this study, since legal theory uses these expressions in different senses.

The multilevel protection of fundamental rights seeks to express the idea that fundamental rights protection in the legal space of Europe is currently based on '*three layers of norms and institutions which overlap and intertwine to ensure an advanced degree of protection of fundamental rights*'.[25] In fact, fundamental rights are protected and enforced by national, EU and international (in this study only the ECHR will be taken into account) norms and institutions, each layer having a substantive catalogue of fun-

[24] Besselink proposed solving the accession with a 'Notwithstanding Protocol' that should read: '*The Union shall accede to the European Convention for the Protection of Human Rights and Fundamental Freedoms, notwithstanding Article 6(2) Treaty on European Union, Protocol (No 8) relating to Article 6(2) of the Treaty on European Union and Opinion 2/13 of the Court of Justice of 18 December 2014.*' In Besselink, 'Acceding to the ECHR Notwithstanding the Court of Justice Opinion 2/13' (n 11).

[25] F. Fabbrini, *Fundamental Rights in Europe – Challenges and Transformations in Comparative Perspective* (Oxford, Oxford University Press, 2014) 4.

damental rights and institutional remedies (with special emphasis on judicial review by courts).

The multilevel protection of fundamental rights is supposed to bring many benefits to individuals. First of all, it may 'prevent gaps occurring in legal protection that may arise from the increasing complexity of societal life. (...). Secondly, the plurality of jurisdictions brings with it many advantages. Additional courts can give innovation impetus to a deadlocked jurisprudence and break new ground.'[26]

The relationship between national (*maxime* constitutional), EU and ECHR law has never been simple and it is not expected to become easier with the accession.[27]

As the Advocate General Kokott pointed out in her opinion:

> [T]he proposed accession of the EU to the ECHR will create a special, possibly even unique, constellation in which an international, supranational organisation – the EU – submits to the control of another international organisation – the Council of Europe – as regards compliance with basic standards of fundamental rights. As a result, in areas governed by EU law, not only national courts and tribunals and the EU Courts, but also the European Court of Human Rights (ECtHR) will be called upon to oversee the observance of fundamental rights.[28]

The EU's accession to the ECHR would certainly have permitted a better multilevel protection of fundamental rights in Europe. As Adam Łazowski and Ramses A. Wessel claim, in examining the way the political power of the EU might affect the fundamental rights of human beings (EU citizens and foreigners), these rights '*will be better guaranteed when the acts of the EU institutions are subjected to the same scrutiny as the acts of Member*

[26] A Voßkuhle, 'Protection of Human Rights in the European Union. Multilevel Cooperation on Human Rights between the European Constitutional Courts' 3-4, see *Our Common Future,* Hannover/Essen, 2-6 November 2010, available at www.ourcommonfuture.de.

[27] In this direction: M Claes and Š Imamovic, 'National Courts in the New European Fundamental Rights Architecture' (n 9) 159.

[28] View of the Advocate General Kokott relating to Opinion 2/13, ECLI:EU:C:2014:2475, para 25.

States' organs. (...) the current state of constitutional development of the EU legal order not only allows, but perhaps even demands, external scrutiny'.[29]

B. Multilevel Constitutionalism

European multilevel protection of fundamental rights is anything but an element of the *constitutionalism beyond the state* theory. Some scholars have long tried to integrate the European Communities and their respective treaties into a broader constitutional theory that could not be solely anchored in the state. New concepts, like transnational constitutionalism,[30] constitutional pluralism,[31] multilevel constitutionalism,[32] or, more recently, global constitutionalism,[33] have emerged and have rapidly circulated in the post-Westphalian world, not without being criticised by those who

[29] Łazowski and Wessel, 'When Caveats Turn into Locks' (n 10) 212.

[30] See M Neves, *Transconstitucionalismo* (São Paulo, WMF Martins Fonseca, 2009) 83 et seq; AMG Martins, *A natureza jurídica da revisão do Tratado da União Europeia* (Lisboa, Lex, 2000) 303 et seq; idem, *Curso de Direito Constitucional da União Europeia* (Coimbra, Almedina, 2004) 119 et seq; idem, *A igualdade e a não discriminação dos nacionais de Estados terceiros legalmente residentes na União Europeia – Da origem na integração económica ao fundamento na dignidade do ser humano* (Coimbra, Almedina, 2010) 22-23; idem, *Manual de Direito da União Europeia* (2nd ed., Lisbon, Almedina, 2017) 37 et seq.

[31] For further reading on constitutional pluralism, see M Avbelj and J Komárek (eds), *Constitutional Pluralism in the European Union and Beyond* (Oxford, Hart Publishing, 2012); JHH Weiler, 'Prologue: Global and Pluralist Constitutionalism – Some Doubts', in G de Búrca and JHH Weiler (eds), *The Worlds of European Constitutionalism* (Cambridge, Cambridge University Press, 2012) 8 et seq; D Halberstam, 'Local, Global and Plural Constitutionalism: Europe Meets the World', in de Búrca and Weiler, *The Worlds of European Constitutionalism* 150 et seq; N Krisch, 'The Case for Pluralism in Postnational Law', in de Búrca and Weiler, *The Worlds of European Constitutionalism* 203 et seq; MP Maduro, *A Constituição Plural – Constitucionalismo e União Europeia* (Cascais, Principia, 2006) 15 et seq.

[32] On multilevel constitutionalism see, above all, I Pernice, 'Multilevel Constitutionalism and the Crisis of Democracy in Europe' (2015) 11 *European Constitutional Law Review* 541 et seq; idem, 'The Treaty of Lisbon: Multilevel Constitutionalism in Action' (2009) 15 (3) *The Columbia Journal of European Law* 349-407; idem, 'Multilevel Constitutionalism in the European Union' (2002) 27 (5), *EL Rev* 511-29; idem, 'Multilevel Constitutionalism and the Treaty of Amsterdam: European Constitution-Making Revisited?' (1999) 36 (4) *CML Rev* 707 et seq.

[33] On global constitutionalism see, above all, N Walker, 'Constitutionalism and Pluralism in Global Context', in Avbelj and Komárek (n 31) 17 et seq.

still remain faithful to state constitutionalism[34] and by those who draw special attention to the limits of these theories.[35]

Although this study is naturally not the appropriate place to elaborate on these issues, we would like to state that our own position is quite close to Ingolf Pernice's multilevel constitutionalism theory. However, in our opinion, the latter should also integrate the ECHR.

Delving further into multilevel constitutionalism theory, we would say that constitutionalism in Europe also includes the EU and, in our view, with regard to the field of fundamental rights, it is also and, at least partially, anchored in the Council of Europe, particularly in the ECHR. As Christian Tomuschat argues, the ECHR '*is not a treaty like another bilateral treaty that the EU concludes with other subjects of international law, especially third States (...) it is a parallel or "neighbor" constitution*'.[36][37]

The concept of multilevel constitutionalism was '*suggested by Ingolf Pernice in 1995 in order to describe and explain the specific constitutional nature of European integration*'.[38] However, Ingolf Pernice's original concept did not emphasise the protection of fundamental rights as it focused mainly on the existence of a European Constitution outside the state,[39] which '*arises from both national and European constitutional levels*',[40] forming two levels of

[34] See R Barents, 'The Fallacy of Multilevel Constitutionalism', in Avbelj and Komárek (n 31) 153 et seq.

[35] Compare R Harmsen, 'The (Geo-) Politics of the EU Accession to the ECHR: Democracy and Distrust in the Wider Europe', in Kosta et al (n 9) 199 et seq; L Lixinski, 'Taming the Fragmentation Monster through Human Rights? International Constitutionalism, "Pluralism Lite" and the Common Territory of the Two European Legal Orders', in Kosta et al (n 9) 219 et seq.

[36] C Tomuschat, 'Der Streit um die Auslegungshoheit: Die Autonomie der EU als Heiliger Gral' (2015) 42 (5-8) *Europäische Grundrechte-Zeitschrift* 136.

[37] In the original: 'ist kein Vertrag wie jeder sonstige bilaterale Vertrag, den die EU mit anderen Völkerrechtssubjekten, insbesondere dritten Staaten, abschliebt (...) "Parallel- oder Nebenverfassung"'.

[38] FC Mayer and M Wendel, 'Multilevel Constitutionalism and Constitutional Pluralism – Querelle Allemande or Querelle d'Allemand?' in Avbelj and Komárek (n 31) 127.

[39] Pernice, 'Multilevel Constitutionalism in the European Union' (n 32) 511-29; idem, 'Multilevel Constitutionalism and the Treaty of Amsterdam' (n 32) 707 et seq.

[40] Mayer and Wendel, 'Multilevel Constitutionalism and Constitutional Pluralism' (n 38) 130.

a unitary system – a composed constitutional system (*Verfassungsverbund*,[41] *constitution composée*[42]) – in terms of substance, function and institutions. Multilevel constitutionalism is a process that affects national and European law simultaneously. '*Both constitutional levels are in permanent interdependency*'.[43] The European constitutional process encompasses both national and primary EU law as '*two interdependent, interwoven, and reciprocally influential parts of one unit*'.[44]

In his most recent essays,[45] Ingolf Pernice apparently shifts the focus '*on the correlation of national and European law from the perspective of both states and citizens*'.[46] This means that EU integration has an impact both on the states and their citizens.[47] '*The EU is an instrument of the states and their peoples for meeting new challenges and for achieving certain common political goals*'.[48] Following this line of reasoning, Ingolf Pernice stresses that '*multilevel constitutionalism thus encourages conceptualizing the European Union from the perspective of its citizens*'.[49] This element strengthens '*the need to ensure an effective protection of the rights of the individuals*',[50] which, according to Giancito della Cananea, suggests a very important shift of paradigm.[51]

Nevertheless, as far as we can understand, Ingolf Pernice's definition of multilevel constitutionalism only comprises two layers of normativity and institutions – national law (*rectius*, constitutional law) and EU law.

[41] I Pernice, 'Europäisches und nationales Verfassungsrecht', in *Veröffentlichungen der Vereinigung der Deutscher Staatsrechtslehrer* 60/2000 (Berlin, Walter de Gruyter, 2001) 163 et seq.

[42] I Pernice and FC Mayer, 'De la Constitution composée de l'Europe' (2000) 36 (4) *Revue Trimestrielle de Droit Européen* 623-648.

[43] Pernice, 'The Treaty of Lisbon: Multilevel Constitutionalism in Action' (n 32) 373.

[44] Ibid. 374.

[45] See Pernice, 'Multilevel Constitutionalism and the Crisis of Democracy in Europe' (n 32) 544 et seq.

[46] Pernice, 'The Treaty of Lisbon: Multilevel Constitutionalism in Action' (n 32) 372.

[47] In our PhD thesis, more than fifteen years ago, we characterised the EU as a union of states and people. See Martins, *A natureza jurídica da revisão do Tratado da União Europeia* (n 30) 303 et seq.

[48] Pernice, 'The Treaty of Lisbon: Multilevel Constitutionalism in Action' (n 32) 376.

[49] Ibid.

[50] G della Cananea, 'Is European Constitutionalism Really "Multilevel"?' (2010) 70 (2), *Zeitschrift für ausländisches öffentliches Recht und Völkerrecht* 300.

[51] Ibid.

In our opinion, taking into account the role that individuals currently play in the legitimation of political power, the multilevel protection and enforcement of fundamental rights should be envisaged as anything but a central element of multilevel constitutional theory. Once this premise is accepted, it will be easier to accept that ECHR law is without doubt a relevant source of fundamental rights in Europe. Consequently, multilevel constitutionalism should also integrate that level of normativity and institutional tools.

In other words, in the fundamental rights arena, ECHR law and ECHR institutions – that is to say a third level – would cooperate, collaborate, intervene in and interact with the European constitutional process. Exactly how they would intervene and interact is difficult to say as there is no historical experience of this.[52]

Continuing with the attempt to define multilevel constitutionalism, according to Ingolf Pernice, it includes a vertical relationship between the EU and its Member States and a horizontal cooperation and mutual recognition between the Member States.[53] As it does not presuppose any hierarchical relationship between the national and European levels of law,[54] this relationship is pluralistic and cooperative.[55]

In our opinion, this pluralistic and cooperative relationship should be extended to ECHR law. This means, in terms of fundamental rights, that multilevel constitutionalism presupposes a cooperative and mutual recognition not only within two layers but within three layers of protection and enforcement – national law, EU law and ECHR law.

Considering the fact that the functioning of the system is not based on a hierarchical relationship, but depends on mutual trust between the institutions of each layer, with special emphasis on the courts, every highest court is the guardian of fundamental rights within the layer to which it belongs. As a consequence, multilevel constitutionalism in Europe presupposes the existence of several guardians of fundamental rights that could have different views of the same problem and all aspire to pronounce the last word, which could lead to divergent decisions. So far

[52] Wendel, 'Mehr Offenheit wagen!' (n 11).

[53] Pernice, 'The Treaty of Lisbon: Multilevel Constitutionalism in Action' (n 32) 379-83.

[54] Ibid 383.

[55] Ibid.

no definitive solution has been proposed for this problem, but one of the means to prevent the proliferation of conflicts is judicial dialogue, although this is not the appropriate place to expand upon this issue.[56]

Much more could be said about the protection and enforcement of fundamental rights in the context of multilevel constitutionalism. However, discussion of this issue lies outside the scope of the present study. Now we must turn to Opinion 2/13 itself, starting with a brief summary.

III. Summary of CJEU Opinion 2/13

First of all, we would like to point out that the task of the Court in this case was relatively clear: it had to determine whether the draft agreement was in accordance with Article 6(2) TEU and Protocol 8, which previewed the specific conditions of EU accession to the ECHR.[57]

Secondly, however, it is important to draw attention to the fact that Article 6(2) TEU does not only state that the EU has the power to accede to the ECHR; it also imposes EU accession as a requirement. To put it in other terms, the EU has no choice whether to accede or not.[58] In our opinion, the Court should have paid greater consideration to this duty.

After a rather brief consideration of the issues, the CJEU concluded that:

> [I]t must be held that the agreement envisaged is not compatible with Article 6(2) TEU or with Protocol No 8 EU in that:

[56] For further developments see M Cartabia, 'Fundamental Rights and the Relationship among the Court of Justice, the National Supreme Courts and the Strasbourg Court' in A Tizzano et al (eds), *50ème Anniversaire de l'arrêt Van Gend en Loos* 155 et seq; AMG Martins and MP Roque, 'Judicial Dialogue in a Multilevel Constitutional Network – the Role of the Portuguese Constitutional Court' in M Andenas and D Fairgrieve (eds), *Courts and Comparative Law* (Oxford, Oxford University Press, 2015) 300-28.

[57] These conditions were: i) the accession shall not affect the Union's competences as defined in the Treaties; ii) the accession shall not affect the powers of the institutions; iii) the accession agreement shall make provision for preserving the special characteristics of the Union and Union Law.

[58] For an exposition of the reasons why the Union should accede to the ECHR, *cf.* 'Editorial Comments' (n 12) 4.

> it is liable adversely to affect the specific characteristics and the autonomy of EU law in so far it does not ensure coordination between Article 53 of the ECHR and Article 53 of the Charter, does not avert the risk that the principle of Member States' mutual trust under EU law may be undermined, and makes no provision in respect of the relationship between the mechanism established by Protocol No 16 and the preliminary ruling procedure provided for in Article 267 TFEU;
>
> it is liable to affect Article 344 TFEU in so far as it does not preclude the possibility of disputes between Member States or between Member States and the EU concerning the application of the ECHR within the scope ratione materiae of EU law being brought before the ECtHR;
>
> it does not lay down arrangements for the operation of the co-respondent mechanism and the procedure for the prior involvement of the Court of Justice that enable the specific characteristics of the EU and EU law to be preserved; and
>
> it fails to have regard to the specific characteristics of EU law with regard to the judicial review of acts, actions or omissions on the part of the EU in CFSP matters in that it entrusts the judicial review of some of those acts, actions or omissions exclusively to a non-EU body.[59]

By contrast, the view of Advocate General Kokott seems to be much more constructive, concluding that:

> [T]he draft revised agreement on the accession of the European Union to the European Convention for the Protection of Human Rights and Fundamental Freedoms presented in Strasbourg on 10 June 2013 is compatible with the Treaties, provided it is ensured, in such a way as to be binding under international law, that:
>
> having regard to the possibility that they may request to participate in proceedings as co-respondents pursuant to Article 3(5) of the draft agreement, the European Union and its Member States are systematically and without exception informed of all applications pending before the ECtHR, in so far and as soon as these have been served on the relevant respondent;

[59] Opinion 2/13, para 258.

requests by the European Union and its Member States pursuant to Article 3(5) of the draft agreement for leave to become co-respondents are not subjected to any form of plausibility assessment by the ECtHR;

the prior involvement of the Court of Justice of the European Union pursuant to Article 3(6) of the draft agreement extends to all legal issues relating to the interpretation, in conformity with the ECHR, of EU primary law and EU secondary law;

the conduct of a prior involvement procedure pursuant to Article 3(6) of the draft agreement may be dispensed with only when it is obvious that the Court of Justice of the European Union has already dealt with the specific legal issue raised by the application pending before the ECtHR;

the principle of joint responsibility of respondent and co-respondent under Article 3(7) of the draft agreement does not affect any reservations made by contracting parties within the meaning of Article 57 ECHR; and

the ECtHR may not otherwise, under any circumstances, derogate from the principle, as laid down in Article 3(7) of the draft agreement, of the joint responsibility of respondent and co-respondent for violations of the ECHR found by the ECtHR.[60]

In this study we will concentrate on analysing the Court's Opinion. The view of Advocate General Kokott will also be referred to where appropriate.[61]

[60] View of Advocate General in Opinion 2/13, para 280.

[61] For an overview of the position of the Advocate General and Opinion 2/13 of the CJEU, see, among many others, Nergelius (n 20) 17 et seq; M Berger and C Rauchegger, 'Opinion 2/13: Multiple Obstacles to the Accession of the EU to the ECHR' (2015) *European Yearbook on Human Rights* 61-73; 'Editorial Comments' (n 12) 7-11; Peers, 'The EU's Accession to the ECHR: the Dream Becomes a Nightmare' (n 13) 215-17; J Odermatt, 'Working Paper: A Giant Step Backwards? *Opinion 2/13* on the EU's Accession to the European Convention on Human Rights' 5-10, available at www.fp7-frame.eu/wp-content/materiale/w-papers/WP150-Odermatt.pdf; E Spaventa, 'A Very Fearful Court? The Protection of Human Rights in the European Union after Opinion 2/13' 12-21, available at www.corteappello.milano.it/allegato_corsi.aspx?File_id_allegato=1862; P Gragl, 'The Reasonableness of Jealousy' (n 17) 31-36; S Douglas-Scott, 'Opinion 2/13 on EU Accession to the ECHR' (n 14).

A closer look at the Court's Opinion permits us to identify three groups of objections. The first group concerns the possibility that EU accession to the ECHR may generally violate the integrity and autonomy of EU law; the second one concerns the institutional innovations, and the last one concerns the jurisdiction of the CJEU over Common Foreign and Security Policy (CFSP).

To be honest, we have to admit that throughout the negotiations[62] over the draft agreement[63], scholarship[64] and some European institu-

[62] On the negotiations over the draft agreement see Korenica, *The EU Accession to the ECHR* (n 18) 106 et seq; A Drzemczewski, 'EU Accession to the ECHR: The Negotiation Process', in Kosta et al (n 9) 17 et seq; O De Schutter, 'L'adhésion de l'Union européenne à la Convention européenne des droits de l'homme: feuille de route de la négotiation' (2010) 21 (83) *Revue trimestrielle des droits de l'homme* 540 et seq; SS Caballero, 'Crónica de una adhesión anunciada: algunas notas sobre la negociación de la adhesión de la Unión Europea al Convénio Europeo de Derechos Humanos' (2011) 15 (38) *Revista de Derecho Comunitario Europeo* 99-128.

[63] On the draft agreement itself see Korenica (n 18) 108 et seq; P Gragl, 'A Giant Leap for European Union Human Rights? The Final Agreement on the European Union's Accession to the European Convention on Human Rights', available at www.academia.edu (2014/12/29) 1 et seq; T Lock, 'Walking on a Tightrope' (n 5) 1025 et seq.

[64] See, among many others, P Gragl, 'A Giant Leap for European Union Human Rights?' (n 63) 3 et seq; P Craig, 'EU Accession to the ECHR' (n 5) 1115 et seq; JMP de Nanclares, 'The Accession of the European Union to the ECHR: More than Just a Legal Issue', *Working Papers on European Law and Regional Integration* No 15/2013, 1 et seq; Terhechte, 'Autonomie und Kohärenz' in J Iliopoulos-Strangas et al (n 5) 37 et seq; AMG Martins, 'A Portuguese Perspective of the Accession to the European Union to the European Convention of Human Rights' in J Iliopoulos-Strangas et al (n 5) 205 et seq; MJR de Mesquita, 'Remarques sur la "valeur ajoutée" de l'adhésion de l'Union européenne à la Convention européenne de Droits de l'Homme pour la protection des droits fondamentaux des particuliers en Europe' in J Iliopoulos-Strangas et al (n 5) 277 et seq; W Obwexer, 'Der Beitritt der EU zur EMRK: Rechtsgrundlage, Rechtsfragen und Rechtsfolgen' (2012) 47 (2) *Europarecht* 119 et seq;_P Gragl, *The Accession of the European Union to the European Convention on Human Rights* (n 5) *maxime,* 87 et seq;_JP Jacqué, 'The Accession of the European Union to the European Convention on Human Rights and Fundamental Freedoms' 2011 48 (4) *CML Rev* 1012 et seq; B Bertrand, 'Cohérence normative et contentieux – à propos de l'adhésion de l'Union européenne à la Convention européenne des droits de l'Homme' (2012) 128 (1) *Revue du Droit Public* 190 et seq; T Lock, 'Walking on a Tightrope' (n 5) 1025 et seq; N O'Meara, 'A More Secure Europe of Rights? The European Court of Human Rights, the Court of Justice of the European Union and EU Accession to the ECHR' (2011) *German Law Journal* 1818 et seq; De Schutter, 'L'adhésion de l'Union européenne à la Convention européenne des droits de l'homme' (n 62) 547 et seq; C Ladenburger, 'Vers l'adhésion de l'Union européenne à la Convention

tions[65] had frequently pointed out several difficulties and potential incompatibilities between that draft agreement and EU primary law. In this study we will not return to this subject.[66] We will concentrate on the objections of the CJEU.

A. Violation of the integrity and autonomy of EU Law

The first concern of the CJEU relates to Article 53 ECHR, which gives authorisation for Member States to have higher rights than the Charter on Fundamental Rights of the EU (CFREU), once the law has been fully harmonised by the EU. According to the Court, Article 53 ECHR should be coordinated with Article 53 of the Charter, as interpreted by the Court in *Melloni*.[67] This means that where the EU legal act calls for national implementing measures, national authorities and courts remain free to apply national standards of protection of fundamental rights, provided that the level of protection provided by the Charter, as interpreted by the Court, and the primacy, unity and effectiveness of EU law are not thereby compromised. The Court considered that EU Member States could use

européenne des droits de l'homme' (2011) 47 (1) *Revue trimestrielle de droit européen* 21 et seq; T Lock, 'EU Accession to the ECHR: Implications for Judicial Review in Strasbourg' (2010) *EL Rev* 777 et seq.

[65] Cf. *Discussion document of the Court of Justice of the European Union on certain aspects of the accession of the European Union to the European Convention for the Protection of Human Rights and Fundamental Freedoms* of 5 May 2010, available at curia.europa.eu.jcms/jcms/P_64268 and *Joint communication from Presidents Costa and Skouris* of 24 January 2011, available at www.echr.coe.int/Documents/UE_Communication_Costa_Skouris_ENG.pdf. See also the European Parliament Resolution of 19 May 2010 on the institutional aspects of the accession of the European Union to the European Convention for the Protection of Human Rights and Fundamental Freedoms (OJEU C 2011/C 161 E/12). On the position of the European Parliament see R Passos, 'The Protection of Fundamental Rights in Europe Before and After the Accession of the European Convention on Human Rights: A View from the European Parliament' in J Iliopoulos-Strangas et al (n 5) 125 et seq.

[66] We have already written on this subject: AMG Martins, 'O Parecer nº 2/13 do Tribunal de Justiça relativo à compatibilidade do projeto de acordo de adesão da União Europeia à Convenção Europeia dos Direitos do Homem', in Marcelo Rebelo de Sousa/Eduardo Vera--Cruz Pinto (coordenadores), *Liber Amicorum Fausto de Quadros*, vol. I, Coimbra, Almedina, 2016, p. 97-129.

[67] C-399/11 *Melloni* Judgment of 26 February 2013, ECLI:EU:C:2013:107, para 60.

Article 53 ECHR to adopt higher standards of fundamental rights in matters covered by harmonised Union law. For the Court, it was necessary to ensure coordination between Article 53 CFREU and Article 53 ECHR, as long as the autonomy of EU law was not affected.[68]

The second objection of the Court concerns the principle of 'mutual trust' between EU Member States in the Area of Freedom, Security and Justice (AFSJ), which obliges the Member States to presume that all other Member States are in compliance with EU law and particularly with the fundamental rights recognised by EU law, except in exceptional circumstances, as interpreted by the CJEU.[69] EU accession to the ECHR, according to the Court, would require a Member State to check that another Member State had observed fundamental rights, which would undermine the autonomy of EU law.[70]

The Court's third concern relates to Protocol 16, which was opened to signature in 2013 and has not yet entered into force. This protocol gives the highest national courts of High Contracting Parties the power to submit queries to the ECtHR concerning interpretation of the ECHR. The CJEU was particularly concerned about the impact that this procedure might have on the autonomy and effectiveness of the preliminary ruling procedure.[71]

The fourth concern of the CJEU was that Article 33 ECHR allows for inter-state disputes between ECHR High Contracting Parties regarding alleged breaches of the Convention. The Court found that this possibility violated Article 344 TFUE, which prohibits the EU Member States to submit a dispute concerning the interpretation or application of the Treaties to any method of settlement other than those provided for in the EU Treaties. This possibility could undermine the autonomy of EU law. Only the express exclusion of the possibility of EU Member States bringing disputes connected with EU Law before the ECtHR would be compatible with Article 344 TFUE.[72]

[68] See Opinion 2/13, paras 187-89.

[69] See CJEU, Joined cases C-411/10 and C-493/10 *N.S. and M.E.* Judgment of 21 December 2011, ECLI:EU:C:2011:865, paras 78-80.

[70] See Opinion 2/13, paras 190-95.

[71] See Opinion 2/13, paras 196-200.

[72] See Opinion 2/13, paras 201-14.

B. Institutional Innovations

Concerning institutional innovations, the Court was particularly concerned about the co-respondent mechanism that created a new procedure whereby the EU and a Member State could be parties to an ECtHR case. The Court found this procedure incompatible with EU law for several reasons. First, it would give the ECtHR the power to interpret EU law when assessing the admissibility of requests to apply this procedure, and consequently, the ECtHR would be able to assess rules of EU law concerning the division of powers between the EU and the Member States; secondly, a ruling by the ECtHR on the joint responsibility of the EU and its Member States could impinge on Member State reservations to the Convention, and the ECtHR should not have the power to allocate responsibility for breach of the ECHR between EU and Member States, since only the CJEU can rule on EU law.[73]

The other institutional innovation that disturbed the Court was the prior involvement procedure that was included in the draft agreement to take into account the concerns of the Presidents of both Courts in their Joint Communication. The Court found the form of this procedure would violate EU law if it did not reserve to the EU the power to rule on whether the CJEU had already dealt with an issue or not. Alternatively, the ECtHR would be called on to decide whether the CJEU had already ruled on the same question of law. In addition, this procedure would permit the ECtHR to rule on the interpretation of the EU Treaties and the case law of the CJEU[74].

C. CJEU Jurisdiction over Common Foreign and Security Policy

The last point of the draft agreement that the Court considered incompatible with EU primary law – and this was perhaps the most complex issue faced by the Court – was the potential jurisdiction of the ECtHR over some CFSP acts.

As a matter of fact, the Court of Justice does not have jurisdiction in CFSP matters except in certain narrow and strictly-defined cases provided for in Article 275 TFEU. Otherwise, the draft agreement would have

[73] See Opinion 2/13, paras 215-35.

[74] See Opinion 2/13, paras 236-48.

created a situation whereby the ECtHR would have jurisdiction over certain acts that are not reviewable by the CJEU.

According to the Court, this possibility would violate EU law as a non--EU court could not be given the power of judicial review over EU acts, even though the CJEU had no jurisdiction itself regarding the majority of CFSP issues.[75]

After this brief overview, we will now look at Opinion 2/13 from the perspective of multilevel constitutionalism.

IV. Opinion 2/13 from the perspective of multilevel constitutionalism

A. General Framework

Recalling that, in its Opinion, the Court drew attention to the constitutional structure of the EU,[76] accepting the fact that the EU has a new kind of legal order, the nature of which is peculiar to the EU, its own constitutional framework and founding principles, a particularly sophisticated institutional structure and a full set of legal rules to ensure its operation, has consequences as regards the procedure for and conditions of accession to the ECHR[77] and also recalling the fact that some scholars have even suggested that the Court's reasoning might be justified by an attempt to defend the constitutional nature of the Union[78], we will begin by clarifying what, in our opinion, the consequences of multilevel cons-

[75] See Opinion 2/13, paras 249-57.

[76] See para 157 of the Opinion – 'As the Court of Justice has repeatedly held, the founding treaties of the EU, unlike ordinary international treaties, established a new legal order, possessing its own institutions, for the benefit of which the Member States thereof have limited their sovereign rights, in ever wider fields, and the subjects of which comprise not only those States but also their nationals' (see, in particular, the judgments in C-26/62 van Gend&Loos EU:C:1963:1, 12, C-6/64 Costa EU:C:1964:66, 593 and Opinion 1/09 EU:C:2011:123 para 65).

[77] Para 158 of the Opinion.

[78] E Dubout, 'Une question de confiance: nature juridique de l'Union européenne et adhésion à la Convention européenne des droits de l'homme' 75; H Labayle and F Sudre, 'L'avis 2/13 de la Cour de Justice sur l'adhésion de l'Union européenne à la Convention des droits de l'homme: pavane pour une adhésion défunte?' (2015) 31 (1) *Revue française de droit administratif* 4-9, 15.

titutionalism are within the scope of the protection and enforcement of fundamental rights.

Only then will we be able to assess, firstly, whether the CJEU had actually any kind of constitutionalism in mind and, secondly, whether it took into consideration multilevel constitutionalism theory.

In our point of view – which does not intend to be indisputable[79] – the protection and enforcement of the fundamental rights of individuals should currently be the *noyau dur* of every constitution. Even within the state, the political decisions of a parliamentary majority should respect the fundamental rights. That means the fundamental rights could be seen as trumps against the majority.[80] Taking this into account, the EU and the ECHR can only be understood and accepted by individuals, as long as they add something to the effectiveness of the protection of fundamental rights, and, from there, draw legitimacy. As a matter of fact, the states are not always able and prepared to respect fundamental rights, to preserve peace and to face the common challenges posed by globalisation. If the multilevel constitutional system, both, the EU and the ECHR, would have the effect of placing less and not more importance on fundamental rights, it would be very hard to convince individuals to adhere to and to legitimate a constitutional network that undermined their rights.[81] We cannot accept that these new instruments have been established with the opposite effect, i.e., a lower standard of protection. Therefore, in our opinion, a multilevel constitutional system should achieve a higher standard of protection and enforcement of fundamental rights than that achieved by any single constitutional layer on its own.

As a result, each constitutional layer should respect the fundamental rights protected and enforced by other constitutional layers. That is to say, EU law and the CJEU should respect the fundamental rights protected and enforced by national constitutional layers and ECHR law, and vice

[79] Contra, see among many others, R Medeiros, *A Constituição Portuguesa num Contexto Global* (Lisbon, UCP, 2015) 91 et seq.

[80] R Dworkin, *Taking Rights Seriously* (London, Duckworth, 1977) xi.

[81] In a similar direction, but without mentioning multilevel constitutionalism, see C Franzius, 'Strategien der Grundrechtsoptimierung in Europa' (2015) 42 (5-8) *Europäische Grundrechte Zeitschrift* 152.

versa. This is actually the meaning of Article 53 CFREU and of Article 53 ECHR. We will return to this argument later.

In conclusion, since the protection of fundamental rights in Europe is currently based on national law, EU law and (to a lesser extent) ECHR law, a comprehensive multilevel constitutional theory should be able to guarantee a better enforcement and effectiveness of fundamental rights and a higher standard of fundamental rights' protection.[82]

It would be possible to achieve this goal in multilevel constitutionalism if national law, EU law and ECHR law were all founded on common values and principles. In fact, in Europe the values of respect for human dignity, freedom, democracy, equality, the rule of law and respect for human rights are shared by the EU and its Member States, as can be clearly seen in Article 2 TEU[83], and also by the Council of Europe, as is clear in the following excerpt from the preamble to the ECHR:

> [R]*eaffirming their profound belief in those fundamental freedoms which are the foundation of justice and peace in the world and are best maintained on the one hand by an effective political democracy and on the other by a common understanding and observance of the human rights upon which they depend*; (...) *the governments of European countries which are like-minded and have a common heritage of political traditions, ideals, freedom and the rule of law (...).*

That is to say, national law, EU law and ECHR law are all based on similar values, which favours a mutual interpenetration, interdependence, interaction and reciprocal influence between the three bodies of law and a progressive convergence of fundamental rights. Otherwise, conflicts would arise so often that they would become the norm rather than the exception and they would destroy the constitutional order in a relatively

82 In the same vein: H Labayle and F Sudre, 'L'avis 2/13 de la Cour de Justice sur l'adhésion de l'Union européenne à la Convention des droits de l'homme: pavane pour une adhesion défunte?' (n 78) 20.

83 Article 2 TEU reads: 'The Union is founded on the values of respect for human dignity, freedom, democracy, equality, the rule of law and respect for human rights, including the rights of persons belonging to minorities. These values are common to the Member States in a society in which pluralism, non-discrimination, tolerance, justice, solidarity and equality between women and men prevail.'.

short time. This does not mean that there are no punctual divergences, but such divergences are not the rule.

Actually, the mutual interpenetration, interdependence, interaction and reciprocal influence between the different levels of normativity and judiciary should be envisaged as another characteristic of multilevel constitutionalism in the field of fundamental rights. This means that the participation either of a state or the EU in the international human rights law system necessarily implies an interference of this system in the domestic affairs of that state and a fortiori in the affairs of the EU.[84]

To put it in other words, if the EU accedes to the ECHR, no-one can seriously expect that EU law will remain untouched as long as the treaties on human rights continue to aim at filling the gaps in the level of protection provided by individual states. '*There is no doubt that being bound by the ECHR under international law will impose restrictions on the exercise of its existing competences*'.[85] The accession of the EU to the ECHR, one consequence of which would be the EU's submission to the jurisdiction of the ECtHR, would naturally affect the autonomy of the EU legal order, as it affects the autonomy of the domestic legal order of every single Member State.[86]

In addition, the accession to a human rights treaty by a state always implies interference in the domestic affairs of that state. That is to say, the international law principle of non-interference in internal affairs does not apply to human rights matters. Otherwise, the states could prevent the enforcement of international laws on human rights.[87] If the EU accedes to the ECHR, it will be subject to the same rules as individual states.

[84] According to Johan Callewaert, 'Beim Beitritt der EU geht es also darum, dass auch die EU es akzepetiert, sich von Zeit zu Zeit etwas "stören" bzw. Ihre Handlungen und Konzepte hinterfragen lassen' (EU accession to the ECHR means that from time to time the EU should let the ECtHR 'trouble' her, that is to say their actions and concepts may be questioned by the ECtHR): J Callewaert 'Der Beitritt der EU zur EMRK: Eine Schicksalsfrage für den europäischen Grundrechtsschutz' (2014) 8 Strafverteidiger 505.

[85] View of the Advocate General Kokott relating to Opinion 2/13, EU:C:2014, para 40.

[86] Christoph Krenn considers that it is not only the EU which is concerned about this but domestic systems are also autonomous and care about their autonomy: see C Krenn, 'Autonomy and Effectiveness as a Common Concern: A Path to ECHR Accession After Opinion 2/13' 162.

[87] See O De Schutter, *International Human Rights Law: Cases, Materials, Commentary*, 2nd edn (Cambridge, Cambridge University Press, 2015) 113 et seq.

In the case of the European Union, this interference would not be so deep as in other cases because, according to the case law of the CJEU, fundamental rights, as guaranteed by the ECHR (and as they result from the constitutional traditions common to the Member States) 'shall constitute general principles of the Union's law' (Article 6(3) TEU).[88]

As a consequence, the EU would currently have to apply (albeit only substantially) the fundamental rights contained in the ECHR and in its protocols and, in addition, under the terms of Article 52 (3) CFREU, in so far as the Charter contains rights guaranteed by the ECHR, the meaning and scope of those rights would be the same as those laid down by the ECHR, admitting, however, that Union law provides more extensive protection.

In other words, the material scope of the draft agreement is much more restrictive – the EU would accede solely to the ECHR, the Protocol, and Protocol No 6, that is to say, to the two protocols to which all Member States are already parties. Consequently, the impact of the ECHR on the EU would be less significant than if the EU had never established any relationship with the ECHR.

Furthermore, the *jus cogens*[89] nature of some human rights provisions, such as the prohibition of torture[90] (Article 3 ECHR) or the prohibition of slavery (Article 4 [1] ECHR), bind either the states or the EU. This means

[88] Before the Treaty of Lisbon, the CJEU had already built up a firm and consistent case law in this direction. See, among many others, CJEU, C-4/73 *Nold* judgment of 14 May 1974 ECLI:EU:C:1974:51; C-36/75 *Rutili* judgment of 28 October 1975 ECLI:EU:C:1975:137; C-44/79 *Hauer* judgment of 13 December 1979 ECLI:EU:C:1979:290; C-222/84 *Johnston* judgment of 15 June 1986 ECLI:EU:C:1986:206; C-299/95 *Kremzow* judgment of 29 May 1997 ECLI:EU:C:1997:254.

[89] According to Article 53 of the Vienna Convention on the Law of Treaties (1969) and Article 53 of the Vienna Convention on the Law of Treaties between States and International Organizations or between International Organizations (1986), a jus cogens norm is a peremptory norm of general international law accepted and recognised by the international community of States as a whole as a norm from which no derogation is permitted and which can be modified only by a subsequent norm of general international law having the same character.

[90] De Schutter, *International Human Rights Law* (n 85) 299 et seq.

that, independently of the EU's accession to the ECHR, the EU is already bound by these provisions.[91]

Finally, the real binding effect of international human rights law depends on the submission of states, in the fields regulated by the human rights treaties, to an international jurisdiction, with each state relinquishing the monopoly of its own jurisdiction.[92] In other words, if this applies to individual states, it cannot be different in the case of the EU.

Nevertheless, multilevel constitutionalism does not imply either a hierarchy of legal orders that participate therein or a hierarchy of judiciaries. Consequently, there are several courts that control the enforcement of fundamental rights and none of them can be considered as having the last word. Andreas Voßkuhle has introduced a legal concept, inspired by the multilevel constitutionalism theory, in order to explain this reality. This is the concept of '*europäische Verfassungsgerichtverbund*'[93] ('multilevel cooperation of the European constitutional courts'), which 'refers to the cooperative, non-hierarchical handling of multilevel constitutional issues by several constitutional courts, i.e., a composite multilevel structure of constitutional jurisdictions which entertain complementary and comparative relationships'.[94]

Taking this situation into account, the cooperative judicial dialogue between the highest national courts (especially the constitutional courts), the CJEU and the ECtHR assumes a huge importance in respect of the prevention of conflicts between the different highest courts.[95] In fact, the

[91] It is debatable whether a regional *jus cogens* does actually exist. This is not the right place to discuss this issue.

[92] For further developments, see AMG Martins and MP Roque, 'Chapter 18 – Universality and Binding Effect of Human Rights from a Portuguese Perspective' in R Arnold (ed), *The Universalism of Human Rights*, Jus Gentium: Comparative Perspectives on Law and Justice 16, (Dordrecht, Springer, 2013) 310 et seq.

[93] This expression has recently been used by the *Bundesverfassungsgericht* in a Decision of the Second Senate of 21 June 2016 (para. 140), known as the Decision OMT, para. 140).

[94] A Voßkuhle, 'Multilevel Cooperation of the European Constitutional Courts – *Der Europäische Verfassungsgerichtsverbund*', (2010) 6 (1) *European Constitutional Law Review* 184.

[95] Stressing the role of judicial dialogue in the fundamental rights context, cf. C Grabenwarter, 'The Cooperation of Constitutional Courts in Europe – Current Situation and Perspectives', in *XVIe Congrès de la Conférence des Cours Constitutionnelles européennes – La coopération entre les Cours Constitutionnelles en Europe – Situation actuelle et perspectives*, vol. I, (Vienna, Verlag

principle of cooperative judicial dialogue between constitutional courts, the CJEU and the ECtHR has already been applied for a long time[96] and the CJEU has always contributed to and benefited from this dialogue. However, this dialogue will only be fruitful if the Courts trust each other. That is to say, cooperative judicial dialogue implies a mutual judicial trust between the highest courts. Moreover, multilevel constitutionalism presupposes a sincere cooperation between all the players, and not only between the EU and its Member States.

Having said this, it needs to be emphasised that the obligations of the EU Member States founded on EU law will not change as a result of EU accession to the ECHR. In other words, EU Member States – as Contracting Parties of the ECHR – will not be authorised by EU accession to violate EU law. As a consequence, the EU Member States' obligations towards the EU will remain unaffected, unless EU law rules otherwise.

To conclude, in the field of the protection and enforcement of fundamental rights, in our view, multilevel constitutionalism implies respect for the following principles:

a) the principle of a higher protection of fundamental rights;
b) the principle of common values between the Member States, the EU and the Council of Europe and its Member States;
c) the principle of cooperative judicial dialogue;
d) the principle of sincere cooperation and mutual trust.

In the next few sections, we will examine Opinion 2/13 on the basis of these principles.

Österreich, 2014) 35 et seq; A Popov, 'L'avis 2/13 de la CJUE complique l'adhésion de l'Union européenne à la CEDH' (2015) *Revue des Droits de l'Homme* 8, available at http://revdh.revues.org/1065; A Voßkuhle, 'Multilevel Cooperation of the European Constitutional Courts – *Der Europäische Verfassungsgerichtsverbund*', (2010) 6 (1) *European Constitutional Law Review* 175 et seq; M Cartabia, 'Europe and Rights: Taking Dialogue Seriously' (2009) 5 (1) *European Constitutional Law Review* 21 et seq.

[96] On judicial dialogue see our study: Martins and Roque, 'Judicial Dialogue in a Multilevel Constitutional Network' (n 56) 300-328.

1. Principle of a Higher Protection of Fundamental Rights

Starting with the principle of a higher protection of fundamental rights, in our view, the Court does not follow this constitutional perspective in Opinion 2/13 and this is quite clear in several parts of the Opinion. The Court seems to be stuck in a more traditional constitutional view that does not establish sufficient, if any, bridges between the three levels of norms and institutions that interact with each other in the field of fundamental rights in Europe.

In other words, the Court seems to adhere to an 'exclusivist' constitutionalism that envisages the EU as a rather formal entity which is almost isolated in the legal world and not a multilevel constitutionalism that views the EU legal order as part of a wider and multi-layered constitutional order.

As Henri Labayle and Frédéric Sudre have argued, '*since the hierarchical path is closed, the Court of Justice reasons in terms of exclusivity*'.[97] In fact, Opinion 2/13 is anchored in a rather formalistic, restrictive and exclusivist constitutional vision of the EU, which will be hardly acceptable to other players such as the ECtHR and the constitutional courts, which seem to be the privileged interlocutors of the CJEU.

In our opinion, this perspective explains why the Court is so concerned with its own interpretation of the CFREU, the primacy and autonomy of EU law and apparently less engaged in the protection and enforcement of fundamental rights.[98] To quote Piet Eeckhout, 'the CJEU hardly mentions that objective of strengthening the fundamental rights protection of real human beings'.[99]

We are not arguing that the Court does not care about the enforcement of fundamental rights, as some have claimed since the beginning of

[97] '*La voie hiérarchique étant fermée, la Cour de Justice raisonne en termes d'exclusivité*', H Labayle and F Sudre, 'L'avis 2/13 de la Cour de Justice sur l'adhésion de l'Union européenne à la Convention des droits de l'homme: pavane pour une adhésion défunte?' (n 78) 15.

[98] Adam Łazowski and Ramses A. Wessel counter-argue that the Court took fundamental rights seriously, but it needed more time to explore the Charter and its potential. According to these authors, '*it seized the opportunity to start building a wall of case law based on the Charter before the European Union accedes to the ECHR. Looked at from this perspective, Opinion 2/13 is undoubtedly an important element in this jigsaw puzzle*', Łazowski and Wessel (n 10) 209.

[99] Eeckhout, 'Opinion 2/13 on EU Accession to the ECHR' (n 15) 7.

European integration. The point we would like to make is another one: the multilevel constitutionalism principle of a higher level of protection of fundamental rights would, in principle, have permitted an interpretation of the draft agreement in conformity with EU law in the following cases.

a) Coordination between Article 53 of the Charter and Article 53 ECHR

As for the coordination between Article 53 of the Charter and Article 53 ECHR, the CJEU considered that the EU Member States could use Article 53 ECHR to adopt higher standards of fundamental rights in matters covered by harmonised Union law, which runs counter to the primacy of EU Law. Therefore, Article 53 ECHR, which permits the Contracting Parties to have a higher level of protection of fundamental rights than that provided by the ECHR, could be in conflict with Article 53 of the Charter, as interpreted by the Court in *Melloni.*

First of all, it should be emphasised that the factual and legal situation in the *Melloni* case was of a rather particular nature, since it concerned the interpretation and, if necessary, the validity of Article 4a(1) of Council Framework Decision 2002/584/JHA of 13 June 2002 on the European arrest warrant and the surrender procedures between Member States,[100] as amended by Council Framework Decision 2009/299/JHA of 26 February 2009 ('Framework Decision 2002/584').[101] It also concerned, if necessary, an examination of the issue of whether a Member State may refuse to execute a European arrest warrant on the basis of Article 53 of the CFREU, on the grounds that such an action would infringe the fundamental rights – rights guaranteed by the national constitution – of the person concerned.

Apart from the fact that the interpretation of Article 53 of the Charter in *Melloni* is far from being peaceful,[102] the truth is that, according to the Court:

> "[T]his interpretation of Articles 47 and 48(2) of the Charter is in keeping with the scope that has been recognised for the rights gua-

[100] OJ 2002 L 190, 1.

[101] OJ 2009 L 81, 24.

[102] For a rather critical view see Nergelius (n 20) 28 et seq.

ranteed by Article 6(1) and (3) of the ECHR by the case-law of the European Court of Human Rights (see, inter alia, ECtHR, Medenica v. Switzerland, no. 20491/92, § 56 to 59, ECHR 2001-VI; Sejdovic v. Italy [GC], no. 56581/00, § 84, 86 and 98, ECHR 2006-II; and Haralampiev v. Bulgaria, no. 29648/03, § 32 and 33, 24 April 2012)".[103]

This means that it is unreasonable to allege that the Court did not take into account the multilevel protection of fundamental rights in Europe. However, in our opinion, the Court adopted a rather rigid position concerning the relationship between fundamental rights and the primacy of EU law that is understandable in the context of the European arrest warrant and the surrender procedures between Member States, but this rigid stance should not have been extended to other areas. The principle of a higher protection of fundamental rights should be viewed as an existential requirement, like the principle of primacy.

In fact, Article 53 of the CFREU clearly states that 'nothing in this Charter shall be interpreted as restricting or adversely affecting human rights and fundamental freedoms, as recognised (...), including the European Convention for the Protection of Human Rights and Fundamental Freedoms, and by the Member States' constitutions'. In our opinion, the Court could have interpreted Article 53 of the Charter differently, as long as it was ready to accept higher standards of fundamental rights emanating from the ECHR and the constitutions of Member States.[104]

To be honest, this is not the first time that the Court has sacrificed fundamental rights in favour of the primacy of EU law.[105] In fact, this question focuses on an old and well-known dispute between the constitutional courts of the Member States and the Court of Justice that has not yet been resolved. This dispute concerns who should be regarded as the final arbiter of fundamental rights in Europe,[106] an issue which lies outside the scope of this study.

[103] C-399/11 *Melloni* Judgment of 26 February 2013, ECLI:EU:C:2013:107 para 50.

[104] In the same vein: Popov (n 91) 5.

[105] At the very beginning of the European integration process, the Court of Justice refused to accept that fundamental rights were part of EC law (see C-1/58 *Stork*), although this would soon change (see C-26/69 *Stauder*, C-11/70 *Internationale Handelsgesellschaft*).

[106] For further developments: M Kumm, 'The Jurisprudence of Constitutional Conflict: Constitutional Supremacy in Europe Before and After the Constitutional Treaty' (2005) 11

This position of the Court may trigger new adverse reactions from the constitutional courts of the Member States and may open a 'Pandora's box', which everyone has reason to fear, including the Court of Justice itself.

As has already been stated in an editorial comment:

> "[T]he somewhat inflexible defence of its judicial powers at the expense of an accession of the EU to the ECHR may, unfortunately, lead to an (unexpected) backlash in the relationship between the ECJ and the constitutional courts of the Member States, who may, paradoxically, draw some inspiration from the ECJ's attitude. Constitutional Courts may be willing to defend their judicial powers (with regard to fundamental rights) vis-à-vis the ECJ in a fashion parallel to the ECJ vis-à-vis the ECtHR".[107]

b) Area of Freedom, Security and Justice

Another objection of the Court that, in our opinion, could have been avoided if the Court had used the tools of multilevel constitutionalism, concerns the AFSJ. In fact, in a field that is rather conducive to the violation of fundamental rights, extreme situations, such as those involving individuals who fear being repatriated or sent to countries they do not wish to go to because they are likely to be arrested or detained, require the highest level of protection of fundamental rights.[108]

However, in Opinion 2/13 the Court maintained its traditional 'exclusivist' constitutional view, appearing to be more preoccupied with the autonomy of EU law and with the preservation of its own interpretation of EU law than with the protection of fundamental rights.

The Court's emphasis on the principle of 'mutual trust' between EU Member States in the AFSJ, founded on the Dublin rules on asylum responsibility, led the Court to reaffirm its own jurisprudence and to fear interaction with a more protective system of fundamental rights for

(3) *European Law Journal* 262 et seq; idem, 'Who is the Final Arbiter of Constitutionality in Europe?' (1999) 36 (2) *CML Rev* 351 et seq.

[107] 'Editorial Comments' (n 12) 15. In a similar vein: Łazowski and Wessel (n 10) 212; Nergelius (n 20) 48.

[108] In the same vein: E Spaventa, 'A Very Fearful Court?' (n 61) 19.

asylum-seekers than the Dublin system, such as the recent case law of the ECtHR.[109]

If the Court had taken the principle of a higher protection of fundamental rights into account, instead of rigidly adhering to its own jurisprudence and to the principle of autonomy of EU law, the fact that a Member State could check that another Member State had observed fundamental rights, would not constitute an insurmountable problem.[110]

In our view, the scope of the principle of 'mutual trust' (or mutual recognition) is not so narrow that it applies only between EU Member States. As we will see below, it should apply in all directions and between every single constitutional player.

c) Jurisdiction over Common Foreign and Security Policy

Finally, although the lack of jurisdiction over the CFSP was perhaps the most difficult question that the Court had to consider, the Court could have benefited from the input of multilevel constitutionalism and the principle of a higher protection of fundamental rights.[111] To a certain extent, this was the position of the Advocate General Kokott.[112]

The Court is right when it said that, in order to preserve the specific characteristics of the EU, a non-EU court could not be given the power of judicial review over EU acts, even though the CJEU has no jurisdiction itself in most CFSP issues.

However, in our opinion, this is only a partial view of the problem. In fact, the monopoly of the CJEU's jurisdiction over EU acts is not the most unique feature of EU law. On the contrary, respect for human dignity and respect for fundamental rights in general also constitute specific characteristics of the EU. The Court could have anchored its reasoning in these two points, and it could have accepted this part of the draft agreement. Theoretically, the CFSP could have been the field in which individuals could actually have gained more protection of their fundamental rights

[109] See *Tarakhel v. Switzerland* App. no 29217 Judgment of 4 November 2014, available at www.hudoc.echr.coe.int/.

[110] Cf. E Dubout, 'Une question de confiance: nature juridique de l'Union européenne et adhésion à la Convention européenne des droits de l'homme' 95 et seq.

[111] In the same vein: Popov (n 91) 7.

[112] See paras 82-103 of the Advocate General's View.

with the EU's accession to the ECHR, because this is a field in which the EU has no real jurisdiction. In practice, the direct violation of an individual's rights by an act of the Union that is excluded from the Court's jurisdiction is somewhat rare.

Not wishing to jeopardise the specific characteristics of the EU, the CJEU rejected the conformity of the draft agreement on this matter.

2. Principle of Common Values between the EU Member States, the EU, the Council of Europe and its Member States

Another significant element of multilevel constitutionalism that the Court apparently did not consider concerns the existence of common values within the Member States, the EU, the Council of Europe and its Member States. In fact, the Court of Justice referred only to the common values between the Member States and the EU (Article 2 TEU).[113] This reference is fully understandable, so long as these common values are so relevant that respect for them constitutes a condition for accession to the Union (Article 49 TEU) and the persistent violation of them by a Member State might lead to the suspension of certain rights of that Member State (Article 7 TEU).[114]

However, as mentioned above, the EU and its Member States also share some values (and principles) with the Council of Europe and its Member States.

[113] Para 168 of the Opinion.

[114] On the common values between the Member States and the EU see AMG Martins, 'Os valores da União na Constituição Europeia' (2005) 84 *Colóquio ibérico: Constituição europeia, Boletim da Faculdade de Direito da Universidade de Coimbra, Studia Jurídica* 497 et seq; V Constantinesco, 'Valeurs et contenu de la Constitution européenne' in *Uma Constituição para a Europa*, (Coimbra, Almedina, 2004) 161 et seq; F Sorrentino, 'Brevi reflessione sui valori e sui fini dell'Unione Europea nel progetto di costituzione europea' (2003) 9 *Diritto Pubblico* 810-11; R Bieber, 'Ingérence ou manifestation d'une responsabilité commune? – La protection des valeurs de l'Union européenne à l'égard des Etats-membres', in Institut Suisse de Droit Comparé (ed), *L'intégration européenne: historique et perspectives* (Zurich, Schulthess Verlag 2002) 95 et seq; AMG Martins, 'Les valeurs communes et la place de la Charte en Europe' (2002) 14 (1) *European Review of Public Law* 130 et seq; F Schorkopf, *Homogenität in der Europäischen Union – Ausgestaltung und Gewährleistung durch Art. 6 abs. 1 und Art. 7 EUV* (Berlin, Dunker & Humblot, 2000) 36 et seq.

The Court could have looked at these common values and could have highlighted the influence that each has had on the other in the past, which has progressively led to a convergence in fundamental rights matters, instead of creating the possibility of future divergences.

This approach would have been of greater benefit to EU law than the 'exclusivist' view of the Court. For example, in the field of CFSP, EU accession to the ECHR could have filled the gaps in human rights protection that exist in this area and the same could be said for the field of AFSJ. Furthermore, the objections of the Court concerning Article 53 ECHR in connection with Article 53 CFREU did not take into due consideration the fact that the common values justify the input of many provisions from the ECHR into the CFREU.

3. Principle of Cooperative Judicial Dialogue

Turning to the principle of cooperative judicial dialogue, in our view, this was not taken into due consideration by the CJEU in its formulation of Opinion 2/13. On the contrary, it seems to have been overly influenced by a principle of distrust.

As Eleanor Spaventa has pointed out, Opinion 2/13 'is also disappointing because it shows a Court's profound distrust of both national courts (and their compliance with the principle of loyal cooperation) and of the European Court of Human Rights'.[115]

Many of the Court's objections could have been avoided if the Court had considered a proper cooperative judicial dialogue.

Above all, the tension between Article 53 of the ECHR and 53 of the Charter, as interpreted by the Court of Justice, presupposes that the ECtHR would force an EU Member State to apply a national standard of human rights protection which is higher than the Convention standard. On the other hand, a higher national standard of protection would be imposed not by the ECtHR, but by the Convention itself.[116] The CJEU seems to have feared that the ECtHR would exceed its jurisdiction and start to control national standards of protection and, in an indirect way, the uniform standard imposed by the Charter. However, nothing in the

[115] E Spaventa, 'A Very Fearful Court?' (n 61) 12.

[116] For developing this topic, see Eeckhout (n 15) 10-14.

former jurisprudence of the ECtHR indicates that it would be likely to do this.

Another position of the CJEU that reveals an enormous distrust of all other courts concerns Protocol 16, which would enable the highest courts and tribunals of the Member States to request advisory opinions.[117] As we have already mentioned, the EU would not become a signatory to this protocol as a result of its accession to the ECHR and, anyway, the Protocol has not yet entered into force. Otherwise, such a problem may arise with or without EU accession, whenever all or some EU Member States ratify the Protocol.[118]

Nevertheless, if by chance the highest court of a Member State used the Protocol in a way that violated EU law, this is a problem that would have to be solved by EU law and its remedial mechanisms.

The position of the Court in this case seems to presuppose that 'Member State highest courts cannot be trusted to respect EU law. That is not a position that is conducive to genuine judicial dialogue'.[119] The same Court that interprets the principle of mutual trust between the EU Member States, which does not clearly result from the Treaties, in a rather rigid manner, also fails to take into due consideration the principle of sincere cooperation between the Member States and the Union provided for in Article 4(3) of the TEU.[120]

The Court's objection relating to Article 33 of the ECHR,[121] which permits inter-state disputes, presupposes a climate of suspicion between the CJEU and the ECtHR that is barely credible in a multilevel constitutional system. For the CJEU:

117 For an elaboration of this topic, see ibid 17-18.

118 In the same vein: Korenica (n 18) 416-18.

119 See Eeckhout (n 15) 18.

120 Article 4 (3) TEU reads: 'Pursuant to the principle of sincere cooperation, the Union and the Member States shall, in full mutual respect, assist each other in carrying out tasks which flow from the Treaties.
The Member States shall take any appropriate measure, general or particular, to ensure fulfilment of the obligations arising out of the Treaties or resulting from the acts of the institutions of the Union.
The Member States shall facilitate the achievement of the Union's tasks and refrain from any measure which could jeopardise the attainment of the Union's objectives.'.

121 Especially on this issue see SO Johansen, 'The Reinterpretation of TFEU Article 344 in Opinion 2/13 and its Potential Consequences' (2015) 16 *German Law Journal* 169 et seq.

> "[O]nly the express exclusion of the ECtHR's jurisdiction under Article 33 of the ECHR over disputes between Member States or between Member States and the EU in relation to the application of the ECHR within the scope ratione materiae of EU law would be compatible with Article 344 TFEU".[122]

Actually, this is a step backwards in the judicial dialogue between these two Courts. Even prior to accession, EU primary law has been reviewed in the context of individual applications. In the *Matthews* case,[123] for example, the ECtHR decided that the citizens of Gibraltar should be able to vote in European Parliamentary elections.

Furthermore, 'the purpose of the accession is to enable individuals to complain to the ECtHR about the Convention violations by the EU'.[124]

Even in issues like the co-respondent mechanism and the prior involvement procedure, where the Court and the Advocate General took a similar position and, in our opinion, were right, there is no sign, in the Opinion of the Court, that these obstacles could be better overcome through a permanent, mutual and profound dialogue between the two Courts. Bearing in mind that the ECtHR has mostly respected the competence of the CJEU,[125] the Court could have acknowledged this fact. However, it seemed to be too fearful of the ECtHR's interference in its competence, striving to prevent such a situation.

Finally, several statements made by the CJEU concerning the exclusion of ECtHR jurisdiction over the EU in certain cases, such as in the fields of the CFSP and AFSJ, are hardly compatible with a proper judicial dialogue.

[122] Para 213.

[123] *Matthews v UK* Application no. 24833/94 Judgment of 18 February 1999, available at www.hudoc.echr.coe.int/eng.

[124] See Eeckhout (n 15) 24.

[125] See, for instance, *Bosphorus* application 45036/98 Judgment of 30 June 2005, available at http://hudoc.echr.coe.int/eng, which is an example of a case in which *'the ECtHR and the ECJ are singing in harmony'*, J Klabbers, *Treaty Conflict and European Union* (Cambridge, Cambridge University Press 2009) 172. On the future of the Bosphorus case see O De Schutter, 'Bosphorus Post-Accession: Redefining the Relationships between the European Court of Human Rights and the Parties of the Convention', in Kosta et al (n 9) 177 et seq; P Gragl, *The Accession of the European Union to the European Convention on Human Rights* (n 5) 69-75.

The CJEU could have used the ECtHR's jurisdiction in CFSP matters as an argument to extend its own jurisdiction in this field or to interpret the provisions of the EU treaties in a wider sense. In contrast, it preferred to argue the exclusivity of its own jurisdiction, which is somewhat disputable in this context.

4. Principle of Sincere Cooperation and Mutual Trust

As has just been pointed out, multilevel constitutionalism presupposes a sincere cooperation between all the players, and not only between the EU and its Member States. This sincere cooperation is based on the existence of mutual trust between all the players.

Taking this into consideration, at least two of the CJEU's fears appear to be unfounded.

The first fear relates to Protocol 16. Apart from the fact that this protocol is not included in the draft agreement, it has not yet entered into force and no-one can predict what its future will be. Furthermore, it does not compete with the preliminary ruling based on Article 267 of the TFEU. '*The Protocol no. 16 advisory opinion is different in nature, as it will be limited to the highest national court, it is never obligatory and the opinion itself is not binding*'.[126]

Anyway, if the Court had taken the principle of sincere cooperation into account and had trusted the EU Member States, it could have omitted the reference to Protocol 16. If in future any Member State used the procedure provided for in that protocol, violating its duties under the preliminary reference procedure, EU law has various mechanisms at its disposal, including judicial ones, enabling it to punish the Member State.[127]

The same can be said of Article 33 of the ECHR, which allows for inter-state disputes between ECHR Contracting Parties over alleged breaches of the Convention. If EU Member States decided to submit a dispute concerning the interpretation or application of the EU Treaties to the ECtHR,

[126] Á Mohay, 'Back to the Drawing Board? Opinion 2/13 of the Court of Justice on the Accession of the EU to the ECHR – Case note' (2015) 1 *Pécs Journal of International and European Law* 35.

[127] Apart from the political mechanism foreseen in Article 7 TEU, EU law has judicial remedies against the Member States, such as the infringement procedure (Articles 258-60).

it could constitute a violation of EU law, including a violation of Article 344 of the TFEU itself, and the EU Member States are fully aware of this.

V. Concluding Remarks

From the aforegoing discussion a number of conclusions may be drawn.

Although the Treaty of Lisbon had imposed on the Union an obligation to accede to the ECHR (Article 6 (2) TEU), the Court of Justice, for the second time in the history of its case law, rejected, in Opinion 2/13, EU accession to the ECHR. In the view of the Court, a number of issues in the draft agreement were not compatible with Article 6(2) of the Treaty on European Union nor with Protocol No 8 relating to Article 6(2) TEU.

These issues concerned the coordination of Article 53 ECHR with Article 53 CFREU, as is interpreted by the Court; the principle of mutual trust in the field of AFSJ, which obliges the Member States to presume that all other Member States are in compliance with EU law and particularly with the fundamental rights recognised by EU law, except for exceptional circumstances as interpreted by the CJEU; Protocol 16, which enables the highest national courts of High Contracting Parties to address queries to the ECtHR on matters concerning the interpretation of the ECHR; Article 33 of the ECHR relating to inter-state disputes; the co-respondent mechanism that would create a new procedure whereby the EU and a Member State could become parties to an ECtHR case, the procedure for prior involvement of the CJEU and the judicial review in CFSP matters.

According to the Court, the principle of autonomy and the specific characteristics of EU law, including the Court's monopoly on the interpretation of EU law, were violated by the draft agreement.

Bearing in mind that the issue of the EU's accession to the ECHR has been on the EU's agenda for decades, Opinion 2/13 has had an enormous legal and political impact. In such a sensitive matter, one would have expected the Court to display a more cooperative attitude with the Member States, with the EU institutions that had conducted what were particularly tough negotiations and, last but not least, with other Courts that also form part of the European multilevel system of fundamental rights, such as the highest national courts, including the constitutional courts, and the ECtHR.

In spite of drawing attention to the constitutional structure of the EU, the Court seems to have rejected the multilevel constitutionalism theory, anchoring its position in an 'exclusivist' constitutionalism, in which the EU as a constitutional entity must preserve its own legal autonomy and specific characteristics at any cost.

In our view, the Court could have decided otherwise if it had considered the draft agreement in the context of multilevel constitutionalism, in which the different components – EU law, national laws and ECHR law – need to work together towards a major objective, namely a higher level of protection of fundamental rights. This would have permitted an interpretation of the draft agreement in conformity with EU law in at least three areas – the coordination of Article 53 ECHR with Article 53 CFREU, the principle of mutual trust between EU Member States in the AFSJ, and the jurisdiction over CFSP.

Another constitutive element of multilevel constitutionalism that the Court apparently overlooked was the existence of common values within the Member States, the EU, the Council of Europe and its High Contracting Parties, which could contribute to the convergence of fundamental rights. The Court referred only to the common values of the Member States and the EU.

Furthermore, in Opinion 2/13, the Court seems to be stuck in a view of the EU constitutional system that is more closely related to a hierarchical judicial order than to a cooperative judicial dialogue. In our opinion, the objections concerning Article 53 ECHR, Protocol 16 and Article 33 ECHR are based on a distrust of both national courts and the ECtHR. In other words, without the acceptance of the principle of cooperative judicial dialogue and the principle of sincere cooperation and mutual trust between all players, it is impossible to avoid jurisdictional conflicts, which would not help to reinforce the protection and enforcement of fundamental rights in Europe.

In Opinion 2/13, it is evident that the Court does not trust anyone, except itself. For the Court, the EU Member States, national courts, and the ECtHR can endanger the autonomy of EU law, the specific characteristics of the EU and the monopoly of its jurisdiction.

This position of the Court may be rather problematic, since it may open a 'Pandora's box' of adverse reactions from all the other players, which everyone has reasons to fear, including the Court of Justice itself.

X
Tribunal Europeu dos Direitos do Homem*

1. Introdução

O TEDH é um tribunal internacional especializado em direitos humanos, ao qual os indivíduos têm acesso direto.

Originariamente o sistema de garantia dos direitos consagrados na CEDH era misto, competindo à Comissão Europeia dos Direitos Humanos, ao Comité de Ministros (pré-existente à Convenção) e ao próprio Tribunal Europeu dos Direitos do Homem, criado em 1959. O TEDH proferia a decisão definitiva e obrigatória sobre os processos que lhe eram submetidos pela Comissão Europeia dos Direitos do Homem ou por uma Alta Parte Contratante.

Após várias modificações, e em especial com os protocolos nº 11 (1 de novembro de 1998), e nº 14 (1 de junho de 2010), o sistema tornou-se totalmente jurisdicional e obrigatório.

2. Composição, estrutura e funcionamento do Tribunal Europeu dos Direitos do Homem

O TEDH é composto por um número de juízes igual ao número de Estados Contratantes da CEDH (art. 20º CEDH), ou seja, 47 juízes, os quais são escolhidos de entre as pessoas da mais elevada reputação moral e que reúnam as condições requeridas para o exercício de altas funções judi-

* Este artigo está em vias de publicação na Enciclopédia Luso-Brasileira de Direito Internacional, coordenada por Manuel Almeida Ribeiro e Marcílio França.

ciais ou sejam jurisconsultos de reconhecida competência (art. 21º, nº 1, CEDH). Exercem as suas funções a título individual (art. 21º, nº 2, CEDH).

Os juízes são eleitos pela Assembleia Parlamentar relativamente a cada Alta Parte Contratante, por maioria dos votos expressos, com base numa lista de três candidatos (art. 22º, nº 1, CEDH).

A duração do mandato é de nove anos, não renovável (art. 23º, nº 1, CEDH). Os juízes não podem ter mais de 70 anos (art. 23º, nº 2 CEDH), sendo que, se estiverem em funções, o seu mandato cessará quando atingirem essa idade.

O Tribunal funciona em formação de juiz singular, de comités de 3 juízes, de secções de 7 juízes e em tribunal pleno de 17 juízes (art. 26º CEDH).

O TEDH só funciona em assembleia plenária nos casos previstos no art. 25º CEDH, dos quais se destacam a eleição dos seus Presidente e Vice-Presidentes e a adoção do seu regulamento interno.

3. A competência do Tribunal Europeu dos Direitos do Homem

A competência do TEDH estende-se a todas questões que digam respeito à interpretação e aplicação da CEDH e dos seus protocolos adicionais (art. 32º CEDH).

O TEDH tem competência consultiva e contenciosa.

No âmbito da primeira pode apreciar os pedidos de parecer que lhe forem formulados pelo Comité de Ministros, nos termos do art. 47º, nº 1, CEDH. Esta competência é muito limitada, dado que estão dela excluídas as questões relativas ao conteúdo e extensão dos direitos e liberdades definidos no título I da Convenção e nos protocolos bem como outras questões que possam por outro meio vir a ser submetidas ao TEDH (nº 2 do preceito).

Esta competência alargou-se com a entrada em vigor do protocolo nº 16, na medida em que este prevê pedidos facultativos de parecer dos mais elevados órgãos jurisdicionais nacionais ao TEDH no âmbito de um processo pendente a nível nacional.

Assim sendo, a principal competência do TEDH é contenciosa, pronunciando-se sobre as petições interestaduais (art. 33º CEDH) e individuais (art. 34º CEDH). O recurso ao TEDH pressupõe o esgotamento dos meios internos (art. 35º, nº 1, CEDH).

3.1. Competência *ratione personae*

Segundo o art. 1º CEDH os Estados partes reconhecem a toda a pessoa que esteja sob a sua jurisdição os direitos enunciados na CEDH.

A CEDH não impõe condições de nacionalidade, pelo que a proteção da CEDH pode ser invocada contra um Estado parte pelos nacionais de outros Estados partes ou terceiros à Convenção, por refugiados ou apátridas, desde que a violação invocada tenha tido lugar nos limites da jurisdição do Estado parte da Convenção.

O TEDH desenvolveu uma noção extensiva de jurisdição segundo a qual os Estados membros são responsáveis por todos os atos e omissões dos seus órgãos internos que sejam contrários à CEDH, mesmo que se trate de cumprimento de obrigações internacionais (TEDH, *Beer et Regan c/Allemagne*, 18 de fevereiro de 1999, § 57 – (todos os casos citados estão disponíveis em http://hudoc.echr.coe.int)).

Os principais problemas a este propósito colocam-se em relação à União Europeia. Em primeiro lugar, não sendo a União parte na CEDH, os atos dela emanados não podem ser sindicados perante o TEDH. Em segundo lugar, esses atos também não podem ser imputados aos Estados-Membros, ainda que coletivamente, se estes se limitarem a aplicar o direito da União Europeia. Em terceiro lugar, apesar de o TEDH considerar que um Estado não pode eximir-se às suas obrigações em razão da Convenção, por força da transferência de atribuições para a União Europeia, só em situações muito excecionais o TEDH condenou os Estados por cumprirem o direito da União Europeia (TEDH *Matthews c. Reino Unido,* de 18 de fevereiro de 1999, § 35 – o TEDH condenou o Reino Unido, por violação do art. 3º do protocolo nº 1 da CEDH, devido à aplicação do direito originário da União relativo às eleições para o PE, que excluía os cidadãos de Gibraltar).

3.2. Competência *ratione loci*

A competência *ratione loci* do TEDH coincide com a jurisdição dos Estados parte na CEDH. De acordo com o direito internacional (TEDH, *Gentilhomme et autres c. France,* 14 de maio de 2002, § 20), exerce-se, em princípio, sobre a totalidade do território, só assim não é se o Estado estiver impedido de exercer a sua jurisdição numa parte do território, devido, nomeadamente, ao domínio desse território por um movimento separatista apoiado por outro Estado (TEDH, *Ilaşcu et autres c. Moldova et Russie*, § 311) ou que vá além do território do Estado se os atos emanarem dos seus órgãos e tiverem efeitos fora do seu território (TEDH, *Drozd et Janousek c. France et Espagne* de 26 de junho de1992, § 90).

3.3. Competência *ratione materiae*

A competência *ratione materiae* do TEDH incide sobre a violação dos direitos e obrigações consagrados na CEDH. Mais uma vez a violação da CEDH por parte dos Estados membros da União Europeia devido à sua pertença à União levanta problemas específicos.

O TEDH considera que se o Estado não tem margem de apreciação e se limita a aplicar o direito da União Europeia existe um princípio de equivalência da proteção dos direitos fundamentais, pelo que o TEDH não exercerá a sua competência (TEDH, *Bosphorus Hava Yollari Turizm Ve Ticaret Anonim Şirketi c. Irlande*, de 30 de maio de 2005, § 155 e seguintes). O Estado-Membro é, todavia, inteiramente responsável se tiver exercido alguma margem de apreciação (TEDH, *M.S.S. c. Bélgica e Grécia*, de 21 de janeiro de 2011, §§ 338-339).

3.4. A decisão do TEDH

Cumpridos os requisitos de admissibilidade (art. 35º CEDH) e seguida a tramitação prevista (arts. 36º a 43º CEDH), compete, em exclusivo, ao Tribunal pronunciar-se sobre o fundo do caso. Fá-lo, através de um acórdão fundamentado (art. 45º CEDH), podendo os juízes juntar opiniões individuais dissidentes ou concordantes.

O acórdão do TEDH vai declarar a compatibilidade ou não das medidas nacionais com a Convenção. Trata-se de um contencioso de legalidade e não de anulação. Por vezes, o TEDH, ultrapassando o art. 46º CEDH, indica quais as medidas de alcance geral que o Estado deve adotar.

As decisões definitivas (artigo 44º, nºs 1 e 2, CEDH) do TEDH têm autoridade de caso julgado, não produzindo efeitos *erga omnes* nem valendo como título executivo (art. 46º, nº 1, CEDH).

O Comité de Ministros deve velar pela execução do acórdão (art. 46º, nº 2, CEDH), prevendo-se, atualmente, um processo por incumprimento contra o Estado que não executa o acórdão do TEDH (art. 46º, nº 4, CEDH.

Na prática, a maior parte dos Estados cumpre os acórdãos do TEDH (ver http://www.echr.coe.int/Fr/FDocs/EffectsofJudgements.html), havendo, no entanto, alguns Estados mais recalcitrantes.

O TEDH tem atualmente um problema muito complicado – o elevado número de processos pendentes – para o qual se tem tentado nos últimos anos encontrar uma solução sem grande sucesso.

Bibliografia

BANTEKAS, Elias/OETTE, Lutz – *International Human Rights Law and Practice,* 2ª ed., Cambridge, Cambridge Univ. Press, 2016.

CABRAL BARRETO, Irineu – *A Convenção Europeia dos Direitos do Homem – Anotada,* 4ª ed., Coimbra, Coimbra Editora, 2011.

GRABENWARTER, Christoph/PABEL, Katharina – *Europäische Menschenrechtskonvention,* 6ª ed., Munique, Beck, 2016.

GUERRA MARTINS, Ana Maria – *Direito Internacional dos Direitos Humanos,* Coimbra, Almedina, 2006.

RENUCCI, Jean-François – *Droit Européen des Droits de l'Homme,* 7ª ed. Paris, LGDJ, 2017.

SCHILLING, Theodor – *Internationaler Menschenrechtsschutz,* 3ª ed., Tübingen, Mohr Siebeck, 2016.

SUDRE, Frédéric – *Droit international et européen des droits de l'homme,* 13ª ed., Paris, Puf, 2016.